BRIGANTIA

Map 1   Britain, the Belinus Line and Brigantia

BRIGANTIA

A MYSTERIOGRAPHY

GUY RAGLAND PHILLIPS

ILLUSTRATED BY THE AUTHOR

ROUTLEDGE & KEGAN PAUL
LONDON, HENLEY AND BOSTON

First published in 1976
by Routledge & Kegan Paul Ltd
76 Carter Lane,
London EC4V 5EL,
Reading Road,
Henley-on-Thames,
Oxon RG9 1EN and
9 Park Street,
Boston, Mass. 02108, USA
Set in 12 on 13pt. Photon Bembo
and printed in Great Britain by
The Camelot Press Ltd, Southampton
© Guy Ragland Phillips 1976
No part of this book may be reproduced in
any form without permission from the
publisher, except for the quotation of brief
passages in criticism

ISBN 0 7100 8316 5

CONTENTS

❉

HOW MANY HANDS? vii
1 SACRED BRIDES 1
2 SPIDER'S WEB 14
3 TRAITOR QUEEN 35
4 CLINSCHOR'S KINGDOM 54
5 WHAT THE BUTLER SAW 68
6 THE ELUSIVE KNIGHT 84
7 MOST ACCURSED KIRKS 94
8 THE VERVAIN PATH 109
9 GIANTESSES IN BROAD BONNETS 125
10 MAGIC RAVENS 147
11 VIEW FROM THE ROWAN TREE 168
12 DRAGON'S BLOOD 184
APPENDIX 200
BIBLIOGRAPHY 206
INDEX 210

ILLUSTRATIONS

❋

MAPS

1	Britain, the Belinus Line and Brigantia	frontispiece
2	Brigantia	4
3	Principal nodes and network of alignments in Brigantia	18
4	Node of alignments to or through Clifton, York	20

DRAWINGS

1	Devil's Arrow, Boroughbridge	46
2	Stone head in the church porch at Kirkby Malham	115
3	St Helen's Well, Eshton	116
4	The Bankwell (Giggleswick) figurine	119
5	Part of the hatching on the shield from Tal-y-Llyn, the relevant sections lined heavily	120
6	At Brimham Rocks	127
7	The Wig Stones, Raygill	132
8	Jenny Twigg and her Daughter Tib	135
9	The Bull Stone, Otley Chevin	142
10	The Swastika Stone, Ilkley Moor	144
11	The Tree of Life Stone, Snowden Carr	146
12	The Green Man at Fountains Abbey	156
13	The Black Horse of Bush Howe	191
14	The Horned God of the Brigantes in Aldborough (Isurium) Church	198
15	Aldborough Cross	199

HOW MANY HANDS?

❊

Initial impetus for the writing of this book came originally from Mr W. R. Mitchell, of the magazines *Dalesman* and *Cumbria*, himself author of a number of books; and from that moment onward he was not only a constant source of confidence and inspiration, but also a ready chauffeur who ferried me about from one end of Brigantia to another. He personally, and the two magazines, gave me help without which this work could not have been completed. Many of the illustrations in this book have appeared previously in the magazines *Dalesman* and *Country Life* and are reproduced here by permission.

Nor could it have been even begun without the basic idea – the theme of a vital continuum from the most remote past to the present day – arising from my close study of Dr Anne Ross's classic *Pagan Celtic Britain*, which was almost my Bible until I began to disagree with parts of it. My deep dependence on her book is obvious throughout the following pages, though she might be horrified if conclusions which I draw were imputed to her.

Several institutions have given me great assistance, including York Minster Library and, especially, the expert staff of Tullie House Library, Carlisle. Equally valuable have been the interest and aid given on a personal level by Mr Sam Brewster, of Tadcaster, who guided my baffled feet through the mazes of medieval English literature; Mr Sidney Jackson, of Shipley, the authority on Celtic stone heads; Mrs Margaret Johnston, of

Bloomfield, USA, a descendant of John R. Walbran the Ripon historian; Mr Paul Screeton, editor of the *Ley-Hunter* and author of *Quicksilver Heritage*; Mr S. G. Wildman, author of *The Black Horsemen* and an observer whose eye is closely in line with mine; and my wife Ivy, who has not only taken countless chores off my back but driven me everywhere in the final year of research, read proofs, correlated texts, corrected typescripts, and kept Buster the dog and Freddie the cat out of my grumpy way, all the time keeping my spirits up and my flag flying.

But perhaps there is still another debt of gratitude. A hundred yards from our house, at the northern end of Appleton-le-Moors, stands an ancient 'cross' — simply a large, flat stone with a hole through one side of it. Up to not so long ago, bargains and agreements were sealed not with a hand on the Book, but with a handshake through that hole. I have put my hand through and closed my fingers. With how many hands of the very long past did I make a compact?

G. R. P.

I
SACRED BRIDES

It has been asked of this book – not unreasonably – 'What is it about? Is it a guide book, history, topography, folklore?' It cannot pretend to be any of these things. Many histories of Yorkshire alone, for instance, have been written, some of them of half a dozen thick volumes. Yorkshire is only a part of Brigantia, and history is only a part – even a small part – of the subject matter treated here. He who wants a guide book of northern Britain will find this book useless. Folklore forms an important part of the material examined, but specialists have written expert and detailed surveys which have formed some of the sources for sections of *Brigantia*.

To the questions posed above, another might have been added: 'Why Brigantia at all?' Let this be answered first. Brigantia, its people or peoples and its culture or cultures, are taken in this book as being a unit with significance for humanity as a whole, and for Britain in particular. It is of course commonplace to hear any northerner laying down the law that his native county is the best in Britain and gives the whole country its leadership. For that matter, a Welshman or Scot or Cornishman or Kentish Man or Man of Kent might say the same. But any northerner will read the story of the heresy by Pelagius the fifth-century monk who insisted on man's free will, and – without bothering to think that Pelagius probably spoke only Latin and Welsh and remembering only that he was probably a Yorkshireman – will imagine him in a cloth cap and feel sympathy with him. Brigantia still has a meaning, a something which can perhaps be summed up as a mystique.

That mystique is what makes Brigantia tick, what makes it still significant, what makes Brigantians still distinct from everybody else. And the mystique is compounded of topography, history, folklore, pre-history and a variety of other factors, some of which are extremely elusive. It is not possible, even in tome after tome, to deal with this enormous mass of evidence in any detail. All that could be attempted here was to try to make a reasonable selection from the high-lights and to put them into something as near chronological order as possible, at the same time showing that events of later times carried links with a sometimes remote past.

Perhaps the only single word to describe a study of this kind would have to be a new coinage: this is a mysteriography. By this is meant not merely a collection of unresolved questions (though there are plenty of those), but a survey of the deeper, partly uncategorised and often inexplicable oddities that go into the formation of a human society.

When I was a small boy my father remarked to me with a straight face that the British Empire (as it then was) was the greatest the world had ever seen; that in Britain the greatest county was Yorkshire; that in Yorkshire the greatest city was Leeds; and that in Leeds the best suburb was Headingley, where we lived. This was a lesson in social geography that I never forgot.

In something of the same spirit, but without the tongue in cheek, may be considered Brigantia. This was the kingdom inhabited by peoples collectively called the Brigantes, whom the Roman army found blocking its way right across what was later to become England, from the Wirral Peninsula in the west to the Wash in the east. Brigantia was not, it is true, comparable with the British Empire of 1,700 or 1,800 years later; but it certainly was a kind of 'British Empire', with a relatively small British aristocracy of Celtic invaders ruling over a mass population of indigenous peoples who may have been proto-Celts or pre-Celts.

Brigantia was probably by far the most important section of Celtic-speaking Britain both before and during the Roman occupation. It may be that as a formal institution Brigantia came into political existence not very long, in historical terms, before the Roman invasion. But the peoples of Brigantia, various as they always were, have also always shown certain common characteristics, different from the rest of Britain and from most of the rest of Europe. What grew into Brigantia had a life extending backward in time from the Iron Age which the Celtic newcomers had brought not long before the Romans came, back through several transformations, beyond the Bronze Age to at any rate the New Stone Age. And forwards in time it exerted an influence which is by no means yet extinguished.

Over that time-span some factors persist in curious ways. They form a kind of continuous cord of twisted threads. Pull it, and up may come something from very long ago; perhaps Brigantia herself, the eponymous goddess who may have been the original Bride. That term in this context refers not to some primeval sacrificial maiden for a Stravinsky ballet, but to the ancient, elusive cult-figure known variously as Bride, Brid, Brigid and St Bridget, whose very name may be far older than the Celts.

Brigantia the goddess is vague in outlines, and so is Brigantia the realm. It is not much clarified by the fact that Brigantia the goddess was worshipped by people called Brigantes in what is now Portugal (Braganca) and western Austria (Bregenz, at the eastern end of Lake Constance) as well as in Britain; but tempting sidelights such as these had best be ignored for the purpose of this study: British Brigantia is bad enough. The prehistorians quarrel about its borders – which anyhow must have fluctuated like any frontier. In general, however, it may be accepted that it included Lincolnshire, Yorkshire, Durham, Northumberland (part), Cumberland, Westmorland, Lancashire, part of Derbyshire and Nottinghamshire and Cheshire. In some periods it apparently extended into the Scottish Lowlands.

What all the prehistorians do accept is that the centre of Brigantia was Yorkshire, especially the West Riding. But it is a fundamental mistake to confine one's view on this account to west Yorkshire. The best and most definite monument to Brigantia the goddess was found at Birrens, in Dumfriesshire, and is now in the

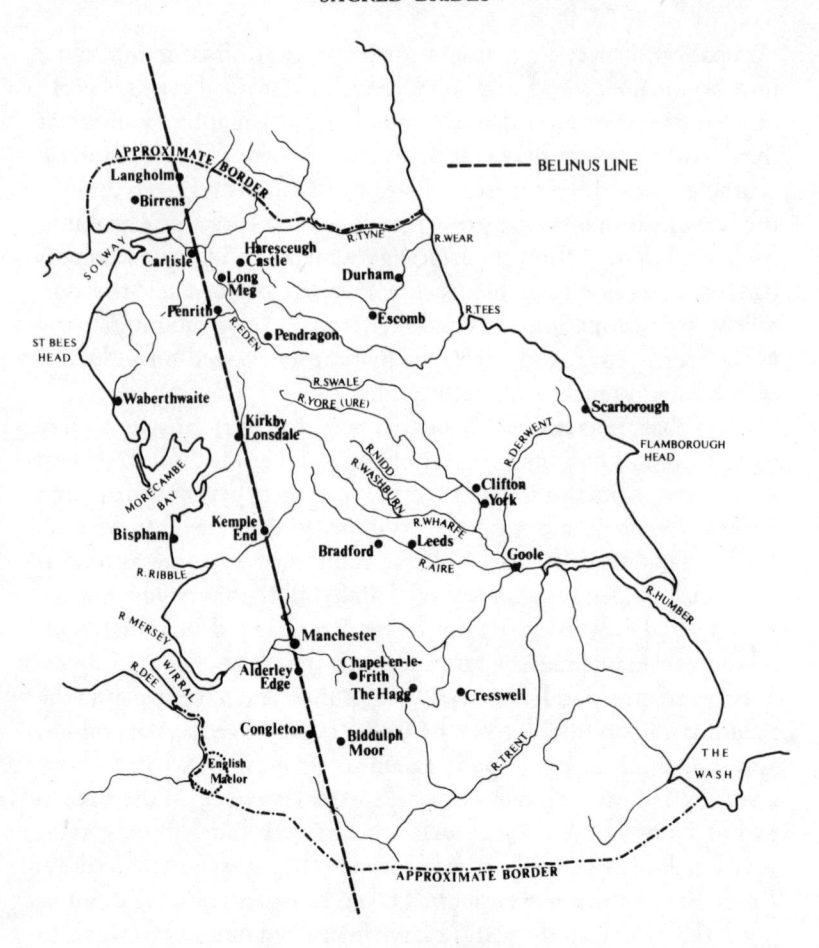

Map 2   Brigantia

National Museum of Antiquities of Scotland. There is a dedication to her from Irthington, east-north-east of Carlisle and not so far from Birrens. An invocation occurs at Corstopitum (Corbridge) on the Tyne. But in Yorkshire, with the exception of a drawing by A. Sutton in Edmund Bogg's *Lower Wharfedale* (1900), no definite monument to Brigantia is known; the drawing, entitled 'Querns found at Wetherby', includes a Roman-type altar which is apparently inscribed 'DEAE V C / TORINE / BRICANT / ADAURS / FAI PLRNV'.

Brigantian objects were included in a hoard recovered from Llyn Cerrig Bach, a lake in Anglesey. The Brigantes established a colony in Ireland. Brigantia the realm cannot be envisaged as widely as this, but obviously it did extend in a very real way far beyond west Yorkshire. Ptolemy, in AD 140, excluded the Brigantes from the territory of the Parisii, corresponding to the East Riding of Yorkshire; but the greater part of the Brigantes were of pre-Celtic stock which certainly covered east Yorkshire before the Parisii arrived; and in any case the Parisii were probably subordinated to Brigantia.

Just as the borders in territory are vague but extensive, so are the borders in time. Nobody can say how long ago Brigantia began, as a divinity or as a political unit; it might be the Bronze Age of, say, 3,000 years ago, or it might be even earlier. It is unlikely to have originated in the Celtic Iron Age that succeeded the Bronze Age in Britain 2,500 years ago. There are some monuments which are virtually peculiar to the territorial Brigantia and which date from the Bronze Age. At the other end of the scale, surprising relics and unconscious remembrances of cultures of long ago are to be found, and are being practised or made, at the present day.

Just off the bottom of Fleet Street, in London, is the famous and beautiful church of St Bride's. At one time King John had a palace here, and in it was a holy well called the Bridewell. Alongside Wren's church in later times there used to be a prison called the Bridewell. From this namesake police cells in other parts of the country – Leeds, for instance – became known as bridewells. There is another Bridewell Prison in Dublin.

Not far from Leeds, to the north-west, ancient tracks cross alongside a ford where one of these tracks goes over the River Washburn; and that point is called the Bride Cross. North-eastward of Leeds, on the other hand, on the North York Moors there are two groups of standing stones, with many miles between the groups, and each group is called the Bride Stones. The group south-east of Chop Gate village marks a former burial chamber. Another group gives its name to Bride Stones Moor, north of

Todmorden on the Yorkshire-Lancashire boundary in the Pennines. Still another group is the Bride Stones at Congleton, Cheshire, which like the Chop Gate group surrounded a barrow burial ground with a long chamber.

In the south-west corner of Brigantia, on a small eminence near Birkenhead called Bidston Hill, are some rocks with strange 'Bride' carvings of which nothing has hitherto appeared in print except a short reference in the book *Mysterious Britain* by Janet and Colin Bord (1973). Bidston Hill is a public open space owned by the National Trust. A long ridge about 250 feet high runs north and south, with a stretch of bare rock 50 yards wide and 500 yards long running along the top. The carvings are at the northern end, and Mr S. G. Wildman, author of *The Black Horsemen*, sends me the following description of them:

> They are (1) a horse executed in dots on a sloping slab of rock. It is certainly older than 1860 for it is referred to in a book of that date as being there and then of unknown age. For various reasons I think it has been there in its present shape since about 1780 but that it was renewed then. It is a conventional horse with an undocked tail. On its lower neck is what seems to be a sun symbol. (2) On another slab of rock a woman also in dots, arms outstretched, something dangling from the right hand, no breasts, but large sexual orifice, and standing on a rayed sun. This I think is Brigid. (3) Near to this but nearly worn away now, a much cruder 'stick woman' of the same type, standing this time on a 'moon'. I think that (2) has been renewed, probably at the same time as (1). (4) A frieze of pictures – man holding knife, headless woman, pleading figure, hand holding wine-bottle. These are on an upright wall of rock, a natural fault. I think this is connected with the Mummers' Play ritual and may not have anything to do with the other figures. (5) Statue (bust) of a woman, said by Mr. Sidney Jackson of Bradford to be definitely Celtic in style.

All over the country are memories of Bride. Sometimes,

especially in Ireland, she becomes St Bridget or Brigid. In Devon there are Bridestow and Bridford, in Dorset there is Bridport. Within Brigantia itself, in Cumberland there is Bridekirk with a church of St Bridget; St Bridget's Beckermet, on the coast; the ancient church of St Bridget at Bassenthwaite; and at Kirkbride a pre-Conquest church described as 'dedicated to St Bride, in honour of a religious Irishwoman, called St. Brydock, corrupted into St. Bride') in the words of the 1881 *Historical Guide to Carlisle and District*). Just across the Solway Firth, but still in Brigantia, is Brydekirk.

It is not only the name that is common to at least some of these widely separated places. With small variations, many of them share a curious and rather sinister legend. The Bride Cross beside the Washburn, like both groups of Bride Stones on the Yorkshire Moors, is said to mark the spot where a man's bride was slain for infidelity and her spirit is said to haunt the locality. The legend, like some others to be found in the same areas, has a ring of human sacrifice long ago. Perhaps we are not so far after all from Stravinsky's *prima ballerina*.

Bridget, Brigid, Bride and other variants – the figures are too full of coincidences to be accidental. These are manifestations of a single individual, who must be regarded as a cult-object. Dr Anne Ross in her authoritative *Pagan Celtic Britain* (1967) points out this fact, accepts Bride as one of the major goddesses of the British Celtic pantheon, and considers that she may be identical with Brigantia the mother-goddess of the Brigantes.

But these Brigantes, the most powerful political unit of Celtic-speaking Britain, who derived their own descent from the womb of Brigantia, were formed only partly of Iron Age Celts. The majority of the rest were people whom the Celts found in Britain and conquered. Broadly speaking, they represented the end of the Bronze Age in Britain; but some may represent an even earlier population originating from the Stone Age.

It is generally believed that Brigantia's pre-Celtic peoples were ruled by a Celtic aristocracy, and that the culture of the realm was mainly Celtic. These assumptions may have been made somewhat too lightly and too sweepingly. There can be little doubt that the language mainly spoken in Brigantia was Celtic; but Dr Ross and others believe that the pre-Celtic language, too, was a kind of proto-Celtic, and was the vehicle of a proto-Celtic culture. If that were so, then there might have been little cultural 'imperialism' on the part of the Celtic newcomers.

It should be remembered, however, that some authorities see the Basques, and perhaps the Albanians and Berbers, as the last relics of an Iberian non-Celtic people who once inhabited most of Europe and North Africa, and their languages as the only surviving representatives of the tongue spoken by that people.

Pre-Roman Celtic culture is designated as La Tène, from a marshy place at the eastern end of Lake Neuchâtel in Switzerland, where the Celts deposited a huge treasure in the lake in sacrificial offerings. It does not appear to have been noticed that at the opposite end of Lake Neuchâtel is a place called Yverdun, which might be read (in Celtic) as Iberian Fort.

Too little attention has been paid so far to the question of the more distant predecessors of the Celts. But Professor Stuart Piggott, in *Ancient Europe* (1965), although he does not mention Brigantia, the Brigantes, Bride or the Basques at all, does say: 'In Iberia [there were] a Celtic population mainly in the centre and west of the peninsula, Iberians (with a non-Indo-European language) in the south and east, and a mixed Celtic-Iberian element resulting from a mingling of the two.' This is his only reference to the Iberians, who are not even indexed. On the previous page, however, he says: 'In the Pictish area of Eastern Scotland linguistic considerations suggest the mingling of a P-Celtic [one of the two groups of Celtic languages] not identical with Old Brittonic and presumptively earlier with a local [what does that mean?] non-Indo-European language.' The Picts are not indexed, either.

In the Celtic expansion the process of cultural development was probably in part two-way, rather than purely a matter of imposition of their own culture by the Celts on the communities whom they conquered. The Celts, when they erupted over Europe, may have absorbed the cults of the Iberians or proto-Celts in addition to their own. Ross mentions an Irish myth according to which the goddess Eriú welcomed the Gaelic Celtic incomers but begged that her name should be that of the island for ever (so it became Eire): 'It would seem that the invaders brought their own god(s) with them, but that the goddess(es) of the conquered tribe must be propitiated or destroyed.' It is well known that when Christianity came to Britain, it 'canonised' pagan divinities, holy places and religious customs. Might not the same thing have happened when the Celts took over the land in northern England and its cult of the goddess Brigantia? It is to be expected. And if that were so, then there would be a continuity of culture backwards in time from, for example, the Leeds police bridewell to a major divinity of the Bronze or Stone Age.

The Iberians indeed have never completely vanished from Brigantia. They have been identified as (to go beyond Brigantia itself) the 'dark Irish beyond Shannon' and similar groups not only in central Wales (and Tacitus in AD 118 described the Silures of south Wales as dark and curly-haired – exactly as the ominous maiden is described in the Welsh *mabinogi* of *Peredur the Son of Evrawc*) but in remote pockets in England.

On the south-west borders of Brigantia, close to the Bride Stones of Congleton, is Biddulph Moor, where there may still be found very dark, short-statured people who are obviously different from Celts, Saxons and Normans. This community used to be noted for its unwelcoming attitude to outsiders – an attitude which may have been only too well justified in past experience. There is or was a similar group at Churchtown near Southport in Lancashire. Mr S. G. Wildman gives me the following list of further places he knows of where the 'dark people' used to be: Lindow End, Heyhead, Rudheath, Sale near Manchester, Monk's Heath, Halton near Runcorn, all in Cheshire. 'Also possibly (at least I think so) the salt-and-sand people of Ruiton near Sedgley in the Black Country.' He adds:

> Most of the people thereabouts (i.e. around Sedgley) think they are gypsies, but I don't. They used to go around selling salt and sand (for sanding stone floors) and had various odd customs. They were called Hyde or Marsh or Watton, but I think they have all gone now.

Mr D. Elliston Allen, in *British Tastes: An Enquiry into the Likes and Dislikes of the Regional Consumer* (1968), sharply distinguishes the urban Midlanders from the rural. He sees the latter as Saxon, while the former are typical 'Brummies', small, slightly built, wiry people with dark hair, narrow heads and sharp, almost chiselled features, their accent 'a faintly sing-song often rasping twang'. He regards them as racial descendants of 'the old native British stock, penned up in the vast wedge of forests – Arden and Needwood, Charnwood and Rockingham – that formerly covered the entire central Midlands, their land unwanted by several waves of invaders because the heavy clay soils made it too intractable for agriculture.' He sees them as having a background of charcoal-burning and tanning and as having become skilled in the fashioning of iron and leather. 'From saddles and stirrups they moved on to saucepans and guns, from these on to bicycle parts, and from these on to cars.' This would accord with the opinion of Mr Beram Saklatvala (*Arthur: Roman Britain's Last Champion*, 1967) that Arthur's sword Excalibur probably came from just that region.

There is a curious piece of evidence, hitherto unremarked, relating to the old Celtic-speaking kingdom of Elmet, which was centred near Leeds and extended from Tadcaster or even York to the central Pennines. Towards the eastern end, between the rivers Nidd and Wharfe, Elmet is traversed from south to north by the A1 road, which crosses the Wharfe at Wetherby and goes northward over the Nidd by Walshford Bridge. Just east of Wetherby is the village of Walton. In such instances Wal- or Walsh- generally stands for Welsh (meaning foreign) as applied not by Celts to themselves but to Celts or Celtic-speaking peoples by Saxons. The implication is that these names were given at a time when the countryside around had become Saxon, but when this pocket of territory was still Celtic-speaking.

Walton, however, was the original seat of the Fairfax family which became famous in the Civil War with its two military leaders of the Parliamentarians, but which achieved distinction in other ways as well. One of its eminent members will figure large and strange later in these pages. Meanwhile the notable fact is its name, Fairfax. It means 'fair-haired'.

The Celts are as fair-haired as the Saxons, and indeed of very similar general characteristics. If the Celtic-speakers of Walton had been tall and fair-haired, it would have been nonsense to surname a family living among them as 'fair-haired'. It makes sense only if the people generally were contrastingly dark. It would be interesting to survey the area now for dark-haired short inhabitants.

North of York, on the eastern side of Ouse and Swale and adjoining the Walton-Walshford pocket, was the King's Forest of Galtres. This name had seemed to me perhaps capable of interpretation as 'Gal-Trees' ('Gal-' can be a variant of 'Wal-'). Mr Geoffrey M. Cowling, the careful and well informed author of *The History of Easingwold and the Forest of Galtres*, assures me that the name is Scandinavian and means 'boars' brushwood' (although boars are the only game of which there is no record in Galtres). It is odd to note, however, that Shakespeare in *Henry IV Part 2*, Act 4, Scene 1, sets the action in 'Yorkshire within the Forest of Gaultree'; and in *Henry VI* at the corresponding spot – *Part 2*, Act 4, Scene 1 – he has Whitmore saying that he does not care whether his first name is represented as Gualtier or Walter, which is really the same point.

Dealing with another Walton, Leslie Alcock in *Arthur's Britain* (1971) says: 'Unfortunately a modern Walton may originally have been the *tun*, "farmstead or village," by forest – *weald*; with a wall – *weall*; or belonging to the British – *weala*.'

He adds some pertinent points on population:

> The Old English word *wealh* (plural *weala*) is also significant for the social status of the Britons for it came to mean 'serf' as well as 'Welshman'. In both senses it would seem appropriate to the Britons whom Æthelfrith subjugated.
>
> Yet this was not the only social position which a Briton might occupy. In the late seventh century the laws promulgated by King Ine of Wessex make it clear that

Welshmen might be substantial landowners, at some legal disadvantage compared with Englishmen, but still far from servile in their status. In other words, when the laws of Ine were drawn up, Britons formed a definite and often substantial element in society.

A little later, similarly, he writes that when Edwin of Northumbria took possession of Elmet and drove out Ceretic the King, 'there is no reason to think that anyone was affected beyond the King and his war-band'.

It is as a matter of fact possible that the Normans favoured the Celtic Britons within England (not in Wales) as a counter-balance to the Saxons; and it is in the same way possible that at the earlier stage in history the conquering Saxons made use of a counter-balance to the Celts in the Celtic-speaking, but dark-haired and short-statured people whom they found at Biddulph Moor and perhaps the Walton-Walshford pocket.

In some areas the Celts or proto-Celts and the Iberians may have kept themselves separate with a no-man's-land between them – like the length of Lake Neuchâtel. In some areas the Celts may have dominated and oppressed the others. In some areas, however, the two peoples certainly merged into a particularly strong group such as the 'Celtiberians' around the headwaters of the Tagus and Ebro in Spain. They had a capital at Numantia, and put up a powerful resistance to the Romans. Later, when absorbed into the Empire, they formed perhaps the best soldiers of the whole Roman army. All the same, it was the Ninth (Spanish) Legion that vanished or was withdrawn from Britain in AD 122, shortly after a major revolt of the Brigantes, and disappeared from the Roman army lists. The Ninth was stationed at York, immediately alongside the Walton-Walshford pocket and the Forest of Galtres.

The argument as to whether or not the Bronze Age people of Britain were 'Hallstatt' proto-Celts of the same cultural group as the Iron Age Celts who came later, has little real meaning. It is rather like arguing whether the plays were really written by William Shakespeare or by another man of the same name. The cultural continuity is not affected – and in any case the continuity goes in some respects past the Iron Age La Tène, past Hallstatt, to inhabitants of Brigantia whom it would be stretching terms much too far to designate as Celtic in any way at all – the sort of Stone Age people whom Professor Piggott might describe as speaking a 'local non-Indo-European language'.

2
SPIDER'S WEB

If we are to talk about Brigantia in the Stone Age, then we cannot avoid talking about leys. Even those who deny their existence must admit that the mere idea of the leys is vital to our whole notion of Stone Age man and cannot be ignored.

The name 'leys' was given by the late Alfred Watkins, author of *The Old Straight Track* (1927), to alignments which he believed to indicate Stone Age routes. He argued that since men in those days travelled only on foot, the quickest way between any two points was generally a straight line. This is a feature noted by observers in various 'primitive' societies. For instance, Bernhard Grzimek in his book *He and I and the Elephants*, about his travels in the Ivory Coast of Africa, wrote:

> At last we got to the steep mountain incline. The natives went straight up even when it was so steep we had to go on all fours. . . . There is a difficulty as far as these native paths are concerned. They don't snake their way in curves to follow the slope like ours do, but are as straight as a die. When you are going up hill you feel like going on all fours, and whenever I went downhill I would break into a run and aim at a convenient tree which I could hold on to to slow myself down a bit.

Watkins said that in the Stone Age climate there would be no difficulty in sighting from one eminence to another forty miles away; that between those points the line was marked by artificial features such as mounds, henges, waterflashes, stone circles, tumuli, escarpment notches, menhirs, marker-stones with a top bevel; and that some of these points – especially mounds, and ponds with a central island – became sacred sites, and later came to have churches (or, if enlarged, castles) built on them.

Working mainly on the 1-inch Ordnance Survey maps of Shropshire and Radnorshire, he showed many examples of such alignments, particularly through old churches. On a single OS sheet he put a pencil ring round eighty-seven points marked by the OS in 'Gothic' lettering as indicating an antiquity. On another sheet of the same size, but blank, he marked eighty-seven spots haphazard. Comparing results on the two sheets, he reached the conclusion that an alignment of three points along a two-foot rule (i.e. twenty-four miles) proved nothing, since the frequency was almost exactly the same on both sheets; that an alignment of four points indicated a strong probability of a deliberately surveyed line – a 'ley'; and that five or more amounted to a certainty since they never occurred on the haphazard sheet but often did on the OS.

He was laughed out of court by most of the professional archaeologists. Nevertheless, much of this had already been said in 1904 by Dr Moeller, Director of the Royal Museum in Copenhagen, from observations in Jutland; and later by Col. Kitson Clark, a prominent Leeds industrialist and painstaking archaeologist, who applied Moeller's discoveries to the enormous number of tumuli (a wiseacre has called them 'tumulative evidence') and very long and deep 'entrenchments' in east Yorkshire. In recent years, as new generations of archaeologists have extended and intensified the field of study, there has been a resurgence of sober scientific interest in Watkins's propositions. At the time of writing (Spring 1975), Peter Mabey of Millfield School, and Hugh Burnett, a computer executive of an industrial firm concerned in cash registers, aided by Millfield pupils, are using a computer to test the odds for and against the actual alignments on a number of 'leys' in Somerset and Dorset; Philip

Ledger, of the University College of North Wales, is using a computer for allied research in Anglesey; similar data are to be analysed by computer at Santa Barbara, California, in association with Donald Cyr; Robert Brown, in the *Ley Hunter* magazine No. 62/63, has explained a mathematical formula for calculating the chance-element on a width-tolerance of 100 metres, applied it in an area 7 miles by 11 miles of north Staffordshire, and found 9 leys including one with 6 potential ley-points, one with 7 and one with 12 – the latter giving odds of more than 1,000 million millions to 1 against chance. In addition the mathematical problem is dealt with fully by Peter Furness, of Durham University, in Paul Screeton's book *Quicksilver Heritage* (1975).

There has also been an enormous resurgence of esoteric and occult interest in the leys which scientists are inclined to dismiss as not so sober. Mabey, dealing with this point, wrote: 'We do not intend to make any comment on the possible significance of ley-lines. We leave that to the experts of the various disciplines involved. Our aim is simply to prove or disprove the existence of alignments.'

When applied to Brigantia, Watkins's principles produce practical results that are so clear that they need await no computer answers. Nothing is more tedious than the detailing of leys, but their existence must be demonstrated. For the sake of example let us consider the OS Pickering sheet, no. 92 of the 1-inch series. On this there are hundreds of cairns and tumuli (i.e. mounds often containing one or more burials, and dating from either the Stone or Bronze Age); 'howes' – larger tumuli; stone circles; crosses; scores of churches which are themselves old, or stand on ancient mounds; many castles, each on a mound (some places, such as Pickering or Kirbymoorside, have not one but two 'castles', of which one is the remnant of a Norman castle, the other an Iron Age hill-fort probably built on an earlier site); 'Roman camps', which are commonly suspected of marking pre-Roman cultural centres and which often fall within the angles of a near-confluence of alignments; 'moats' without castles; abbeys and priories; and very many other features which, while on the surface not apparently significant, turn up with such frequency at important points on alignments that they come to attract attention (crossroads, for instance, or 'MS' milestones, or names such as Cold Harbour, Mount Pleasant, Gallows, Whitethorn, Blackthorn or Primrose Hill).

There is one alignment on this sheet which we may call 'A'. It comes southward (in fact through Upleatham Church on the next sheet) at 4 degrees east of Magnetic South (1974) through the Ralph Crosses, along the Blakey Ridge metalled road from SE 683993 to 684986, then parallel to the road for more than a mile up to Stone Haggs beside Pike Howe, then roughly parallel for nearly 3 miles to Barmoors – a junction of metalled roads where in addition the ancient track along line 'A' can be clearly and impressively seen. From here southwards it runs through Bog Hall, Cartoft, Little Edstone, Rook Barugh and White Thorn, Butterwick, a tumulus and down to 'Castle (site of)' at Leppington.

From Wildon Grange another alignment runs through Shandy Hall and Coxwold Church through the remains of Newburgh Priory, along 2 miles of metalled road, through Mowthorpe Hill, Kirkham Priory ruins, the crossroads at Leavening and another triple junction, up some earthworks and through the tumulus at 808616 and on to the Wolds.

Apart from these, however, there are many other strong alignments on this sheet and most of them go from Blakey Topping. They run to Fimber Church; along the eastern side of the 'Roman fort' at Malton; the moat at West Lilling; Crayke Castle and Church; Husthwaite Church; Gregory's Minster at Kirkdale; Kirbymoorside 'Castle (remains of)' and between Helmsley Church and Castle; southern edge of 'camp' 506855; Bee Stone 681931; Three Howes 715948; the holy well of St Helena 683037; and Sil Howe 852028. Details are given in the Appendix.

These by no means exhaust the number of alignments to be found on this one sheet 92, or even of those leading from Blakey Topping. Anybody can check them, and they are amply sufficient to show that they cannot be haphazard accidents but must be the result of deliberate planning. This at once poses the enormous questions: By whom, and when, and why?

Far more baffling; in Brigantia there are many centres or 'nodes'

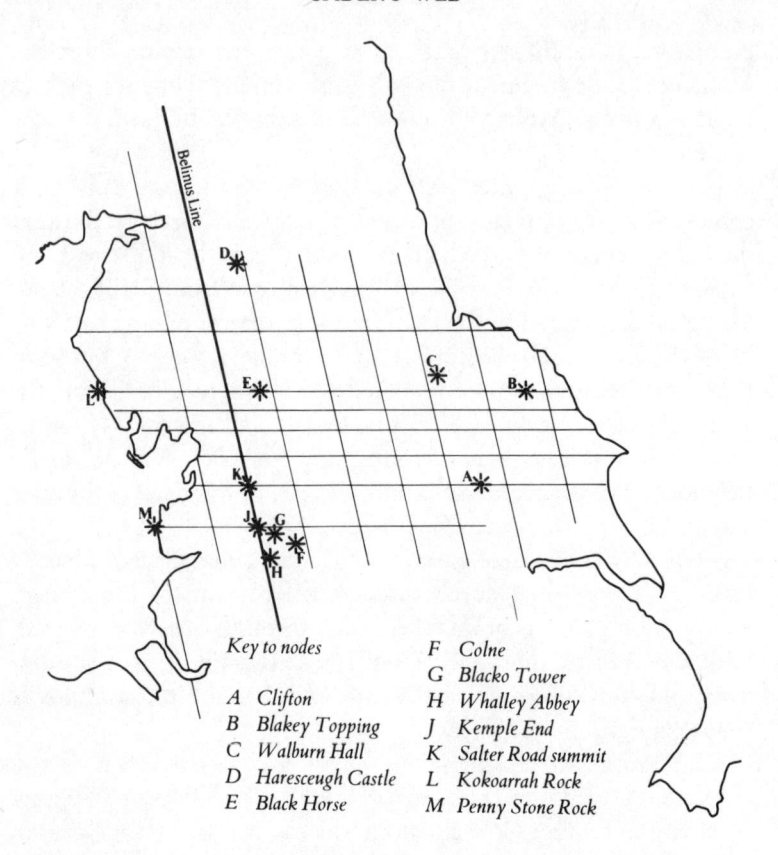

Map 3   Principal nodes and network of alignments in Brigantia

Key to nodes

A Clifton
B Blakey Topping
C Walburn Hall
D Haresceugh Castle
E Black Horse
F Colne
G Blacko Tower
H Whalley Abbey
J Kemple End
K Salter Road summit
L Kokoarrah Rock
M Penny Stone Rock

such as Blakey Topping, some of them with a much larger number of alignments springing from them.

Some of these central points are, like Blakey Topping itself, prominent features which might be expected to have been chosen as pivots in any such prehistoric planning. Other central points leave one wondering why they were selected, and some points that might have been expected to be important in prehistoric times do not appear to be on any such alignments or only on one or two.

These nodes have become a feature familiar to almost anybody who begins seriously investigating alignments in any area. In Brigantia there are undoubtedly many nodes that have escaped notice. Some, however, are Blacko Tower near Colne in Lancashire; Kemple End, near Clitheroe, Lancashire; Walburn Hall, near Richmond, north Yorkshire; the Black Horse, a patch of scree on the slopes of Bush Howe in the Howgill Fells north of Sedbergh; Harescaugh Castle, an insignificant farmhouse where there used to be a small fortress north-east of Penrith; and many others — they are constantly turning up.

Still more perplexing: some of these nodes show no connection with each other, even when they have every other appearance of being linked. For instance, Blakey Topping and Clifton, a mile north of York Minster.

Clifton is a huge enigma in itself. It might have been thought that either York Minster, or the clearly artificial mound of Clifford's Tower nearby, would be a node. In reality not a single ley seems to lead to either of them. This is not so surprising, however, when it is recalled that the earliest relic found in York is the headquarters building of the Roman army, discovered under the foundations of the Minster. The British Kingdom of Brigantia, under its monarch Queen Cartimandua, is believed to have had its capital at York before the Romans came, but no trace of it has been found under the Minster.

A mile to the north is Clifton, where an old ferry across the River Ouse has been replaced by a very busy bridge. Three hundred yards from the ferry the road comes to a triangular village green, a spot of striking beauty surrounded by Victorian housing. On the green is a horse-trough, fed by the culverted Bur Dyke which runs from the enigmatic Burton Stone 300 yards away. The great trees on the green are arranged in two rows at right angles parallel to two of the sides. It is here that scores of alignments converge in what may well be one of the biggest nodes in Britain. The spot has been of such overwhelming importance thousands of years ago that it may have retained sufficient status to be the capital of Cartimandua's Brigantia before the Romans shunted her off upstream to Aldborough. It was not here that the Romans built their army headquarters; but it was here —

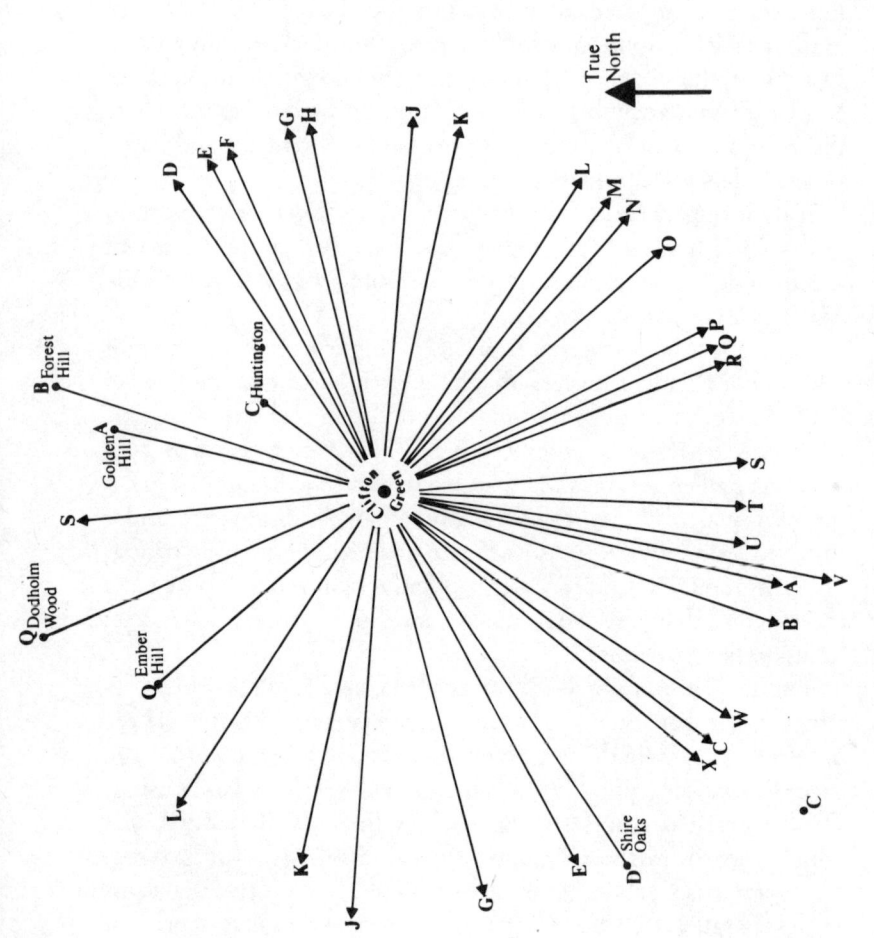

Map 4 Node of alignments to or through Clifton, York

KEY

- AA Golden Hill; Clifton; Temple Hill; Button Hill; Stockbridge; Wood House; Beal.
- BB Forest Hill; Haxby crossroads; Clifton; moat, Appleton Roebuck; Mote Hill, Nun Appleton; Ryther Ferry; moat, Paradise Lodge; Castle Hill, east of Sherburn-in-Elmet, Knottingley; Darrington.
- CC Huntington Church; Clifton; moat, Pallathorpe; Kirkby Wharfe Church; Towton Spring; Saxton Church.
- DD Howsham Church; Willow Bridge; Claxton Church; Clifton; moat, south of Healaugh; Shire Oaks.
- EE (the Fountain Line) Castle site south of Buryhorpe; Mount Pleasant; Clifton; Healaugh Church; Wighill Church; Firgreen Bridge; Clifford Church near Boston Spa. This line extends south-westward to Warrington and north-eastward to Scarborough; it was first noticed in the Oldham area by Mr James Fountain of Shaw.
- F Leppington Castle site; Kirk Gates; Stockton-on-the-Forest; Clifton.
- GG Primrose Hill; Bagthorpe; Skirpenbeck Manor House and Church; another Primrose Hill; Warthill Moat and Church; Clifton; Rufforth Church; Long Marston; Bilton Hall and Manor House; Wetherby Church.
- H Garrowby Hall; Burtonfield Hall; Stamford Bridge; Gate Helmsley Church; Clifton.
- JJ Bolton Moat; Whinberry Hill; Londesborough Lodge; Dunnington Church; Murton Hall; Apple Tree Farm; Clifton; southern edge of Poppleton Villa; Skewkirk Hall.
- KK Kexby Church; Four Lane Ends; Heworth Church; Clifton; Upper Poppleton Church; Whixley crossroads.
- LL Seaton Ross Church; Melbourne Hall; Clifton; Nether Poppleton Church; ferry; Overton Church; Red House; Widdington moat; Aldborough.
- M Storwood moat; Mount Pleasant; Heslington; Siwards How; Clifton.
- N Bursea Lane Ends; Foggathorpe moat; Laytham moat; Heslington Hall; Clifton.
- OO Spaldington Church; Willitoft moat and Hall; Ellerton Church; Thorganby Hall and Church; York Castle; Clifton; Skelton Hall; Ember Hill.
- P Goole; ferry, Boothferry; Aselby Church; Holmes House; Mount Pleasant; Primrose Hill; Clifton.
- QQ Skipwith moat; Fulford Hall; Clifton; Dodholm Wood.
- R Scarff Hall; Hemingbrough Church; Danes Hills tumuli; Escrick Church; Deighton Old Hall; Clifton.
- SS Quosquo Hall; Primrose Hill; Selby Abbey; Wheel Hall; Clifton; Sutton-on-the-Forest Hall and Church.
- T Earth Hill; moats south-east of Chapel Haddlesey; Brayton Barff; Elfhole Farm; Kellfield Manor House; Garth Farm, Acaster Malbis: Bishopthorpe; Clifton.
- U Gateforth; Cawood Bridge; moat north-east of Acaster Selby; Clifton.
- V Wood Hall moat; Hambleton ley-crossroads; Ox Close; Dringhouses; Clifton.
- W Ledston Hall; Lodge; Boot-and-Shoe ley-crossroads (A 63/A 1); Barkston Ash (the tree itself); North Milford Hall; Hornington Bridge; Steeton Hall; Clifton.
- X Lead Church; mounds north-west of Saxton; Towton Hall; Grimston Park tower and flash; Steeton Grange; 1 mile of A 64 to Buckles Inn; Clifton.

somewhere close to the green — that the Romans had their main cemetery.

The point, however, is this: from the great node of alignments at Clifton to the great, although lesser, node at Blakey Topping, there is no trace of a connecting alignment. It is as if they belonged to two distinct systems, perhaps dating from different periods and different cultures. There are other examples of this puzzling disconnection.

The curious will find it easy enough to note plenty of alignments centred on Clifton. On OS 1-inch sheet 97 one may see them, for instance, running to Clifton or through it from Wetherby Church (to Primrose Hill beyond Bugthorpe); Clifford Church (to the Leppington 'Castle site'); the ancient Lead Church (to Huntington Church); Ledston Hall, near Castleford; moat at SE 536206; Gateforth; moat north-west of Brayton at 598308; another Primrose Hill at 620285; Hemingbrough Church; and the point 748231 in the northern angle at the confluence of Dutch River with the Ouse in the middle of Goole Docks. There are many others.

The Goole terminus is a node of peculiar interest. From it an alignment goes through Aberford Church west-north-west right across the country to a node on the Irish Sea coast of Cumbria at Waberthwaite, a small village at the mouth of the River Esk facing the better-known village of Ravenglass on the opposite bank. This alignment passes through many clear marker-points such as, for instance, Settle market-place and the ley-cross in Giggleswick, and in a number of stretches the line may still be traced on the ground. It may indicate a Stone Age route across Britain for continental communication with Ireland.

Worse yet. We have one system of alignments and nodes which includes Blakey Topping, and apparently a quite distinct system of alignments and nodes which includes Clifton and Goole and Waberthwaite. There is also, however, at least one other almost unrelated system. It passes through Blakey Topping and the Goole node, but only as it were in passing. This third system is laid out not on a nodal pattern, but as a web. The alignments run either northward on 4 degrees west of Magnetic North (1974) — i.e. southward on 4 degrees east of Magnetic South — or due east–west according to the latitude. A few of the many points at which the two sets of alignments cross are developed as nodes.

The line 'A' described earlier on, running northward from the 'Castle site' of Leppington to the Ralph Crosses (still on the OS Pickering sheet) belongs to this third system. The network is so important that it is necessary to follow it westwards across Brigantia. Starting from the east, the first line runs northward to terminate at Whitby Abbey. Three miles west of this is a line running from Snainton through Aislaby NZ 858086 (the Aislaby near Whitby, not the one near Pickering). One mile further west comes an indistinct line from a 'Castle mound' at NZ 832118 through Sil Howe and Blakey Topping.

Farther west is a triad of parallel alignments. The first is $11\frac{3}{4}$ miles west of the Whitby line, and runs through Herd Howe, between the public house and the River Seven at Hartoft End, along the metalled road through Cropton Forest, through the Castle Mound at Cropton, across the main A 170 road at Wrelton (where it can clearly be seen in a field on the north side of the road at the western end of the village), and through Kirby Misperton Church.

A mile and a half to the west is a line through Pike Howe, Castleton Church, Botton, Lastingham Church, High Cross and Low Cross at Appleton-le-Moors, Friars Hill and Great Habton. The third alignment, rather more than a mile and a half further west, is our line 'A' from Upleatham, $11\frac{3}{4}$ miles west of the Aislaby line. Most of the north–south lines are about this latter distance apart, and a further 12 miles westwards brings us to a strongly marked line from Mount Pleasant Grange at Stockton-on-Tees through Miley Pike and Coxwold Church; but this is only the second line of a close sequence.

The eastern line is $2\frac{1}{4}$ miles away, running through Stainton and Thornton-in-Cleveland through Old Byland and forms a track straight across Wass Moor. The third line runs from Yarm by Mount Grace Priory, and thereafter is not very distinct. Fourth, $3\frac{1}{2}$ miles to the west, comes a line from Deighton through the western end of Thirsk by Aldwark Toll Bridge, Healaugh Church, Kellington and Whitley. Two and a half miles west of this is an extremely strong alignment on the ancient bridge at Romanby, Northallerton; the church between Newby Wiske and South Otterington; Kirby Wispe churchyard; Sandhutton; the Topcliffe-Asenby road; Tockwith (really Cowthorpe) Broad Oak; Newton Kyme Hall; Barkston Ash; and South Milford. Two and a half miles west again is a line through Cowton Castle, Arkendale and Bramham Church (in all these cases, of course, only the most important points are mentioned).

Twelve miles west of the Northallerton line is one on Constable Burton Hall, Ellingstring, Lobley Hall, Birstwith, Castley, Arthington, the centre of Leeds, and Howe Hill south of Wakefield. Exactly 12 miles west again is a line running through earthworks on Addingham Moor, East Riddlesden Hall, the 'Fairfax Entrenchments' above Keighley, Harden Hall, the major crossroads at Queensbury, Southowram Church, and the middle of Huddersfield. This is the centre line of another triad. A line 3 miles to the east goes through Maidenkirk SE 095550 and Upper Hapton Church 198185, and the western line through Thorpe Fell summit 598007 to Golcar Church 097008.

From the central line of this triad $11\frac{1}{2}$ miles west is a line from Hellifield crossroads through Barnoldswick Church, Foulridge Church, an earthwork near Thursden SD 902352, the centre of the ridge of Black Hameldon (a hill-name constantly found on leys), Lydgate Church, Butcher Hill Church, and Calderbrook Church. Twelve miles west is the next alignment, which is to be known as the Belinus Line for reasons to be explained later. On sheet 95 it runs from the gate at the summit of the unpaved Salter Road at SD 652588 through Sugar Loaf Hill near Dunsop Bridge, exactly across the central entrance hall of Browsholm Hall 683453, a node at Kemple End 695402, and Old Langho.

Twelve miles west again is a line running across Morecambe Bay from Guides Farm to Morecambe (the bay was dry land in the Stone Age), through Garstang to Castle Hill at Penwortham and on by Leyland to the major crossroads in the centre of Warrington. West once more $11\frac{3}{4}$ miles is an alignment the northern end of which is at the Penny Stone, a rock with an iron ring in it, which stands nearly a mile to seaward off the Bispham

Promenade at Blackpool. Visible only at very low tides, it stands beside the site of the inn at Singletonthorpe, a village which was swallowed up by the sea a century or so ago.

From the same Penny Stone an alignment runs due east on latitude 53 degrees 51·5 minutes through Kemple End on the Belinus Line (where it is a very distinct public path), by Colne Church (another node), Long Lee just east of Keighley, through Esholt Hall, Slaid Hill, Bramham crossroads (a node), and just north of Beverley to the sea half-way between Aldbrough and Mappleton.

Nearly 8½ miles north of this alignment is another going due east from Cockersand Abbey through Hammerton Hall SD 719538, Embsay, Harlow Hill near Harrogate, Ribston Hall, Upper Poppleton Church (a node), Holtby Church and to the coast close to Skipsea Castle. One mile south of this line, however, is a parallel from Cockerham through Top of Blaze Moss SD 619525, Slaidburn (it is very clear here), Flambers Hill SD 877523, southern edge of Copy Hill 952523, Draughton (extremely clear), Beamsley Gibbeter and Beamsley Beacon, Heligar Pike, Scow Hall 203523, Little Almscliffe Crag, Tockwith Church and on to the coast. This line turns out to be the centre of another triad, the third alignment lying just a mile to the south. It runs between Holdron Castle and Longden Castle, immediately south of Sugar Loaf on the Belinus Line (where it is very noticeable), Castle Haugh SD 830508, Marton Church, yet another Primrose Hill SD 937508, the 'Tree of Life' carved 'cup-and-ring' stone on Snowden Carr at SD 180504, Sunrise Farm 330504, Kirk Deighton Church, Long Marston Church, Keasby Church, Wilberfoss Church and to the coast.

Probably included in this system is an alignment which runs almost, but not quite, due east from Waberthwaite, the little coastal village near Ravenglass in Cumberland. Starting off at 54 degrees 20·5 minutes north, it runs across the country to Blakey Topping at 54 degrees 19·5 minutes. At SE 725938 it runs through Ana (or 'One Howe') Cross, a large tumulus. One mile east-south-east across the moor from Ana Cross is another tumulus known as Abraham's Hut. Between Ana Cross and Abraham's

Hut it is possible to find on the surface of the moor (Redman Plain) pieces of magnetite.

This moor overlooks the valley of the River Seven in Rosedale. Kendall and Wroot in their classical work *The Geology of Yorkshire* (1924) point out that at Rosedale the 'dogger' iron ore underlying the North York Moors changes to what was formerly a very rich deposit of magnetite, now worked out. Magnetite is the iron ore otherwise known as lodestone; if a long, narrow piece of it is suspended on a thread or (as the Arab navigators used to do) floated on water, it will point to Magnetic North.

The Rosedale rock may still be found in small pieces, but some geologists tend to describe it as not true magnetite. It is a hard, heavy, dark blue, shaly rock which splinters and powders easily into crumbs, whereas the 'true' magnetite is brown, with a sheen resulting from a micro-crystalline structure. It has been suggested that the Rosedale material would not act as a lodestone. In reality it does, with considerable strength. If, for example, a fragment $\frac{1}{4}$ inch long and $\frac{1}{8}$ inch wide be placed on a piece of flat but pointed wood which is then floated on a saucer of water, it will within a minute or so settle down to point the wood north and south. Not only this: the powdered crumbs of the rock, laid lengthwise along a similar piece of wood, and arranged in ionised formation by moving a magnet under the wood, will have the same effect. Very small pieces of the stone can thus be used as easily portable compasses. Indeed, a fragment $\frac{3}{16}$ inch long and $\frac{1}{16}$ inch wide will rest on the surface tension of water, and will instantly point north–south. And one of our north–south parallel alignments lies precisely on the source of the stone.

The whinstone which forms a ridge right across Brigantia (and extends to the Isle of Mull) is also said to be magnetic, sometimes more strongly so than the Rosedale magnetite. This is not correct. It may be slightly magnetic, but too weakly to be usable as a lodestone. By a curious circumstance, a prominent outcrop of the whinstone at Egton is only seven miles from the Rosedale magnetite deposit.

Over a period of 120 years Magnetic North is known to have swung through no less than 35 degrees, from 24 degrees east of

True North to 11 degrees west of it. The movement is believed to be cyclical.

Magnetic North is now moving slowly back eastwards towards True North, but is still (1974) nearly $9\frac{1}{2}$ degrees west. If the movement is indeed cyclical, then the north–south alignments such as the Belinus Line, which are 4 degrees west of Magnetic North, would on many occasions since the Stone Age have fallen exactly on Magnetic North. There are many alignments which nearly, but not quite, fall on the 'Belinus' orientation. They might have been laid down with the aid of lodestones, but not at the same period as the general network. That general network could have been laid down by lodestones, but all more or less in the same period of a few years at most.

The east–west lines could have been laid down at any period by the equinoctial sunrise or sunset, spring or autumn, but might be affected by the intervention of high land; and some of these lines might show some distortion as they pass over the Pennines.

The web network of alignments came to light only as a result of the intensive plotting of lines in Brigantia. Its implications, however, are of great importance. The system may be said to pivot on what has been here termed the Belinus Line. That alignment is capable of extension southwards to Lee-on-Solent and northwards to Inverhope on the north coast of Scotland. The next line to the west, which crosses Morecambe Bay, can also be extended across the Solway Firth by a still existing ford with an 'Altar Stone' in mid-passage; but the Firth, like the Bay, was dry land in the Stone Age. Northwards this line would lead to Cape Wrath, southwards to the Channel a little east of Bournemouth. None other but these two of the north–south alignments could be regarded as a 'through route' the length of the island. Of the two, the easterly one is the more strongly marked and the more central and that is why this alignment, quite arbitrarily, has been assigned a name which bids fair to become a type designation.

Like Alfred Watkins, another researcher who long aroused the angry scorn of academic experts was the monk known as Geoffrey of Monmouth, who in 1136 completed writing a *History of the Kings of Britain* (*Historia Regum Britanniae*). Lewis Thorpe's translation and introduction to this extraordinary work is one of the most important instances of the new serious scholarly attitude to it. It has previously been generally accepted that up to the Saxon period, Geoffrey had simply invented all his kings and their deeds.

Geoffrey was an official of the Church at Oxford, and a man of some considerable authority. Professionally, however, he came under the dominion of Walter, Archdeacon of Oxford, a man whose learning and integrity are admitted. Geoffrey claims in his text that he obtained his material for the pre-Saxon history from an ancient book, written in Welsh and given to him by Walter. One of the several dedications of his *History* was to Walter, and the powerful Walter not long afterwards secured the Bishopric of St Asaph's in Wales for Geoffrey.

The scoffers always pointed out that there was no other record of that ancient Welsh book. Surely, however, Geoffrey – an obviously astute careerist – would never have been such a fool as to pretend that his patron had given him a unique source, and then dedicated his own work to that same patron. Nor, if he had done so, can it be imagined that Walter would have so rewarded him with the see of St Asaph's. On the face of it, the likelihood is that Geoffrey was telling the truth.

Again, the scoffers remarked that one of Geoffrey's main characters, a King Belinus who reigned over all Britain about 500 BC, never existed, and that there was no such kingdom anyhow at that time. In reality, Geoffrey's story has quite startling implications. What he says is that the kingdom was shared between two brothers, Brennius, the younger, who ruled from the Humber to Caithness, and Belinus, who ruled the rest and was superior to Brennius. Together they sacked Rome 'about 500 years before Caesar'. At another period they quarrelled and fought (perhaps in the Forest of Galtres near York), and Belinus won and established his rule over the whole island, later making it up with his brother. The classical historians record that in 390 BC – that is, about a century later than Geoffrey's date – Rome was sacked by a Gaulish (i.e. Celtic) chieftain named not Brennius but Brennus.

Either of these variants would be a normal Latinised version of a Celtic name Bren, just as Belinus is accepted to be a Latinisation of

Celtic Bel or Beli. Bel or Beli was the oldest and chief god of all the Celts, and may have been taken over by them from peoples and cultures which they conquered and displaced. The Bren who truly did sack Rome would have been a worshipper of Beli. The tradition recorded by Geoffrey is therefore very close to the probable fact. It is also worth suggesting that so powerful a chieftain as Bren, who ravaged Rome, was likely to have found his own way into folklore, and may be the origin of the gigantic, semi-divine Celtic hero Bran the Blessed (Bendigeidfran).

But it may also be thought that Geoffrey's account describes a period in which all Celts acknowledged the supreme divinity of Beli, but in which the authority of his priesthood was challenged by a chieftain who, though powerful enough to raid Rome, was acknowledged as ruler by only a part of the Celts.

Belinus and Brennius, according to Geoffrey, were the sons of King Dunvallo Molmutius. This monarch, in the Lewis Thorpe translation, 'decreed that the temples of the gods and the cities should be so privileged that anyone who escaped to them as a fugitive or when accused of some crime must be pardoned by his accuser when he came out'. He also decreed 'that the roads which led to these temples and cities should be included in the same law'.

This law goes far beyond the medieval idea of sanctuary, which protected a person only as long as he remained in the specified building, and which did not include the road to it. But if it be supposed — as has been suggested — that the nodes of leys mark the sites of ancient temples or cities, then the Molmutine or Mamutine Laws, as they became known, would have given fugitives extraordinarily numerous means of permanent escape.

Perhaps the priesthood of Beli had to make some concessions to the chieftains in order to beat back Bren's challenge. Geoffrey says that when Belinus had defeated Brennius and assumed the rule of the whole island he ratified the Molmutine Laws, especially that 'cities and the roads leading to cities' should have the right of sanctuary which Dunvallo had established. The roads themselves were a bone of contention, for no one knew just where their boundaries should be.

'The King was very keen to remove every ambiguity from this law,' continues the Thorpe translation. 'He summoned workmen from all over the island and ordered them to construct a road of stones and mortar which should bisect the island longitudinally from the Cornish sea to the shore of Caithness and should lead in a straight line to each of the cities on the route.' He ordered a second road to be built from St David's (Pembrokeshire) to Hamo's Port (Southampton), and two other roads diagonally across the island. The presumption is that the right of sanctuary was confined to these four roads specifically, and perhaps left uncertain on all the others.

Geoffrey's denigrators insisted that only the Romans built straight roads (this idea has now been thoroughly discarded) and that only the Romans built roads of stone and mortar. They also pointed out that on the map it was demonstrably impossible to build a straight road from Cornwall to Caithness except over unacceptably wide stretches of sea.

Rachel Bromwich, however, in her *Trioedd Ynys Prydein: The Welsh Triads* (1961) points out that as late as the Middle Ages the term 'Cornwall' referred to the whole Dumnonian Peninsula up to Gloucester, and earlier appeared to include everything south of the Severn and Thames, and that 'Caithness' covered the whole north coast of Scotland. Two strong alignments in the Brigantian area can be extended all the way within those limits, and of the two the eastern is the stronger. It seemed only fair to name this the Belinus Line.

The Belinus Line is probably sufficiently authenticated by observations on the field, above all where it passes through Brigantia.

Between Hollowgate Farm, near Shap, and Kemple End, near Clitheroe, the Line passes through at least forty 'potential ley points' which have been checked in the field. The distance is 40 miles. That is an average of one per mile, which is also very close to the highest average obtained by Mr Brown in north Staffordshire (twelve points in about 12 miles on a ley assumed to be 100 yards wide). The odds against that alignment being random were calculated by Mr Brown at more than 1,000 million millions to one. The odds against a similar incidence occurring on a single alignment not 12 but 40 miles long are enormously higher.

This is not the place to examine that line in all its astonishing detail from one end to the other. It is sufficient to remark that, going southwards, it passes through a very large prehistoric settlement at Lairg; through the remarkable Church of Insh near Kincraig; along a street right through Pitlochry; precisely over the Forth Railway Bridge(!); through the middle of Langholm; Carlisle (Stanwix); precisely along almost the whole route of the Haweswater–Manchester water pipeline(!); through Salford, Alderley Edge, various roads and streets through the western half of Birmingham, the great crossroads at Moreton-in-the-Marsh (coinciding for a mile here with the railway!), Carterton (coinciding for 2 miles with a main road), the exact centre of Winchester, and down to the Solent.

This begins to make sense of Geoffrey's account. The Thorpe edition avoids a reading in the earlier Giles version which explicitly stated that the law of sanctuary was thereafter limited to these new roads; nevertheless, it is scarcely possible to imagine any other reason for them – except one, and that one calls for the establishment of many other routes parallel to these four new ones. The fact is that if a chief priest of Beli had his seat at, say, Clifton, and if he had a courier stationed at each intersection of the web of north–south and east–west routes, then he could send orders to, or receive information from, any part of Britain within twenty-four hours, each courier having to run only 10 or 12 miles. That is much better than our modern Post Office can manage.

As it happens, however, Clifton is not on any of the leys that form the web. Indeed, within Brigantia at any rate few of the more important nodes are on the web, although some of the web junctions such as Kemple End are minor nodes. It looks rather as if the web system may belong to a different date from the big nodes. Geoffrey's account may contain an explanation. According to him, Belinus laid down his four roads about 500 BC. That was in fact about the time when the Iron Age Celts came to Britain. It is thought by modern archaeologists that in Europe as a whole they subdued Celts of the Bronze Age. If that is correct, it might be suggested that the hero of the 'Bronze' Celts was the original of Bran the Blessed, that he was overcome by other followers of Beli but allowed a tributary dominion and that later in alliance the forces of both factions were united in the raid on Rome. In this case the great ley-nodes such as Clifton would belong to an earlier culture (the 'cities and temples' and the roads leading to them) than the web; and since there appeared to be two distinct sets of nodes, one of these may be older than the other; as for instance that the nodes on Blakey Topping and the Howgill Black Horse (natural features) pre-date those of Clifton (a ferry) or Kendal Castle, and originate in times before the Celts altogether. But this is pure conjecture, and many of the sites linked by the supposedly late Belinus Line are themselves apparently early, such as the Lairg settlement.

One difficulty is that all the leys, whether of the web or of the nodes, appear today very similar. The Belinus Line itself, and the parallel to the west of it, are both cobbled in parts (though evidence of mortaring has yet to be discerned, and the date of the cobbles cannot be established) and they are both indistinguishable in other stretches. The same is true for nodal leys. All three sets of leys — the two nodal sets and the web — have similar marking-points, among which old churches and church-sites are probably the strongest.

Another strange fact is that many human monuments of comparable antiquity do not appear to fall on more than one ley or indeed on any ley at all. The famous Swastika Stone on Ilkley Moor — a very striking example of the 'cup-and-ring' type of carving — seems to lie on only one alignment, which passes also through the similarly carved Badger Stone on the same moor. The three Devil's Arrows at Boroughbridge are in alignment with one ley and are the initial point of another, but that seems to be all.

Some outstanding natural features which cannot fail to have impressed men of all times are no more prominent in the ley pattern. The natural rock 'giantesses' Jenny Twigg and her Daughter Tib, on the escarpment above Ramsgill in Upper Nidderdale, seem to be merely the initial point of two leys. The mind-bending Brimham Rocks, not far away, and their attendant prehistoric cemetery of Graffa Plains, and the near-by Brimham Beacon, appear to be all on a single alignment – and one of not much importance. And yet that patch of scree in the Howgills, the Black Horse – so evanescent that some people can deny its existence at all – is a ley-node as important as Blakey Topping if not Clifton (incidentally nobody appears to have noticed that there is an almost identically shaped scree almost opposite the Black Horse on the other side of the valley).

These are all puzzles. Bigger than any, perhaps, is the baffling problem of how the leys were laid down, constructed and marked out. To carry out this huge operation would have been beyond the economic resources of Britain at the height of the prosperity of the British Empire. Indeed, it is a heartening thought that the despoilers of Britain's countryside may do their worst – they could make little impression on the traces of the thousands of miles of leys that remain even within Brigantia alone.

The other main question is: Why? What was the purpose of these lines? That some of them, at least, were tracks as Watkins thought can scarcely be doubted. That the web-leys were a means of administration and a brilliant cohesive device seems difficult to evade. But that leaves a huge number of alignments which on the face of it would not be necessary politically or economically, and which would be a wild extravagance on religious grounds. Various far-fetched explanations are being put forward, a favourite one being that they are, or represent, some sort of gigantic gadget planted on the earth by visitors from outer space for re-charging their 'batteries'. One may laugh; but it might be considered that whatever the answer to the question is, it is almost bound to be far-fetched.

It is not pretended here that the leys are peculiar to Brigantia. They are an extremely significant feature throughout Britain, and it is not to be doubted that important nuclei or nodes (and other ley-phenomena) may be examined in many other parts of the country – Stonehenge, Avebury and Glastonbury at once spring to mind. What is true, however, is that Brigantia is at the centre of all three (if there are three) ley-systems. It is obvious that the 'administrative' web would be of most use if the 'administrator' were sitting, like the spider, in the middle of it. It might be remembered that the oldest trace of the culture of *homo sapiens* in Britain is probably that of the Cresswell caves, on the southern border of Brigantia; and a few miles from those caves one of the strangest relics of most ancient paganism – an oak that was reputed to scream and bleed if a bough was torn off it – died only a century ago. But if a nucleus of the web system is to be sought, the most probable area might be thought to be the Rosedale valley of the River Seven and the magnetite deposit.

A rather more detailed account of the Belinus Line where it falls within Brigantia may be found in the Appendix.

3

TRAITOR QUEEN

❖

When Dr Ross's *Pagan Celtic Britain* was on the point of publication, a remarkable series of carved stone heads began to be unearthed from all parts of Brigantia, especially west Yorkshire, and was collected together by Mr Sidney Jackson, the then Keeper of the Cartwright Hall Museum, Bradford, where he organised an exhibition of them. Some of these heads were undoubtedly typical Celtic cult-objects, dating from the Roman occupation or before it. Others, though showing considerable similarity, were of more doubtful origin, and some of these were even found to date from modern times. An official of a Yorkshire museum is said to have alleged that Mr Jackson carved the heads himself – which would make Mr Jackson a genius of gigantic stature. But it was perhaps the modern heads that especially appealed to Dr Ross when, as the leading authority, she visited the collection. Afterwards she said:

> What strikes me as above all significant is not so much whether this head or that is genuinely Celtic or not, but the extraordinary continuity of culture shown by this collection. Presumably without knowing it, there are local craftsmen of this very century in these Yorkshire industrial valleys, carving heads with specific Celtic characteristics such as the 'Celtic eye'. I had always imagined the West Riding to be an industrial hotchpotch in which all traces of past cultures

would have been obliterated. I had failed to realise that each mill-town and village was, almost to this day, largely cut off from the others and isolated. It is a treasure-house of continuity.

In *Pagan Celtic Britain* Ross avoids over-stressing this continuity feature. She says in her introduction: 'It is a side-issue rather than the main theme of the work.' In this study of Brigantia, on the other hand, continuity of tradition is precisely the main theme pursued, especially because it is such a treasure house. It may only be appropriate to add that a survey of Brigantian continuity would not have been possible without the previous work of dedicated archaeologists, historians and prehistorians, among whom Ross is one of the leaders.

The treasure preserved in Brigantia has some peculiar aspects, including some going back far before the coming of the La Tène Celts and the Halstatt Celts, representatives of whom also established themselves in northern Britain. An instance is given by Colin Burgess in *Bronze Age Metalwork in Northern England c. 1000 to 700 B.C.* (1968), where he and his metallurgist colleague Dr R. F. Tylecote show that in northern England (i.e. Brigantia) in the Middle and Late Bronze Age there was a considerable time-lag as compared with southern England in the adoption of new bronze-making techniques. In this area the smiths were still making tin-bronze long after those in the south had gone over to lead-bronze; and what lead-bronze objects occurred in northern England had been imported from the south. This was in spite of the fact that plenty of lead was available in the north in the deposits of the Pennines – and at any rate not long afterwards must have been known to be there, since the Romans no sooner entered Brigantia than they began lead-mining there. Yet the tin had to be imported to the north from south-western England – where the tin-miners may have been glad to find that the Brigantian market for their product still continued when other bronze-makers were no longer using it. The cairns known as the Three Men of Gragareth, near the summit of Gragareth Mountain west of Ingleborough, are said to mark a route formerly followed by tin-miners. There is no tin to be mined anywhere near. Perhaps it was the route by which prehistoric tin was carried from Cornwall to the north.

Even so, Brigantia still did not truly belong to the Iron Age even at the time when the Romans arrived. A. L. F. Rivet says (*Town and Country in Roman Britain*, 1958):

> Compared with the southern tribes they [the Brigantes] were a backward people and so far as it is known their economy was still largely that of the Bronze Age, Iron Age influences being represented by a few hill forts and chariot burials; the latter are clearly related to those of the Parisi of the East Riding. Brigantia is divided by nature into a number of well-defined areas, and this fact seems to have been reflected politically.

This is much the same point as struck Dr Ross.

An earlier authority, R. G. Collingwood (*Roman Britain and the English Settlements*, 1937), says that in northern England by the time of the Roman coming

> the descendants of the Middle La Tène invaders had by now grown into a Celtic warrior-caste ruling over a populace of primitive culture hardly differing from that of a poor and ill-furnished Late Bronze Age; and thus had come into existence the state of the Brigantes.

Illumination on the relationships between the Celtic overlords and their subjugated predecessors is perhaps cast by a beautiful piece of folk tradition which is still extant in Co. Cork in the Irish Republic. A young bride is stolen away by the fairies. One year later she is seen sitting on a mound, nursing her baby and singing to it what purports to be a lullaby. The words she sings, however, are really instructions to her non-fairy husband on how to release her – he must quickly bring his black-handled knife and so on – or she will for ever have to stay with her captors 'as their queen'. The legend and the song were broadcast by the BBC Radio 3 in December 1972.

The implications of this story and of the Gaelic song itself are several. First, the primitive tribal practice of 'marriage by capture' is seen in operation. Second, it operates across the 'national' boundaries – like the human prince capturing the fairy swan-princess, only the other way round. Third, the girl clearly does not expect her possession of a half-fairy baby to affect her human husband's desire to win her back – and nobody else expects it either. Fourth, the 'fairies' are clearly human enough to be able to cross-breed (which they could not if, for instance, the fairies were tiny butterfly-like creatures). Fifth – and this is perhaps the most important point – it is taken for granted that the fairies could not understand Gaelic Celtic, even to the extent of realising that a 'lullaby' was talking about a black-handled knife, so their own language can hardly be thought of as even 'proto-Celtic'. The fact that this is an Irish legend does not invalidate these points for the British context, although in Britain the conditions indicated would have to be referred to a somewhat earlier period. Considering the legend's survival to the present time in Ireland, it can scarcely be unreasonable to suppose that these conditions may have been largely the current relationships in Brigantia 2,000 years ago.

Something like this, then, was the structure of the Brigantia which the Romans met when they entered Britain. There were Iron Age Celtic aristocrats, proud and warlike, with a tradition of imperial conquest that had taken them far afield from central Europe where their La Tène culture had developed. Their religion was regulated by the caste of Druids, who were by no means the benevolent old white-bearded gentlemen in white robes of the popular picture, but the guardians of a ritual and faith which had features so horrifying that the Romans, in their conquest of Gaul, destroyed two major Celtic cemeteries at Entremont and Roquepertuse in order to suppress the ceremonies practised there.

In general the Romans loathed the Druids while they tolerated Celtic worship of the Celts' own gods – although this discrimination may have reflected a fear that the Druids might (as indeed they did) provide a focus and ideological buttress for Celtic resistance to Rome. But the ferocity and brutality of much of

Celtic religion is evidenced both by archaeological discoveries, such as pits at the bottom of each of which was a stake bearing traces of hair and blood, and by Celtic legend. The stories are not confined to the charming vision of Tir nan Og, the Land of Youth, but describe a divinity as approaching in a chariot with a single shaft, which runs from back to front clean through the horse that draws the vehicle.

This was the kind of surpassing cruelty that inspired Boudicca, the Queen of the Celtic Iceni of southern England, in her appalling vengeance after the tribe's rising against the Romans in AD 61. Ross quotes Dio's account of how Boudicca tortured women by having them skewered lengthwise on sharp stakes – a similar fate to that suffered in the Celtic Gaulish temples by captured enemies. The Romans subsequently annihilated Boudicca's power, and she committed suicide.

The La Tène Celts in Brigantia were not confined to their Queen, Cartimandua, and her entourage, or to the nobles scattered over the wide realm, but also included farmers who had in part dispossessed and displaced the people who were in Brigantia before. These Iron Age farmers used the labour of the earlier people, presumably in the form at least partly of slavery or for payment in kind (although Brigantia had its own gold coinage). It may be that such arrangements are reflected in the much later Saxon legends of a 'hob' – generally described as a fairy – who threshed the farmer's grain harvest overnight, and was paid with a bowl of milk or gruel only.

The earlier inhabitants would also live partly by farming; but they would not have such good or – more important – so many of the tools necessary for clearing and cultivating boggy or wooded ground, as the new overlords had. They would therefore tend to stay where they had been before, or to move farther up the contours of the hills, while the iron-users would tend to take up the more fertile areas nearer the valley-bottoms. Both populations would use hunting and stock-raising as further sources of livelihood. For both, stock-farming was probably much more important than field-tilling (except, especially in the case of the iron-users, for growing cattle-feed); but the bronze-users would obtain a higher proportion of their food from hunting and from gathering wild plants, roots and fruits than the iron-users.

In 1688 Thomas Denton quoted the *Chronicle of Lanercost* as saying that the Forest of Inglewood (in north-west Brigantia between Penrith and Carlisle) was a forest before the Norman Conquest. He added that in the reign of William Rufus the whole of this forest, except in the immediate neighbourhood of Carlisle, remained uncultivated and neglected. Rufus therefore sent a team of advisers from the south of England to teach the natives of Cumberland the art of cultivating the soil and making it contribute to their subsistence.

This evidence is quite startling, since not only the Saxons but the Celts were agriculturists. It would appear that as late as the end of the eleventh century Inglewood Forest was inhabited by 'pre-Celtic' people who lived not by agriculture but by hunting the King's venison and by gathering wild vegetable products.

The bronze-users would have known many cross-country routes (including leys) long before the iron-users came, and may well have kept some of those routes secret. As a result the iron-users may have established routes of their own – it would have been risky for them to follow one of the more ancient paths even if they knew where those paths lay. The bronze-users' routes may be seen to this day for short stretches, where they came down with their cattle from the moors to a watering place or a stream-crossing and wore down the well known 'hollow-ways'. Largely, it appears likely that the bronze-users and the iron-users kept their communities separate, while maintaining the iron-users' superiority. For much of the time, perhaps, they were thus able to preserve fairly peaceful relations – there are not many legends suggesting any large-scale attacks on the 'Celts' by the 'little people'. But that does not mean that the bronze-users did not find the presence of the others a perpetually sore point, and one which from time to time might erupt into violence. More often, hostility would find its expression in more subtle ways, such as stealing a girl – or a baby – and whisking them off (as the raggle-taggle gypsies were later accused of doing) by secret ways to distant places before a search could be made.

Perhaps the bronze-users were themselves 'proto-Celts' who had been in Britain only a couple of centuries or so before the iron-users followed in their tracks, and who spoke a form of Celtic. If that were so, it would not necessarily follow that relations between the two groups were amicable. But if it were so, then the indications are that there was also a considerable population of a still earlier people who were not Celtic, who did not speak Celtic (or originally did not), and who lived in a more primitive and poverty-ridden manner and were exploited by both the other groups.

Brigantia at the time was therefore divided up 'vertically', socially between overlords (who were divided into aristocrats and farmers) and underlings (who may have been divided into mainly stock-rearing proto-Celts and mainly hunting and wild plant gathering non-Celts). It was far from being a homogeneous society. But the country was also divided up 'horizontally' into petty kingdoms which were united loosely in the Brigantian federation, but which nevertheless were constantly on the look-out for the advantage of the various ruling groups.

One major such kingdom within Brigantia, it is thought, may have been situated in what might roughly be called north Yorkshire, with its administrative centre at Stanwick, near Richmond. At the time when the Romans invaded southern England, that north Yorkshire area was ruled by a man whom the Romans called Venutius. He was in alliance – perhaps as a result of the growing Roman menace in Gaul before the legions actually crossed the Channel – with Cartimandua, Queen of the area to his south, whose capital was probably at York (that city's '1,900th anniversary of its foundation', celebrated in 1971, referred only to the supposed date of the foundation of the Roman fortress – but the very name of it as adapted by the Romans, Eboracum or Eburacum, has no meaning except in a pre-Roman context). Cartimandua and Venutius married, and together they were amply strong enough to control Brigantia. It was Cartimandua who was the sovereign of the whole, and it was her name that appeared on the coinage. She is believed to have succeeded her father Dumnoveros or Dumnocoveros and grandfather Volisios as ruler of Brigantia.

Brigantia had long been in contact with the Roman Empire, trading with it and copying some of the Roman institutions – such as the gold coinage. Brigantian coins of Cartimandua, Dumnocoveros and Volisios have been found with Roman silver coins of dates corresponding to the period between 209 and 41 BC. This must not be taken to mean that Brigantia had been trading with Rome for 200 years before Julius Caesar – only that the older coins were still in circulation. It is probable that Brigantia exported wool, woollen products such as the hooded capes which were prized all over the Empire, and lead which was mined in the Pennines. Imports would largely consist of Roman pottery, wine and other luxury products. This trade would therefore benefit almost solely the Brigantian aristocracy, while it was made possible by the labour of the Brigantian farmers and by the miners who were unlikely to include Celts of the ruling caste.

The more productive areas of Brigantia, from the viewpoint of this foreign trade, were therefore the uplands of the Pennines, whereas the consumption of and demand for the imports lay primarily in the more civilised and 'luxurious' towns of the lowlands, particularly Cartimandua's capital. The trade was thus a divisive influence, even between the Queen and her upland-based husband.

Julius Caesar was the first Roman to invade Britain in 55 BC and again in 54; but he did not aim at conquest, his troops did not penetrate beyond the Thames, and after no more than a reconnaissance expedition he withdrew. It was ninety-seven years later, in AD 43, that the Romans returned in strength and rapidly conquered the south of England. The main resistance came from Caratacus or Caractacus, the history-book British hero who was the leader of those dark-haired south Welshmen, the Silures. The name is a Romanisation of the Celtic Caradoc, Ceretic, Cerdig or Cerdic.

Four or five years after the first landing, the Romans under Ostorius Scapula pushed north-westward towards Chester to separate Caratacus' Silures from Brigantia. Ostorius had meanwhile also obtained from Cartimandua some sort of pact by which she would support the Romans and, it transpired, they would support her – that is, they would maintain her primacy among the Brigantian Celtic aristocracy.

After a great defeat in which he lost his army but himself managed to escape, Caratacus by secret roads made his way to Brigantia, the only remaining powerful Celtic state, to try to rally further resistance to the Romans (he seems not to have been aware of Cartimandua's pact). Cartimandua clapped him in chains and handed him over to Ostorius. The Romans kept him in his chains to parade through Rome as a distinguished prisoner, and he lived out the remainder of his days in restricted but honourable conditions in the capital of the Empire, along with his family – while his memory was preserved in heroic legends of the Celts for many centuries afterwards.

His fate indeed turned out to be much more glorious than that of the Brigantian Queen. It may be wondered whether Cartimandua saw the Silurian leader as a representative not of the tall, fair, imperial and imperious Celts to whom she herself belonged, but of the shorter, dark-haired people within her own realm who were the lowest section of the population, the most oppressed and so in a critical political situation perhaps the most dangerous to herself.

At any rate, her treatment of Caratacus brought to a head the smouldering split within her kingdom. Venutius had already identified himself with the growing anti-Roman section, which extended not only through the lower layers of society but also to the ruling groups. Cartimandua had taken his brothers and other relatives as hostages, but in the same year of AD 51, after the betrayal of Caratacus, Venutius put himself openly at the head of the anti-Roman resistance movement, and left Cartimandua – who divorced him and insultingly married his armour-bearer or chief aide.

It is perfectly possible, of course, to see things from Cartimandua's point of view. She knew how powerful was the Roman Empire, how vast were its resources in military manpower and material. She may have found it impossible to conceive of any resistance to Roman arms having any result other than destruction of those who resisted. The revolt of Boudicca and her Iceni in southern England, and the Roman revenge, had not yet taken place – it was ten years after Cartimandua had handed Caratacus over – but she may well have believed, not without reason, that she was saving not only herself but the Brigantes as a whole from great suffering by her policy of collaboration. But such a policy would look less and less attractive the farther down the social scale one went. Within Brigantia, the local kinglets enjoyed a great deal of independent power, which would be that much diminished if they became no longer the second but only the third social layer. Below them, the Celtic farmers might see themselves being turned into slaves except where they were conscripted into the Roman army and posted to serve anywhere except in Britain. The proto-Celts or non-Celts who were already subordinated to the lowest ranks of the Celts, and who probably lived in conditions of extreme hardship, would fear the end of what freedom they had, and for many of them slavery or sheer starvation.

Venutius therefore found a growing response to his call for resistance. Something like civil war raged through Brigantia for about a dozen years. Eventually Venutius captured Eboracum and Cartimandua fled for refuge to her Roman protectors. All Brigantia now followed Venutius' standard, and forces from as far away as southern Scotland joined him. It was about this time that Boudicca led her revolt in the south, when the Roman presence in London and St Albans was overnight wiped out. Venutius had known all along that in the end the Romans would have to make war on him, and he had for years been building great defensive earthworks in his own part of Brigantia – some at Grassington, some above Kettlewell (the huge Ta Dyke across the head of Park Rash, where the way to Wensleydale goes over from Wharfedale), some on the summits of Ingleborough, and especially an enormous fortification at Stanwick, Venutius' capital.

The Roman attack on the north came in AD 74, when Agricola moved up the western side of the Pennines from Chester, and Petillius Cerialis stormed up the eastern side. Tacitus, the Roman historian, described Venutius as outstanding in the art of warfare; but he may be suspected of stressing the Brigantian leader's ability in order to magnify the Romans' achievement in utterly defeating him at Stanwick: Tacitus was a near relation of Agricola who, however, took no part in this Roman victory. Venutius retreated into the Pennines, but the threat to the Roman army had been broken. Almost immediately, the prisoners were set to work building roads and mining lead for the Romans, and the rest of the population were levied to supply slaves for the same purposes.

Brigantia, however, was a useful unit for the Romans. Pursuing the policy of indirect rule, they maintained it as a client kingdom, while seeking to ensure that it could no longer move against Rome and that its actual or potential power was greatly reduced.

Eboracum was seized by the Romans, who turned it into a great legionary fortress – one of the greatest in the Empire. The capital of Brigantia *civitas* was set instead at Isurium Brigantum, at the confluence of the Swale and the Ure or Yore (the river which flows through Wensleydale).

It is commonly stated that the Romans under Petillius built Isurium at Aldborough, which is about half a mile east of Boroughbridge. The impression is thereby given that there was no Brigantian town there before Petillius kindly built it for them. In reality Isurium does appear to have been more Roman than Brigantian, but its name, like that of Eboracum, is Brigantian – it is based on the Celtic *Is Ure* – i.e. River Ure. What Petillius did was to build typical Roman amenities there, complete with villas with tessellated pavements, and to drive a Roman road – the main one, the Watling Street – through it from south to north. But that road kept just to the east of these strange monuments, the Devil's Arrows, which were close to Isurium and much older than Celtic Brigantia itself. North-north-west of Boroughbridge, the road also kept about the same distance away to the east of the earthen henges which lie in line with the Arrows to pass Ripon. It is likely that any Celtic pre-Roman town at Boroughbridge was nearer the Arrows.

Venutius was defeated at Stanwick in AD 74. Forty years later the north revolted, so successfully at first that many of the Roman forts in Brigantia were destroyed. This was when the Ninth Legion disappeared from the Roman army, to be replaced at York by the

Sixth *Victrix* Legion. Seven years later, in AD 122, Hadrian built the Wall from the Tyne to the Solway – roughly across the northern frontier of Brigantia, although a large area south of the Wall was removed from the purview of the Brigantian client-kingdom and placed under direct military government. It has usually been assumed that the Wall was built to keep the tribes from Scotland out, but its purpose may have been as much to keep the Brigantes in. One of the original purposes of the Roman invasion of Britain was to stop the flow of Celtic refugees from Gaul; and now that the Romans had reached the Solway, the same problem was that much farther northward.

1 Devil's Arrow, Boroughbridge

Forty years after the disaster to the Ninth Legion, the Brigantes again rose in rebellion in AD 154, this time in alliance with the peoples of southern Scotland. The rebellion was put down, but as Raistrick points out (*The Romans in Yorkshire*, 1972), one result seems to have been the end of Roman lead-mining in Brigantia. The mines were handed over to the Brigantes to work. On the other hand the country between York and Aldborough (Eboracum and Isurium) was more or less cleared of Brigantes and parcelled out to Roman or Romanised Brigantian farmers. On the east side of the river, this was precisely the area that later became the Forest of Galtres.

Again a little more than forty years, and in AD 197 some of the Brigantes revolted along with tribes from southern Scotland. After this there was a prolonged period of quietness and prosperity, and it was eighty or ninety years before further rebellion broke out and continued sporadically to the end of the third century. By that time the Roman Empire everywhere was beginning to show signs of decay from within. Before the rot had become disastrous, however, Constantine the son of Constantius was proclaimed western Roman Emperor by his troops while he was at York, and he went on to become Constantine the Great, the builder of Constantinople and the man who legalised Christianity in the Roman Empire. He had an enormous effect throughout the Empire, and certain special effects in Brigantia.

Christianity was already practised in Brigantia before that time, and – thanks to the protection of Constantius, who was lord of Britain – escaped the worst rigours of the persecution of the Christians by Diocletian, to whom Constantius was subordinate. A possible link with the Brigantian Christianity of that time lies in the beautiful little Saxon church at Escomb, near Bishop Auckland, County Durham. This was erected in about AD 677, fifty years after King Edwin the Saxon, the ruler of all Northumbria, had become Christian and his kingdom with him, and the Saxon heathen idols had been destroyed.

The well known story is that Coifi, High Priest of the pagan religion, himself advised King Edwin (whose wife was already a Christian) to adopt Christianity, and himself desecrated the temple at Goodmanham and threw down the idols. Not only was a Christian church built on the spot (so that it cannot now be excavated) but it may be that Coifi thereby ensured his own job. Geoffrey of Monmouth, unreliably describing the conversion of Britain to Christianity, ambiguously says (Thorpe edition, 1966):

> At that time there were twenty-eight flamens [pagan priests – but Geoffrey probably meant priests of high rank] in Britain and three archflamens, to whose jurisdiction the other spiritual leaders and judges of public morals were subject. Where there were flamens they placed bishops, and where there were archflamens they appointed archbishops. The seats of the archflamens had been . . . in London, York, and the City of the Legions, the site of which last, by the river Usk in Glamorgan, is still shown by its ancient walls and

buildings. The twenty-eight bishops were placed under the jurisdiction of these three cities, once the superstitions practised there had been purged away. Parishes were apportioned off, Deira being placed under the Metropolitan of York, along with Albany ... Loegria [the rest of England] was placed under the Metropolitan of London, together with Cornwall ... Kambria or Wales was placed under the City of the Legions.

Thus His Grace of Ebor, for example, perhaps is in a line of succession going back far before Christ through Coifi.

When Escomb Church was built, Arthur had been dead for about 140 years, and it was nearly 280 years since the Romans had left Britain. At a time when churches – and for that matter royal palaces – were generally being built of wood, three churches in Durham were more or less simultaneously built – and most carefully built – of stone; the churches of Escomb, Monk Wearmouth and Jarrow in the abbey alongside which Bede wrote his *Ecclesiastical History*. The building material used was at once an emphatic declaration of importance. But Escomb Church was something very special indeed. It was built of no ordinary stone.

Escomb (the name of which is not Saxon but Celtic) stands beside the River Wear. Two miles downstream was the Roman town of Vinovia, the modern Binchester. The stone for this church, expertly worked ashlar, was all brought from the ruins of Vinovia. On very many of the stone blocks the typical marks of the Roman masons can still be clearly seen.

The chancel is divided from the nave by a high, narrow opening, topped by a perfect Roman arch. It is an impressive structure. When one examines it it seems difficult to believe that it could have been so exactly assembled from stones that had been brought to this spot haphazardly – not only the arch itself but the big, splendidly alternating stones that make the high support on either side.

Why was so much trouble taken? Why, in this instance, did the builders ignore the usual custom of leaving Roman ruins severely alone? Why was this church not built, like those of Wearmouth and Jarrow, from stone cut and trimmed for the particular job? Why is the result nevertheless by far the most beautiful of the three? Was it because those stones were already consecrated? Were the Escomb builders re-erecting a church that had stood in the Roman town less than four centuries after the Crucifixion? There was a church at Glastonbury very early indeed – perhaps even before the Romans came to Britain – but it was built of wattle.

In Brigantia the official toleration of Christianity after Constantine's measures had certain special effects. They have to do with the identity of Helen, Constantine's mother who (unlike his father Constantius) was a Christian and who admittedly wielded great influence over her son in favour of Christianity. So far as is known, Constantine never publicly embraced the faith himself: but he did inscribe his victorious battle-banners with the Christian *Chi-Ro* monogram. It was she who went out to Palestine, discovered what was stated to be the True Cross, and – very justly – later became St Helen.

For a long time she was stated to have been a Brigantian princess. In recent years it has been asserted by contrast that she was the daughter of a Greek innkeeper on the eastern coast of the Adriatic, whom Constantius picked up on his travels – in other words, that she was a prostitute.

This derivation fails to explain one remarkable thing. When Christianity was legalised in the Empire, and when pagan cult-centres were hastily 'canonised' throughout Brigantia, a great number of pagan holy wells became re-dedicated as St Helen's Well. In eastern Brigantia to this day, where a well bears a saint's name that saint almost always is Helen; and this phenomenon is far commoner in Brigantia than anywhere else. This suggests that the early Christian authorities considered, or knew that the people considered, Helen to be a Brigantian. Often a church or chapel was built in association with the well, in which case it, too, would have Helen as its patron saint. Near Liverpool such a site has grown into the important town of St Helens. Brigantia claims Helen for its own.

So much is this so that it may be wondered whether the wells had previously been sacred to the goddess Brigantia – Bride Wells, in fact. Many of these wells have until the present century been the scene of regular beautiful 'decoration' ceremonies such as are still carried out annually with much pomp and circumstance at Tideswell, Eyam and other villages in the limestone country in south-east Brigantia.

The *Chronicle of Lanercost* under 1282 says that Edward I defeated the Welsh under Llewellyn, and then

> possessed himself of the ancient and secret treasures of that people [dating], as is believed, from the time of Arthur; among which he found a most beautiful piece of the Holy Cross, carved into a portable cross, which was the glory of their dominion and [carried] the presage of their doom. Which [cross], it is said, Helena kept after the Invention [the finding of the True Cross by Helena, celebrated on 3 May] as a special portion, and brought with her when she returned to Britain with her husband. The Welsh had been accustomed to call it . . . 'Crosnaith'.

C. W. Scott-Giles in *The Road Goes On* (1946) says:

> In Wales are ancient roads known as Sarn Helen, or Helen's Causeway [but some believe Sarn Helen to be a corruption of Sarn y Lleng – 'the Legions' Road'] associated with the British maiden, daughter of Eudav [but by some identified with Helena, daughter of King Coel], whom the Emperor Maxen [Maximus] first saw in a dream, and later found and married.

The *mabinogi The Dream of Maxen Wledig* says:

> Helen bethought her to make high roads from one castle to another throughout the Island of Britain. And the roads were made. And for this cause are they called the roads of Helen Luyddawc, that she was sprung from a native of this island, and the men of the Island of Britain would not have made these great roads save for her.

Among the traces of earlier faiths found in Britain is a shrine of the Romano-British period to a Celtic god called Vinotonus. His name is supposed to come from a root meaning 'wine' but in this shrine he appears to be identified with the Roman god Silvanus; and it is suggested that the wild country around (the spot is on the shoulder of Great Whernside) is apt for a god of hunting. Perhaps it was so in Romano-Celtic times, although nowadays there is precious little to hunt on those bare moors. But it may be worth considering whether the dedication to Vinotonus owes anything to the memory of Venutius, who built the Ta Dyke at the other end of Great Whernside.

A curious echo of Cartimandua's dismal betrayal of Caratacus seems to come from the equally dismal end of the Celtic kingdom of Elmet — in effect, all that was left politically of Brigantia — long after the Romans had gone. Christian Elmet faced pagan Saxons to the north, east and south. It was ruled by a king named Cerdig or Ceretic — the same name in Celtic as Caratacus. His court, being Christian, was sought as a refuge by a Christian Saxon king who had been overthrown by the pagan Saxons. Cerdig betrayed him, and soon afterwards was himself destroyed when his kingdom was swallowed up in the Saxon tide.

One other figure remains from the Roman tradition of Brigantia. This is Pelagius, a monk who has been described as Irish but who probably came from Brigantia. He left Britain in about AD 380, travelled in North Africa and the Middle East and settled in Rome in about AD 400. He was shocked by the profligacy and immorality in the capital of the collapsing Empire and said so.

His character and philosophical views have been described as typically British. They might be thought typical of northern England but that there was no such concept at that time. Northern England — Brigantia — was in effect Welsh, and Pelagius should be thought of as having Old Welsh for his mother tongue. His Latin name means 'islander', and it was probably a translation from the Welsh 'Morgan'. Nevertheless, his attitude strikes a chord that might harmonise with the feelings of many Brigantians of our own day.

His main theme was that every man had a free will and

51

consequently full personal responsibility for his conduct. Pelagius could not accept the idea of original sin into which every man was born. Nor would he allow that before a man could choose the right path, his will must first be moved in that direction by God. In effect, he proclaimed that a man had a right to be wrong, if he would take the consequences. Worst of all, perhaps, he declared that the freedom to choose between good and evil also belonged to heathens.

This set of doctrines is still known as the Pelagian Heresy, and is still – 1,500 years later – regarded as a dangerous deviation. His teachings were condemned, and in AD 418 he was banished from Rome by the Emperor Honorius – just as his Empire was falling about his ears. Pelagius moved to the Middle East where he found the Eastern Church readier to tolerate him. Most of his writings were destroyed, except for some which were saved by being attributed to St Jerome. But the condemnation of him and his views had one odd effect. Of Pelagius's countless followers (including many bishops) who had to leave Rome and its See, many came to Britain in AD 421 and Pelagianism spread rapidly here.

Eight years before banishing Pelagius, the same Emperor Honorius had received a message, in AD 410 from the Britons asking him to send back the Roman troops which had all been withdrawn, as Britain was being beset by Saxon invaders. He replied that the Britons would have to see to their own defences. He himself had none to spare.

Not many years later, however, when the Empire had collapsed, some hierarchs of the Christian Church in Britain asked the Pope of Rome for help in combating Pelagianism. In reply in 429 he sent Germanus – later St Germanus – the Bishop of Auxerre, who had formerly been an officer of the Roman army. He not only stamped out heresy in those British centres to which he went, but also took command of a British force and defeated an enemy army which may have been partly or wholly heathen, but more probably was partly or wholly Pelagian. He was able to prevent the heresy from winning final control of the Church in Britain, but he could not wipe out Pelagian views and Pelagian stubbornness themselves. Morgan the monk left a deep impression on his native Britain, and perhaps most of all on the Brigantia from which wave after wave of passionate Nonconformity has sprung.

Pelagius and Germanus more or less end the story of Roman Britain and Roman Brigantia. What came next were the Dark Ages, with little written record and most of that obscure or unreliable. That is the period of the mysterious Arthurian legend, in which not the least mysterious part is played by Brigantia. It is the period when real political and military struggles of the post-Roman chaos and the Saxon advance become fused with lore and magic born among the Celts and other peoples centuries before and perhaps in distant lands.

4
CLINSCHOR'S KINGDOM

❋

The Dark Ages are at once the despair of historians and a challenge to them. From the withdrawal of the Roman troops from Britain in about AD 400 to the Norman Conquest more than six centuries later, the documentary sources are extremely meagre. There were brief accounts in Welsh of the period from 453 to 954, called the *Annales Cambriae*; the *Anglo-Saxon Chronicle*, begun during the reign of King Alfred in the ninth century, and partly attributed to him; the *Ecclesiastical History* of the Venerable Bede, written in the eighth century; *The Destruction and Conquest of Britain*, written in the fifth century by the British monk Gildas; the *History of the Britons*, attributed to Nennius and written about AD 800; the *Life of Germanus*, written about forty years after the saint-general's second (AD 448) visit to Britain; and that is practically the lot until the Doomsday Book, except for a mass of Celtic — mainly Welsh and Breton — folklore and legend, and the medieval *History of the Kings of Britain* by Geoffrey of Monmouth, who certainly used a prolific imagination but who has probably been extravagantly denigrated.

That same period, however, saw a succession of conflicts between various British realms, including Brigantia or its successors; a gradually increasing pressure against all British political units from the incoming Saxons; and many instances in which some Saxons and some Britons were in alliance against other Saxons and Britons. These events may have found little reflection in written history, but that is only because written history at that time hardly existed. The events themselves were important, so important that they must have found reflection in other ways. The folklore and legend therefore has been and is being combed and recombed to find indications of historical facts.

Of all this material, by far the most outstanding in interest and significance is that contained in or relating to the Arthurian legend. Things have moved a long way from the idea that Arthur was nothing but a fairy-tale figure, and have swung perhaps to an opposite extreme with the well reasoned picture of him as a man in the Roman succession who strove to unite the British people against the Saxons. This latter picture may be correct in so far as it concerns the real, physical Arthur; but whoever he was, he made such a profound impact on the ideology of the British people of his own and subsequent times, that a great deal of Celtic myth – some of it extremely ancient – came to be attached to him and his entourage.

Arthur seems to have been in truth a war-leader of some or most of the British peoples, though not accepted as such by all. It is very difficult to identify the places where the main events of his campaign occurred, but what is certain is that many of them must have been in Brigantia. Saklatvala (1967) considers that Camelot may be found not at Cadbury Castle in Somerset, but at Almondbury, the hill-fort near Brigantian Huddersfield which under the Romans bore the Celtic name of Camulodunum (not to be confused with Colchester in Essex, which had the same name). It is the kind of problem which may be solved, if at all, only by the most careful and extensive field work on the spot – or all the possible spots. Other people have put Camelot at Carlisle; and indeed Sir Thomas Malory in *Morte Darthur* sometimes appears to put Camelot either at or near to Carlisle.

The passage concerned is that in Book XII, Chapter 14, in which Sir Tristram and Sir Palamides fight, but then decide to be friends. Sir Palamides has until this point been described as a heathen Saracen. 'Saracen' in Malory (in whose time in the fifteenth century the tradition of the Crusades was still strong) should perhaps be read instead as 'Saxon'; and in the times of Arthur and

Tristram – that is the sixth century – Saxons were in fact mostly heathen; but so also were some British Celtic kingdoms, and these, or political units which were Christian but leaned towards Pelagianism, might have been equated with 'Saracens'. Sir Palamides asks Sir Tristram to have him baptised, and Sir Tristram says that within a mile is 'the suffragan of Carlisle, that shall give you the sacrament of baptism'. After the ceremony they depart, 'riding towards Camelot'.

Here, then, are three possible sites for the Arthurian city: Almondbury and Carlisle, both in Brigantia, and Cadbury, far to the south. There are several other possible candidates as well; Wildman (*The Black Horsemen*, 1971) puts forward a persuasive case for considering that 'Camelot' was a composite of a number of different centres. As far as Brigantia is concerned, however, it is notable that most Arthúrian references are on the western side. If Almondbury had really been Camelot or taken a major role in Arthur's campaign one might have expected the eastern half of Brigantia to have exhibited a considerable Arthurian influence on place-names.

Arthuret, a parish north of Carlisle, looks like a good western example. In reality it is probably a corruption of Arderydd or Arfderydd, the site of a battle which occurred in 573, rather later than what is believed to be the Arthurian period. Farther south, a mile or two beyond Penrith, is a place named 'King Arthur's Round Table'. In fact, it is a prehistoric henge – a nearly circular platform, surrounded by a ditch and embankment presumably constructed for ritual or ceremonial use. A few miles to the south-west from here, frowning down on the eastern shore of Ullswater, is a mountain called Arthur's Pike; but it may have acquired that name in corrupted form from a farm just below the Pike and above the lake, called Auterstone. Many Arthurian references in western Brigantia are like this: examined closely, they dissolve into indistinctness. What remains is little more than the fact that in eastern Brigantia there is little Arthurian tradition, whereas in western Brigantia such a tradition is so insistent that it should be taken seriously though not literally. Exceptions in the east are the Sneep in Durham; Arthur's Chair, a rock formation in the King's

Crags near Sewingshields in Northumberland (outside Brigantia); and Richmond Castle in Yorkshire, where there is said to be a cave in which Arthur and his knights are sleeping. North of the border, however, there are 'Arthurian' place-names and legends up the middle of the Lowlands and to Arthur's Seat at Edinburgh.

Geoffrey Ashe, one of the most authoritative writers on Arthurian matters, puts Arthur's homeland firmly as in the West Country – Cornwall and Somerset. But he points out that the poems (Celtic British) which mention him were composed in Cumberland. (That is, so far as is known. There is good reason to think that earlier compositions about him may have existed. The Cumberland bards' references to Arthur are too obscure to be quoted.) The poets or bards concerned were Taliesin, Aneurin, and Myrddin, whom Geoffrey of Monmouth in the twelfth century transmuted into Merlin. All of them lived in the period immediately after the presumed lifetime of Arthur – which was from about AD 470 (when the Roman tradition was still fairly strong) to about AD 537 – or may have been born before he died.

A poem called *Gododdin* by Aneurin describes a disastrous expedition, in which Aneurin took part, by a force of 363 Britons from near Edinburgh to a battle against the Anglo-Saxons near Catterick (perhaps at the old Stanwick fortifications) in Yorkshire. There were only a few British survivors, including the poet himself. He makes the oldest known reference to Arthur by name, as the greatest British warrior, but it is only a passing mention.

There is a problem, however, about Arthur's period. If he lived and was active in the time suggested above, then he fitted in with some genuine historical personages who come into the Arthurian legend, but not with others. To get round this difficulty it has been suggested that he really lived about fifty years later than had been supposed; in that case he fits in with the second group but no longer with the first.

An example may lie in the two Brigantian figures of Urien and his son Owain of Rheged, who lived too late to have been associated with Arthur in the early sixth century. Both of them are prominent in the Arthurian legend, and moreover in both aspects of it – what might be called the historical aspect, and the legendary. In Malory's fifteenth-century *Morte Darthur* Urien appears first as one of the bitter opponents of Arthur the young 'king' (in reality Arthur never seems to have borne the title of King, or at any rate King of anything more than a small dominion in the south-west), and as having taken part in the wars against Arthur's claim to superiority. There was from then on recurrent trouble in north-west Britain which Arthur had to deal with. On the other hand, in later times Urien himself, and Owain, appear among Arthur's Knights of the Round Table.

Urien is married to Morgan le Fay, Arthur's half-sister who in Malory, though much less so in earlier works, is a very negative character. She repeatedly tries to arrange the death of Arthur; and she is prevented from murdering the sleeping Urien himself only by the forcible intervention of Owain. This appears to be all folklore in theme and treatment; but in the Arthurian 'matter' it is never safe to say that an episode is purely folklore and never possible to say that it is purely historical. Commonly the same episode may recur with different actors. Morgan le Fay switches roles with the Lady of the Lake. Arthur changes places with his chief rival Sir Lancelot. What has to be constantly kept in mind is that where Urien or Owain is concerned — and therefore Morgan le Fay, and possibly the Lady of the Lake — the area of Brigantia is or may be involved. The same may also be true of other figures, both in Malory and in earlier sources, Continental or Welsh (Welsh, of course, including Rheged).

Not very much attention has until recent years been paid to this north-western connection with the Arthurian story. The tendency has been too much to concentrate on the West Country, which was almost certainly Arthur's own personal realm, and on Wales as it now exists, and to forget that at one time the whole of what is now 'England' was literally 'Wales', and that most of Brigantia in Arthur's time still was Welsh. This imbalance in the inquiry is now being partially remedied.

One student who has been impressed with the western preponderance of Arthurian references is Mr Sam Brewster, of Tadcaster. He began one line of quest with the story of the 'Castle of Wonders', 'Land of Wonders' and 'Bed of Wonders' which form a major theme in the Parsifal (Perceval, Parzifal) legend on which Wagner based his great opera. It occurs in two twelfth-century poems of the Romance in medieval French by Chrétien de Troyes, and in medieval German by Wolfram von Eschenbach. The King of the Land of Wonders is a great magician (who never makes a 'personal appearance' in either poem) named Clinschor, rendered by Wagner as Klingsor.

Many researchers have hitherto accepted the Castle of Wonders as located at Gloucester. Mr Brewster noted that in the legend there was a constant sense of looking *up* to the Castle from the environs. This and other circumstances left him feeling that Gloucester did not fit, partly because it had no high hills near. Another odd fact was that the way to the Castle led over a river-crossing called the Ford Perilous (*li gweiz prelljus*) in Von Eschenbach's version or the Ford or Fords *de Galvoie* – which appeared to mean 'of Galloway' unless it was a corruption of 'Gallois' meaning 'Welsh' – in Chrétien's. Galloway is a long way from Gloucester.

Mr Brewster pondered the possibility of a British, non-Roman, road running up the western side of England, starting perhaps somewhere near Glastonbury or Stonehenge and leading to Galloway. He noticed that such a route would probably run close to Ingleborough, which has a major British fort on top of it. That fort, the late Professor Sir Ian Richmond thought, was probably the Rigodunum mentioned by Ptolemy. Rigodunum is presumably a Romanisation of something like Rig Dun, Celtic for King's Castle. From near Ingleton, at the south-western foot of Ingleborough, running northward between Whernside and Gragareth is the valley called Kingsdale, with an ancient non-Roman way going up it and over into Deepdale and down to Dent. From Dent going east and then north over the moors to the head of the valley of the Eden, is another ancient track called Galloway Gate. It was worth investigating.

The relevant section of the legend concerns directly not Percival himself but another redoubtable champion of the Round Table. It is Sir Gawain who leaped *li gweiz prelljus* in the Land of Wonders. 'He heard the roar of a waterfall; it has worn away a ravine wide and deep and impassable,' says the translation of Von Eschenbach by Helen M. Mustard and Charles E. Passage. 'The valiant Gawan dug in his spurs and urged the horse on to the leap.' This makes it appear that the crossing-place was not really a ford but a prodigious leap.

Approaching from the south, where Mr Brewster thought the track might come from the Forest of Bowland by Cross o' Greet, it would not be easy to pass the River Greta below the point where it is formed by the confluence of the Doe and the Twiss, or indeed lower than a point somewhat higher than that. The track coming southwards down Kingsdale (the Doe valley), which is now a metalled road, turns off sharp left (east) along what is still a 'green road' called Twistleton Lane. A branch off to the right turns down beside the Doe, with an easy ford across the top of Thornton Force – but it does not lead anywhere. If Twistleton Lane is followed further, it crosses the upper Doe, passes below the southern escarpment of Twistleton Scar, goes over the Ribchester–Bainbridge Roman road, and divides at Beezley Farm. The upper arm runs higher up the Twiss valley, crosses towards Ingleborough and doubles back southwards. The lower arm drops immediately to Beezley Falls, where the stream is spectacular.

It was Pecca Falls, on the Doe, that first aroused Mr Brewster's curiosity. They are a charming place to visit even without an excuse. The search for a possible *gweiz* made them still more pleasant. From Ingleton the path ascends beside the Doe through gorges of impressive height and gloom, and alongside thundering waterfalls, one above another. They are beautiful. But above the sheer sides of the ravine are deep banks so steep that it is impossible to imagine even a fabulous horse leaping across. Only above Thornton Force is there a possible place – and here a horse could cross without wetting its hooves. The report to Mr Brewster had to be a reluctant negative.

In this search, however, the Galloway Gate kept coming into question; and then it turned out that there was a place actually on that old road where people traditionally leaped across a chasm (Nevison the highwayman was said to be one of them). But it was far beyond Dent: at Hell Gill, where the infant River Eden forms the border between Yorkshire and Cumbria in Mallerstang. The road runs just above Hell Gill Farm. This is the track along which Anne Clifford, Countess of Pembroke, travelled in her coach from Skipton Castle to Pendragon and on to Brougham. How did her coach cross Hell Gill? It is a yard wide, but 100 feet deep.

Her retinue must have made a temporary wood bridge. Nowadays there is a substantial stone arch, but to look over the parapet into the gloomy gulf is startling. If Hell Gill were the *gweiz prelljus*, however, the Castle of Wonders would have to be Pendragon, which is about six miles away. Pendragon did not seem sufficiently impressive; and instead of looking *up* to it, from Hell Gill one would look down. The Gill can also be jumped on foot if one has the nerve. Perhaps still more important, Pendragon Castle does figure in Arthurian legend in another story but under its own name, as we shall see later.

Again the hunt had drawn a blank. On the return from Hell Gill through Ribblehead towards Ingleton, once again there is the sight of Ingleborough looming majestically overhead. Why, of course, the old road crossed first the Doe and then – nearer Ingleborough – the Twiss. The two valleys run into one and are collectively known as 'Ingleton Waterfalls'. It was time to go up the eastern branch, through Twistleton Glen.

From the first dramatic footbridge onwards, one after another were places where it was just possible to think of a fabulous knight on a fabulous horse making a huge leap across the chasm and being able to climb up the far side. The river itself was much more impressive – more worth while leaping over. Well up the glen, the path climbs a concrete but discreet staircase beside a gorge of great beauty. A roaring cascade comes down in tumbling white foam beside the track. At the top of the staircase the path edges round a crag, and emerges high above a great bowl. On the far side is a narrow rift where the water forces a way between two great rocks. Below is a whirlpool and shelving beach. From there the stream vanishes into a thunderous cascade.

What was it Sam Brewster had written? 'It would be necessary to find a place near a high waterfall where the tops of the ravine on each side are level enough and not too far apart.' In addition – since Gawain and his great horse fell into the water at the first attempt – the leap could not itself be across a deep chasm. The horse was swept by the whirlpool to a sloping bank where the knight was able to pull it out. This spot seemed to fit every requirement. Just below, there was even a great yew tree spanning the ravine – just such a tree as the one from which Gawain had to break a bough for a wreath for the duchess whom he was escorting on his adventure.

If this is indeed *li gweiz prelljus* – and Mr Brewster is extremely cautious about it – then Ingleborough is the magician Clinschor's castle where he kept many ladies imprisoned (Gawain in unexplained manner set them free by means of the Bed of Wonders), and the whole area around is the Land of Wonders. Once the map is drawn up from that point of view, it is remarkable how well the jigsaw of clues seems to fall into shape.

The story told by Chrétien and Von Eschenbach shows signs of having a source or sources earlier than both poets. For instance, while Von Eschenbach writes in German, he gives the ford a name in French – but it is not the same as the one given in French by the French poet. Moreover, considerable similarities exist between their versions and the probably somewhat earlier story of *Peredur Son of Evrawc* in the collection of Welsh tales called the *Mabinogion*. It might be worth the while of specialists in Old Welsh to consider whether 'Clinschor' could be compounded of Celtic elements – Linsgurr, for instance.

An odd instance of continuity of culture stands near Ingleton at the entrance to the gorge of the Ingleton waterfalls. At this point, alongside the path, an artificial 'well' has been built, complete with a little Jack-and-Jill gabled roof, a circular wall and, within it, an incongruously square depression containing a square tin full of water. The passers-by are invited to throw coins into this and to make a wish.

On the well is a plaque saying: 'May your wish be for happiness. Proceeds from this well will be donated by Bentham and District Round Table No. 346 to local charities.' Not only would the ancient gods perhaps appreciate this revival of the holy-well cult, but Sir Gawain – if he came a bit further downstream from *li gweiz prelljus* – would no doubt feel at home with the Tablers.

Five miles southward from this 'wishing well' along the route which may be the postulated ancient British track, the way to Cross o' Greet passes alongside a highly conspicuous 'erratic' boulder, deposited by a retreating glacier at the end of the Ice Age. This rock, up which steps were cut in the long past, bears the name of the Great Stone of Fourstones. Near it is a farm called Fourstones.

In Malory's *Morte Darthur*, during the tragic story of the brothers Balin and Balan the two knights 'from Northumberland', after a long separation during which Balin had been imprisoned for a while at the court of Arthur (an oddly negative sidelight on Arthur), he sets out on an adventure and is found by Balan. Balan tells his brother: 'A man told me in the castle of Four Stones that ye were delivered, and therefore I came hither into this country, for here I supposed to find you.'

At the place near Cross o' Greet no remains of a castle have been noticed, and the three other stones of the Four are missing: a tradition says they were broken up to make whetstones for scythes, but they would presumably have contained enough material to keep all England mowing for centuries. Within Brigantia, however, in the northern frontier region on the southern marches of Northumberland, there is another place called 'Fourstones', and with a 'castle' near it in the shape of a hill-fort. It is near Hexham, south of the Wall, and in the area which has been put forward as the site of Arthur's last, fatal battle against Mordred by the Wood of Celidon. Another Fourstones stands on the south-western ridge of Whernside, west-north-west of the Hill Inn at Chapel-le-Dale (Grid reference SD 731779).

The Galloway Gate is an old drovers' road, along which until quite recent times, in historical terms, livestock used to be herded from Scotland down to the meat-markets of the industrialised West Riding of Yorkshire, the Midlands and eventually London. The name 'Galloway Gate' may have arisen in connection with that traffic; or with the road's use by pedlars – 'Scotties' as they were commonly known – and packhorse men, who usually rode and drove small horses called 'Galloways'. It may therefore be suggested that the name 'Galloway Gate' has no connection with an Arthurian legend that dates from at the latest the twelfth century and may be much older. This suggestion, however, again smacks of the claim that the Shakespearean plays were written by someone else of the same name: it is a distinction which really makes little difference. No one has ever proposed that the pedlars and packhorse men made the roads that they used. Nobody knows how old this road is, though Raistrick (*Green Tracks on the Pennines*, 1962) describes it as very ancient. The old road called the High Way down the east side of the Mallerstang valley, to which the Galloway Gate leads, is pre-Celtic.

If Sir Gawain – having liberated all the ladies held prisoner by Clinschor in the Castle of Wonders, and having given the duchess the bough from the tree for a garland to avenge her for a wrong done by another knight – then continued on his way northward towards Galloway, he would after a couple of hours' riding or so (assuming the Castle of Wonders to be Ingleborough) find himself going along that remarkably level High Way down Mallerstang. After negotiating Hell Gill, he would see the track dropping gradually to the bottom of the valley under the huge and menacing fang of what is now called Wild Boar Fell (perhaps a corruption of Wilbert Fell) until at The Thrang he crossed the River Eden, and shortly afterwards arrived at Pendragon Castle.

Its name would be familiar enough to him. Arthur's father was known as Uther Pendragon, because he adopted the Welsh national emblem of a dragon's head as his personal device. But the Pendragon Castle that exists today was built in Norman times, and nothing of it – or at any rate very little – would have been seen by Sir Gawain. On the other hand, it is quite likely that he would have seen something there.

Nobody has ever sought to explain why this Norman castle should have borne such an un-Norman name. Lady Anne Clifford, who in 1663 journeyed along the High Way, owned the building. She stayed in it, and repaired it; and she called it 'Pendragon's Castle'. There must at some time have been a Celtic Welsh establishment here, and one of some importance. The rock on which the Norman castle was erected stands in a commanding position controlling all passage along the valley.

There is something else special about it. In the Arthurian and general Celtic tradition a regular feature is that of a building standing on an island. Commonly the site was either very sacred (in a pagan or Christian sense), or the centre of a kingdom, or both. The tradition is a very ancient one, to be found not only in the Celtic world but, for instance, in the ancient Egyptian and Babylonian myths. Sometimes the island was in the sea – generally the western sea (where Atlantis was). Sometimes it was in a lake. Sometimes it might be in a river.

There is a deep moat-like ditch around Pendragon Castle; the tradition in Mallerstang says that part of the River Eden was diverted to flow around the castle, but the Eden insisted on returning to its own course. The local couplet is:

> Uther Pendragon may do what he can –
> Eden will run where Eden ran.

The castle's name has long been assumed to indicate that an original stronghold on this rock was built by Uther. It may be otherwise. The Celtic Welsh kingdom of Rheged, which existed in Arthur's day and considerably later, is believed to have had its southern frontier at one time at or about Hell Gill. Anybody coming northwards along the High Way would therefore meet something like a border-fortress where the castle's remains now stand. If its name refers not to Uther but to the national emblem of the Celtic Welsh, that might indicate that after Arthur's death, the leadership of the British resistance to the Saxon invasion was taken up or claimed by Rheged; and in fact King Urien of Rheged and his son Owain did fight valiantly against the invaders, taking a prominent part in battles as far away as Lindisfarne.

It is a remarkable fact that Pendragon Castle figures in Malory's *Morte Darthur*, and even more remarkable that throughout the relevant section, no reference whatever is made to any possible connection of the castle either with Arthur and his Round Table (except inimically) or with Uther Pendragon himself. The circumstances, indeed, would seem to bear out the proposition that this was a border strongpoint which it was necessary for Arthur's forces to subdue.

The episode is the final one in the adventure of the 'Badly Dressed Knight' – La Cote Male Taile. This was the nickname bestowed by the boorish Sir Kay on the newly knighted Sir Breunor le Noire, who had to escort the contemptuous damsel Maledisant. Sir Lancelot was riding to overtake them. La Cote Male Taile came to Pendragon Castle, and was attacked and taken prisoner by six knights. Sir Lancelot came into the vicinity and was warned by one of his own companions, Sir Nerovens, not to go by Pendragon Castle, 'for there is a lord, a mighty knight, and many knights with him, and this night I heard that they took a knight prisoner yesterday that rode with a damsel, and they say he is a knight of the Round Table'. So of course Sir Lancelot engaged the six knights and overthrew them, and hurtled into the castle where he defeated the lord, Sir Brian de les Isles. Inside the castle Sir Lancelot set free thirty of Arthur's knights (a major gain) and forty ladies, and gave the castle to La Cote Male Taile.

This story occurs later in *Morte Darthur* than Sir Lancelot's defeat of Sir Turquine, which seems to have taken place at the Giant's Cave on the River Eamont according to local traditions; but there is probably little significance in Malory's choice of order.

King Urien of Rheged figures many times in *Morte Darthur*: in the period of Arthur's consolidation as a determined opponent of Arthur, and later as himself one of the Knights of the Round Table, though in reality he probably appeared on the historical scene after Arthur's death; but he seems to have left little impression on the legends and traditions of his own kingdom of Rheged. This is by no means true of his son Owain, who is a character who cannot be ignored.

Owain is a hero of medieval romance comparable with Sir Lancelot, Sir Gawain and 'King' Arthur himself. Chrétien de Troyes in the twelfth century devoted a long poem to him under the name of *Yvain*. As Sir Uwaine le Blanchemains ('White Hands'), he plays a considerable role in *Morte Darthur*: among other incidents he is temporarily expelled from Arthur's court on suspicion of spying for his mother, Morgan le Fay, in her attempts to murder her half-brother Arthur; Urien at the same time is not expelled because Arthur knows of Morgan's attempt to murder Urien too. Since Owain's homeland is Rheged, it may be significant that he is named as one of two knights involved with Sir Galahad in the early stages of the Quest for the Grail – a quest that began in Camelot, identified a few pages earlier in *Morte Darthur* as Carlisle.

In the *Mabinogion*, the tale of *The Lady of the Fountain* has Owain as the hero of a very pagan adventure around a magical tree. It concludes with a passing reference to his followers, 'and those were the army of three hundred ravens which Kenverchyn [Owain's grandfather] had left him'. Another *mabinogi*, *The Dream of Rhonabwy*, introduces a game of chess between Owain and Arthur, which at first is three times interrupted because Arthur's men are attacking Owain's ravens. At last Owain raises his banner, whereupon the ravens are revived and turn the tables until Arthur begs for mercy. All this has reference to very ancient pagan Celtic motifs which may have been interwoven with historical events. Both the magical tree and the magical birds are themes which will be considered later.

5

WHAT THE BUTLER SAW

❖

Owain in his own historical homeland of Rheged left a mark under the name of Hewen. The citadel of Owain and his father Urien is believed to have been not at Carlisle but among the low hills on the east side of the Penrith–Carlisle Roman road (the modern A 6), between that road and the River Eden, near High Hesket. Leland, in the time of Henry VIII, wrote that 'in the forest of Ynglewood, a VI miles fro Carluel, appere ruines of a castel cawled Castel Lewen' – otherwise Castle Hewen. T. F. Bulmer in 1884 wrote:

> The foundations, which were visible a few years ago, show the castle to have been 233 feet by 147 feet, with walls in some places eight feet thick. Here dwelt, according to popular legend, Ewan Caesario, a man of gigantic stature who ruled over 'rocky Cumberland'.

Broadly the legend, *The Marriage of Sir Gawain*, is that Arthur, while holding court at Christmas at Carlisle, sets out to punish Hewen/Owain/Ewan (or the 'Carle of Carlisle', or the giant baron of Tarn Wadling – a lake which until last century existed immediately south of Castle Hewen) for misusing a maiden. When he approaches the magic ground on which the castle stands, however (it is very close to the site of a huge oak known as the 'last tree in Inglewood Forest' which stood until the nineteenth century), his courage vanishes and his sword-arm is helpless. Hewen lets Arthur go, on condition that on New Year's Day he should return and answer the question: 'What does a woman love best?' The members of his court cannot provide the reply, but an ugly old hag (the 'Loathly Lady' theme) offers to help if he will grant her request, to which he agrees. She tells him: 'Woman loves her own way best', and then demands to marry one of his knights. He gives Hewen the answer; and Arthur's nephew Sir Gawain offers to marry the hag. During the wedding night a spell on her is broken and she is transformed into a beautiful young woman. The Gawain element will be considered later.

Another variant describes 'Sir Ewan Caesario' as a slayer of robbers and wild boars, who lived during the time of a Saxon king called John in the fifth century. Of this legend, the early date mentioned is particularly interesting.

On the south-east side of Blaze Fell, south of Castle Hewen, is a farm called Ewan Close, and this is traditionally associated with Urien's giant son. In the churchyard at Penrith is what is called the Giant's Grave, said to be Owain's; and there is a tradition that at one time it was opened and some very large human bones were found in it. In reality the 'grave' has a high Saxon cross-shaft at each end, and two Danish hog's-back gravestones are arranged along each side. The 'Giant's Thumb' near by is another Saxon cross. All these stones are believed to be of about the tenth century, some 350 years after Owain; but the Owain tradition is there.

So it is also just south of Penrith, at the River Eamont. The present A 6 road crosses it by Eamont Bridge, alongside the prehistoric henges of Mayborough and King Arthur's Round Table; but about a mile upstream, to the west, is the village of Yanwath, which has been described as derived from Ewan-wath, i.e. Ewan's ford. Downstream from Eamont Bridge, near the confluence of the Eamont with the Eden at Edenhall, is a cave in the red sandstone cliff. This cave, probably formed by the scouring of the water when the bank on that side lay much lower, is known as Giant's Cave, and is stated to have been Ewan's or Owain's. The local tradition which calls him Ewan Caesario or Caesarius is curious. If Rheged did seek to take the leadership of the Britons after Arthur's death – especially if Saklatvala is correct in believing Arthur to have claimed to be *Dux Britanniae* in the Roman succession – it might not be surprising if Rheged's warrior-king adopted such a pseudo-Roman imperial title.

Undoubtedly, however, pagan mysteries are bound up with this giant-Ewan as much as historical memories. Customs and ceremonies associated with this cave and other points in the surrounding area are a confused mass of Arthuriana and Celtic or pre-Celtic mythology, almost certainly connected in some ways with local prehistoric earthworks and megaliths.

William Furness (*History of Penrith*, 1894) says that the dweller in the cave is first represented as a giant, then as a dubious knight-errant, and lastly as a monster killing men and beasts and devouring them in his den. He quotes a legend of a damsel who did not know about the monster and went walking near the river. The monster rushed out, and the terrified damsel took a flying leap across a cleft in the bank. The monster missed his step, fell into the river and was killed. 'This opening bears the name of "The Maiden's Step", and near it is the figure of a maiden, sculptured in the rock, in a running posture, but the head, etc., have been disfigured by thoughtless visitors.' I lived in Penrith from 1929 to 1934 and several times went to the cave. I also examined it in 1973. I have never seen any trace of this figure. One may wonder if this was another representation of Bride-Brigid. Nicolson and Burn (*History of Cumberland*, 1777) in describing the caves (there is a smaller one next door) make no mention of the carving – but this omission, in that particular work, means nothing. The statement that the head of the maiden had been disfigured is reminiscent of the statue of 'St Margaret' or 'Peg o' th' Well' at Waddow Hall, mentioned later.

It may be thought that Furness's monster variant, judging by comparative mythology, would be more likely to be the earliest of the three rather than the last. It is this human-devouring monster that recalls the very pagan child-eating giant of St Michael's Mount whom in *Morte Darthur* Arthur fought and slew.

Even more curiously, Furness refers to

an ancient ballad which associates one Tarquin with these caves, who held there three-score and four of the knights of the Round Table as prisoners, and very obligingly kept a copper basin hanging near his den to be used as a bell. Sir Lancelot du Lac slew the monster and delivered the knights.

This is the story in *Morte Darthur*, Book VI, Chapters 7 to 9, about Sir Turquine, brother of Sir Carados (one of Arthur's most consistent and powerful foes – who Saklatvala thinks was identical with Cerdic the West Saxons' king, the earliest known ancestor of the existing British Royal Family). This Sir Turquine kept three-score and four Round Table knights prisoner, and had a basin hanging from a tree to act as a challenge-bell. Sir Lancelot beat the basin, slew Sir Turquine and freed the sixty-four knights. It may be added, however, that if sixty-four knights were squashed into this cave and the smaller one next to it, there would be no room for Sir Turquine himself. The copper basin seems to have reference to the magical bronze cauldron which figures in many Celtic legends; a number of highly decorated cauldrons have been recovered from Celtic sacrificial hoards.

Had the maker of the ballad quoted by Furness read *Morte Darthur*? Had Malory, on the other hand, read or heard the ballad? As we shall see, Malory's family possessed a manor quite near the cave. Or did both the ballad and Malory's story come from a song sung by Taliesin or Aneurin or Myrddin at the court of Rheged, also not far away?

The cave itself is memorable. It is approached from the top of the cliff by a flight of steps cut in the sandstone rock face. From the entrance, the inside of the cave glows partly red, the colour of the rock, and partly emerald green, from a rare alga which puts up millions of tiny chlorophyll-packed plates all facing the same way to catch the maximum light. Looking in the opposite direction, from the entrance one looks down some 40 feet to the swirling Eamont. Downstream is an old, disused ford. Straight across the river is a field, in which is the little church of St Ninian's, known locally as Ninekirks, which Lady Anne Clifford rebuilt but which is said to have been founded by St Ninian in the fourth century –

that is before Arthur and during the Roman occupation. The cave commands an extensive view, but is itself difficult to distinguish.

In 1860 the Rev. B. Porteous, then Vicar of Edenhall, wrote of an annual assembly called 'Giant's Cave Sunday', which was observed on the third Sunday in May when thousands of people would congregate at the cave and ceremonies were held which Porteous did not describe. But in his time 'the custom has dwindled into insignificance, the "shaking bottles" carried by the children at that season being the only remains of what it has been'.

Furness, more than thirty years later, is more explicit. Each of the four Sundays in May was a special occasion for rejoicing, especially among young people. The first of these 'Well Sundays' was held at Skirsgill (on the northern bank of the Yanwath ford over the Eamont) where there was a well known spring reached by a flight of stone steps and furnished with a drinking-cup. Near the well on that day there would be a fair. Next Sunday was the turn of the well at Clifton, on the opposite bank of the Eamont. The third was 'Giant's Cave Sunday', associated with a well at Edenhall, and the fourth was at Dickey Bank.

> The young people filled bottles with water at the respective wells, putting Spanish juice [liquorice] into the bottles, and then shaking them until the froth boiled over, when they sucked the froth [the same practice is recorded at the once very revered 'Ebbing and Flowing Well' at Giggleswick, near Settle in the Yorkshire Pennines]. This was repeated until the bottle was empty. Clifton Sunday was the most popular, and the well there had the repute of being the best in the district. Stalls were numerous, and laden with shortcakes, gingerbread, etc., and the whole aspect was that of a village fair. A ditty was current in that neighbourhood:
>
> > The second Sunday in May
> > Is shaking-bottle day.
>
> These Sundays had to be discontinued through the bad

repute that attached to them from the fighting and other irregularities with which they often ended.

But it is at Edenhall itself that there is a special well around which paganism seems to be mixed with possible references to the Arthurian legend. Between the village and the river is a thirteenth-century church dedicated to St Cuthbert, marking one of the points at which the monks are believed to have rested in their seven years' wandering with the saint's body after the Danish invasion of Northumbria in AD 875. Close by, between the church and the (now demolished) Eden Hall mansion, is a spring known as St Cuthbert's Well.

It has another name, however: Fairy Well. Under this name it figures in a story about the origin of a glass vessel called the Luck of Edenhall.

Edenhall Manor in 1460 came into the hands of the Musgrave family, who trace their descent from one of the followers of William the Conqueror. The story – which is not, however, quite the earliest version recorded – is that the Musgraves' butler went to draw water at the Fairy Well, and happened to find the fairies dancing around the glass cup. He seized it and refused to give it back, whereupon the fairies sang:

> Whene'er this cup shall break or fall,
> Farewell the luck of Edenhall.

Ironically, while there is no longer an Edenhall mansion and the Musgrave family no longer inhabit the manor, the Luck is preserved in the Victoria and Albert Museum in London, which in 1959 bought it for £5,600 (a bargain price) from the administrators of the estate of the late Sir Nigel Courtenay Musgrave.

The cup is of green glass with red, yellow and blue enamel. It was made in Syria – probably at Aleppo – in about 1250, and is thought to have been brought back to England by a Crusader. It is equipped with a finely tooled leather case which was made about a century later either in England or in the Narbonne district of France. On the top of the case appears the Christian monogram

IHS, and the vessel itself was probably at one time used as a chalice. The Museum treasures the case as much as the cup.

The Rev. C. E. Golland, in a paper read in 1914 to the Cumberland and Westmorland Antiquarian and Archaeological Society, suggested that *Isis Parlis*, a name found in reference to the Edenhall and Giant's Cave locality, meant in Celtic 'Jars of the Mound-Folk' and concerned a rite connected with a magical and talismanic vessel. He mentioned the huge concourses on Giant's Cave Sundays and the 'shaking bottles'; and he suggested that although the Luck itself was 'too modern', it was a memory of the old magic vessel of Celtic myth which 'emerged in a Christian disguise as the Holy Grail'.

Nicolson and Burn (vol. 2, p. 405) say of Penrith:

> On the east part of the parish, upon the north bank of the river Eamont, are two caves or grottoes dug out of the solid rock, and sufficient to contain 100 men. The passage to them is very narrow and dangerous, and perhaps its *perilous* access may have given it the name of *Isis Parlis*, tho' the vulgar tell strange stories of one Isis a giant who lived here in former times, and like Cacus of old used to seize men and cattle and draw them into his den to devour them. But it is highly probable that these subterranean chambers were made for a secure retreat in time of sudden danger; and the iron gates, which were taken away not long ago, do not a little to confirm that supposition.

I am aware of no other reference to these iron gates, which sound reminiscent of those alleged once to have guarded the entrance to the hollow at the summit of Castle Sowerby, about 12 miles to the west-north-west. The serious etymology of *Isis Parlis* seems to remain a mystery.

In 1972 the Fairy Well at Edenhall contained some pearl buttons, and an American five-cent piece dated 1970.

Meanwhile, why the butler? What was he doing going to draw water at the Fairy Well?

'Butler' means 'bottler'; but one of the more prominent Knights of the Round Table was called Sir Lucan the Butler, appointed to that post by Arthur in his first disposition of his officers. It did not mean a servitor in striped waistcoat and with a salver in hand. A butler in the Middle Ages was a high officer of a royal household. Sir Lucan was no menial. He was the brother of Sir Bedivere – one of the greatest of the Round Table fellowship – a son of Duke Corneus, and himself described as a mighty duke. In Arthur's early campaigns to establish his authority, Sir Lucan fought valiantly in his support. (In *King Arthur's Death*, a ballad reproduced in Bishop Percy's *Reliques of Ancient English Poetry*, the position is reversed: 'Lukyn' is 'Duke of Gloster', and his brother Bedevere is Arthur's butler; and it is Lukyn, not Bedevere, who at the third time of asking throws Excalibur into the lake).

Lucan's official job may have been that of a kind of quartermaster of supplies, but an alternative title to 'butler' was that of 'cup-bearer'. Saklatvala has suggested that the Grail was a real holy relic which was used officially in Arthur's court for special ceremonies and for the administering of formal oaths. It might then be thought that the official Cup-bearer was responsible for the Grail and, if it were recovered from robbers (Saklatvala thinks it was twice stolen by rebels), it would be he who would take charge of it.

The Luck of Edenhall would be mystery enough by itself, but it might almost be said to be merely the start of the story. The Edenhall cup is only one of a whole collection of similar objects, each of which is a big question-mark.

I was long aware of other 'Lucks' associated with Muncaster Castle (near Ravenglass on the Cumberland coast) and at Burrell Green, a farm in the Eden valley; and of a 'Luck of Levens Hall' consisting of the birth of a white fawn in the Hall's herd of dark fallow deer to mark important events. These may therefore be considered next.

The Muncaster Luck is a glass bowl enamelled in white and gold, which is kept at the castle. It may be of similar origin to that of Edenhall. After the battle of Towton (near York) in 1461 during the Wars of the Roses, King Henry VI fled, and was discovered by a shepherd sheltering on Muncaster Fell. He must have been exhausted by such a long and difficult journey to escape his enemies.

The shepherd led him to Muncaster Castle, where Sir John Pennington gave him refuge. Henry recovered his strength, rallied supporters and eventually departed; in token of his gratitude he gave Sir John the bowl, assuring his host that his family would prosper as long as the vessel was preserved intact.

It is still the property of the Pennington family. On Muncaster Fell is a Henry Chapel, a memorial to the King's escape; and in Muncaster Church is a stone slab inscribed: 'Holie Kynge Harrye gave Sir John a Brauve workyd glass cuppe ... whyllys the famylie shold keep hit unbrecken they shold gretelye thrif.'

The odd fact emerges that King Henry gave Sir John Pennington the Luck of Muncaster in the year after the Musgrave family, in the same king's reign, acquired Edenhall. By a further coincidence, if coincidence it is, the former Castle at Kirkoswald – near Edenhall but on the other bank of the Eden – had a remarkable panelled ceiling, with no less than 145 panels occupied by portraits of the Kings of England from Brutus (traditionally the country's first monarch) to this same Henry VI; the ceiling was later removed to Naworth Castle, where it was destroyed by fire in 1844.

The Luck of Burrell Green was supposed by the late Molly Lefebure, the writer on the Lake District, to have disappeared. In reality it remains where it has been for many years past, and where in 1973 I handled and examined it. It acquires added significance from its provenance. Burrell Green farmhouse is only a mile away from Edenhall, on the same side of the river. The Luck is a brass bowl or dish, more than sixteen inches in diameter, with a central decoration of 'wrython' flutes.

Around this centrepiece, according to an article of December 1879 in the *Art Magazine*, used to be a Latin inscription in black-lettering or late Gothic, translated as 'Hail Mary Mother of Jesus Saviour of Mankind', and outside this another ring, inscribed in later lettering: 'If this dish be sold or gi'en, Farewell the luck of Burrell Green.' The article described the dish as of sixteenth-century style. Both the inscriptions are now quite illegible, allegedly as a result of constant cleaning (and it still gleams). The Luck is also described in vol. 15 of the *Transactions* of the Cumberland and Westmorland Antiquarian and Archaeological Society.

I am indebted, however, to Mr H. G. Gill, of The Manor House, Greystoke, Penrith, for the following information:

> The Luck of Burrell Green is what is termed by antique dealers an alms dish and was probably made in Nuremberg about the year 1500. The motif is what is known as a variation of the 'voluted rose' which appeared at the end of the 15th century and is depicted on many dishes of a later period.
>
> The term 'alms dish' is really a misnomer as it is extremely rare to find one portraying the sacred inscription. The Luck is obviously later than the date of the dish. Gothic letters were extensively used for decoration only and the so-called inscriptions were meaningless, although there are rare instances where these make sense.
>
> Without an examination of the dish, and judging solely from the photograph, it appears to be a genuine product of Nuremberg but could also be of Dinant, or other towns in Flanders or the Rhine noted for medieval brass work.

To Mr Gill's memoir it may be added that his provisional date of 1500 is thirty-nine years after Henry VI gave Sir John the Luck of Muncaster Castle.

The tenants of Burrell Green, Mr and Mrs S. Armstrong, showed me a letter they had received from Mrs G. Rycroft, née Lamb, of Kingston, Tasmania, whose father was born at Burrell Green. 'The luck came into being somewhere about 1417' [that is, four years before Henry VI came to the throne as an infant], she wrote. 'My father told me the story. There was a wedding between a Lamb and the "King of Mardale".' The 'kings' of Mardale were a hardy family who for centuries maintained quasi-independence in the Haweswater area – something like the moss-trooper barons of the Scottish Border.

'When the servants went to draw water from the well just

below Burrell Green house,' Mrs Rycroft continued, 'the hobgoblins came up out of it. They said: "If you bring us wine and food [that is, if they were allowed to take part in the wedding feast], we will bless this wedding [that is, it would receive pagan sanctification]." So the servants fed the hobgoblins, and they left the brass dish as a gift when they went. Our crest is a lamb carrying a two-point pennant and wearing a halo over one ear and standing on a bit of barley-sugar.' The last sentence is irrelevant but irresistible.

The tradition related by Mrs Rycroft has obvious similarities with – and notable differences from – that of the Edenhall Luck. I examined the Burrell Green well, and had no difficulty in envisaging the hobgoblins (one version says a witch, and another Hob Thross) popping up out of it.

So here were four Lucks – Edenhall, Muncaster, Burrell Green and the Levens white fawn. When a query asking for information about them appeared in the magazine *Cumbria*, however, Mr Hugh C. Little of Steeton, near Keighley, wrote mentioning a Luck of Haresceugh Castle. This was something quite unknown.

Haresceugh (pronounced Har-skyewf) Castle is now a farm near Renwick, near the foot of the Hartside Pass that goes over the Pennine ridge from Penrith to Alston. It is $4\frac{1}{2}$ miles from Kirkoswald and 14 miles from Penrith. The 'castle' has by now almost vanished. Its last remaining tower was blown down one night in March 1866 by the Helm Wind, the tempest which from time to time strikes the western side of the Cross Fell range. Alongside is a farmhouse.

The occupants of Haresceugh, Mr Blenkinsop and his father (who in 1973 was over 80 years old and had lived in the locality all his life), had never heard of this Luck. The 1866 newspaper report of the collapse of the tower said nothing of the Luck. Neither did an account of the castle, some 1,500 words long, by 'W.T.M.' in the *Cumberland News* of 7 July 1934. There was no mention of the Luck in the description of the castle in Bulmer's *History and Directory of Cumberland* (1901). Tullie House Museum and Library, Carlisle, has no record of a Haresceugh Castle Luck. Nor was there anything in the *Transactions* of the Cumberland and Westmorland

Antiquarian and Archaeological Society, including Graham's account in 1909 of 'Six Extinct Cumberland Castles'. Mr Little himself had never seen the Luck. Nevertheless, there can be little doubt that his reference is authentic.

He described the vessel as a wooden bowl about 8 inches across, with a silver rim bearing an inscription something like:

> Should this bowl fall in feast or wassail
> Farewell the luck of Haresceugh Castle.

Mr Little recalls reading about this Luck more than forty years ago in a Cumberland newspaper, and a reference to it in some guide later; and he adds that the late Francis Mason, who farmed Sickergill, Renwick, and who died in 1965 at the age of 92, appeared to know something of it.

It may be wondered whether this Luck had any association with a legend of a secret tunnel between Haresceugh Castle and Kirkoswald Castle and of a kail-pot full of guineas buried in the cellars beneath the castle. Such legends of impossibly long tunnels are told of every old castle, abbey or priory – there is supposed to be one, for instance, between Pendragon Castle and Lammersyde Castle, a mile and a half farther down the Eden in Mallerstang. These legends probably relate to secret paths, almost certainly ancient leys. A ley starting at Alston Parish Church passes through Haresceugh Castle and the site of Kirkoswald Castle and on to the hill-fort on Carrock Fell. In medieval times and earlier this area was covered in dense forest.

The kail-pot theme is a common variant of the fundamental Celtic and Scandinavian magic cauldron from which the Grail is thought to have derived; but not far from Haresceugh Castle towards the end of the nineteenth century a triangular silver Saxon ornament of about AD 800 (now in the British Museum) and 700 Saxon coins were found buried. The find is described in the *Victoria County History of Cumberland*, vol. 1, p. 282. The silver ornament – not strictly triangular but a filigree trefoil in Carolingian style – is described and illustrated in the *Proceedings* of the Society of Antiquaries, second series, vol. 23, pp. 304–5.

Mr Little's description of the Haresceugh Castle Luck is quite distinct from that of all the other Lucks. Some indicative matter is contained in *Treen and Other Wooden Bygones* by Edward H. Pinto (1969). 'Treen' he defines as wooden objects which are or were in daily domestic or farm use and in trades and professions, and he adds: 'References to treen are numerous in old English literature, particularly to chalices, cups, bowls, platters and "services of treen".' He quotes the delicious sentence in a sixteenth-century sermon by John Jewel, Bishop of Salisbury: 'In old times we had treen chalices and golden priests, but now we have treen priests and golden chalices.' Still more interestingly, Mr Pinto adds: 'A very similar statement has also been attributed to Archbishop Boniface, 1240–1270.'

Describing treen wassail-bowls, Pinto refers to customs such as the wassailing on Twelfth Night ('Wassail Eve'), and the ceremonial wassailing of the orchard to ensure a good fruit harvest. At this ceremony a rhyme would be chanted such as Herrick's

> Wassaile the trees that they may beare
> You many a plum and many a peare;
> For more or lesse fruits they will bring,
> And you do give them wassailling.

This and other more ancient wassail-songs are somewhat reminiscent of the Haresceugh Castle couplet. Nevertheless, Mr Little's description fits the wassail-bowl less than it fits the mazer. There were two kinds of mazer: the ordinary plain drinking-bowls used by monks, and the larger silver-mounted ceremonial vessels. These latter, says Pinto, were 'the most important drinking-vessels used between about 1250 and 1600'.

The mazer was turned from the burr excrescence formed on some trees – particularly the maple – just above the ground. This was chosen because it withstood frequent changes in temperature and wetness or dryness; but it allowed the making of only a shallow bowl of relatively small diameter. To increase the capacity, important mazers were given deep, outward-projecting silver rims. One of the vessels claimed to have been the Grail, which was kept for many years in a monastery, has been described as a shallow wooden bowl. Certainly wooden mazers were used as chalices as the Grail appears to have been used. It is very much to be hoped that the lost Luck of Haresceugh Castle turns up.

Inquiries have so far failed to bring it to light; but if it were necessary to show further reason to think it existed, such reason might be provided by the fact that the search for the Luck of Haresceugh Castle did result in the discovery of yet another and quite distinct Luck. This one is associated with a farm called Nether Haresceugh – which has its own 'Holy Well' – about $2\frac{1}{2}$ miles from Haresceugh Castle and on the other side of Renwick village. It lies exactly on another ley running from Haresceugh Castle through Calthwaite to the prehistoric 'castle' near Hesket Newmarket. Nether Haresceugh's old name is stated to be Charbuckle Haresceugh. I have never hitherto come across any mention of a 'Luck' there under either name, and the archaeological and antiquarian sources have no reference to it. The only reference that exists, and that so cursory as to be contained in half a sentence, occurs in the late Col. T. Fetherstonhaugh's privately printed and published history of Kirkoswald, *Our Cumberland Village* (1925).

This Luck is kept not at the farm, but elsewhere, in safety. For decades it had rested, screwed up in a wooden case. For my benefit the vessel was gently extracted from the case, and I examined it.

It is a glass bowl or cup of a beautiful deep claret colour, with a white edge (like the Lucks of Edenhall and Muncaster). The cup is quite small, however, only about $2\frac{1}{2}$ inches high and the same in diameter. Its origin and provenance are another mystery. Some antiquarians who have not seen it – who indeed had never heard of it before – thought it might be a specimen of 'Bristol glass', meaning not the white 'milk-glass' made at Bristol in the middle of the eighteenth century but the opal glass with a 'sunset glow' made not only at Bristol but also in the north of England. Such an identification would call for authoritative confirmation. In any case, there was obviously no possibility of confusion of this Luck with the Haresceugh Castle Luck.

Later, still more Lucks came to light. One was very similar to that of Levens Hall – the appearance of a white fawn in a herd of 'black' fallow deer – but this was in the New Forest (one of the very few places apart from Levens that have such dark-coloured fallow). At Levens Hall itself, however, on the River Kent on the southern edge of the Lake District, some glasses known as 'constables' are kept. An annual 'Radish Feast' was held at the Hall on 12 May (corresponding to Shaking-Bottle Sunday), when the 'constables' were filled with a specially brewed and potent 'Morocco beer'. The stranger had to drink the glassful at one breath with the toast: 'Luck to Levens while the Kent flows.'

How many Lucks are there now, then? Four, if we count Edenhall, Muncaster, Burrell Green and Levens Hall's white fawn; five, if we add Nether Haresceugh; six, if the silver-rimmed wooden bowl of Haresceugh Castle can be traced; seven, if we include the New Forest fawn; eight, with the Levens 'constables'. By contrast, the *Encyclopædia Britannica* index, under 'Luck' cites only Edenhall, and the next entry is 'Lucknow'. Many so far insoluble questions remain, however.

Why does each of these objects, except perhaps that of Muncaster, refer not to a person or a family, but to a particular place? Why do all of them, except that of the New Forest, have their homes in Brigantia, and particularly Rheged? Why are all but two of them cups or bowls? Why, of these, are all but one located in the middle of the Eden valley, only a short way from Castle Hewen and Tarn Wadling? Why, in the midst of them, surrounded by Long Meg and her Daughters, the Grey Yauds and many other stone circles and tumuli, are there a St Michael's Well and a ruined Chapel of St Michael – the archangel whose services were especially in demand for combating pagan forces? Luck? Carlisle's Romano-Celtic name was Luguvallium, the city of the god Lugh.

During the correspondence over the Cumbria article, Mr Walter M. Johnston, of Barrow-in-Furness, wrote:

> Whether there is any significance in the word 'Luck' I cannot say. These vessels when they were brought to England were

highly revered and in many cases looked on as sacred objects, and as such were said to have certain properties; but it was an age of holy superstition.

These have been long shots. A much longer one still leads from Edenhall past the Malorys' manor to Brough, then over ancient trackways to Middleton-in-Teesdale, down to Vinovia on the Wear, past another manor of the Malorys and on to Eden Castle. This place has no etymological connection with the River Eden in Cumberland, but derives its name from a British or pre-British hill-fort called Eoden or Yoden on the coast. Here in 1775 a vessel was found far older than the Luck of Edenhall, and it may be thought far more impressive though rather sinister. This vessel, now in the British Museum, is a glass claw-beaker described as Celtic, made in the late fifth or early sixth century AD – precisely Arthur's time. It shows considerable similarities, however, to a green glass beaker found in an 'Anglo-Saxon burial ground' at Broadstairs, exhibited to the Society of Antiquaries by Mr Howard Hurd in 1910.

The very part of Brigantia where most of the Lucks occur will appear in even stranger contexts. One of the traditions about the Grail was that it was a wooden bowl, which for a long time was kept in a monastery but later disappeared – something reminiscent of the Luck of Haresceugh Castle. (A similar wooden 'Grail' is still preserved at Nanteos, near Aberystwyth). The Rev. C. E. Golland, referring to the Edenhall Luck as a possible 'memory' of the Grail, may have been only a few miles out. Dr Todd, the well known Cumberland antiquarian of the eighteenth century, said that in early times the bishops of the diocese permitted not only the parochial clergy, but also the monastic or regular priests, to celebrate Mass in chalices of glass. One of the canons issued in the reign of King Athelstan (ruled AD 925–40) read: '*Sacer Calix fusilis sit, non ligneus*' – 'Let the sacred chalice be fusile, not wooden'.

6

THE ELUSIVE KNIGHT

※

The Lucks lead on by unexpected routes to the problem of the identity of Sir Thomas Malory, the fifteenth-century author of *Morte Darthur* which was one of Caxton's first printed books in English literature. Leland's *Itinerary*, compiled in the sixteenth century, says there are two lordships not far from Ripon. 'Malory hath Hutton Coniers. . . . Malory hath another Place caullyd Highe Studly, a little from Fountaines.' Leland describes Malory — this same Yorkshire Malory — as a 'Welchman'.

Both Hutton Conyers and High Studley are only a few miles from the Walton-Walshford pocket near the old Brigantian capital of Isurium. Perhaps Malory — whose name may indeed be Welsh — was within reach of old Welsh stories about Arthur in addition to those in the Continental romances which he used. As we shall see later, stories and poems of the Arthurian cycle were in fact being written down, if not actually composed, in the Yorkshire-Lancashire-Cheshire area of Brigantia in the Middle Ages about a century — perhaps less — before Malory wrote *Morte Darthur*. One of them was an alliterative poem actually called *Morte Arthur*. There are certainly in Malory's work some puzzling passages which seem to owe nothing to the Romance poets, but to have their origin farther back, even beyond Arthur in Celtic paganism.

A manuscript of the French prose romance *Merlin* exists bearing a note in another hand saying: *Ci comence le livre que Sir Thomas Malori Chr reduce in Engloys et fuist emprente par Willm Caxton*. This note appears at the section dealing with Ygerne and Uther's proposition. The MS was in an old hide trunk together with all the old deeds and seals relating to the property of Ribston Hall back to the twelfth century. The trunk was kept at the Hall, which is halfway between High Studley and Walton. It was suggested by the former owner, Major J. G. Dent, that Malory or Mallory might be a corruption of Mauleverer, the name of the medieval lords of Ribston; but there are records in, for instance, the Wars of the Roses, of a Malory operating accompanied by a Mauleverer; and later a Cromwellian Mauleverer held Ripon and was routed by a Cavalier Mallory who held Skipton for the King and raided Ripon. Major Dent gave the other deeds in the trunk to Leeds Public Library and the Yorkshire Archaeological and Historical Society. The *Merlin* is now in the safe keeping of Cambridge University Library Manuscripts Department.

John R. Walbran, the historian of Ripon (who seems to have been related to the Mallorys of Studley) wrote a work in 1841 entitled *Genealogical and Biographical Memoir of the Lords of Studley*. He had only twenty copies printed, all for private distribution (what would Caxton have said about that!). Two of these copies, however, are included in the large collection of Walbran's writings and manuscripts owned by York Minster's Library, which went to considerable lengths to enable me to examine the book.

In it Walbran says of William Mallory of Hutton Conyers, who became Lord of Studley through the inheritance of his wife Dionysia Tempest, that he 'was the representative of an ancient and well-allied family. It cannot now be ascertained whence they originally sprung, though probably from some of the southern counties, where families of the same name, though bearing different arms, are often mentioned in records as existing and holding property.'

A valuable sidelight on the past of the Mallory family transpires, however, from the researches of Mr Geoffrey M. Cowling on the Forest of Galtres, stretching northwards from York. He notes that

King Henry III made very numerous gifts of oak timber from Galtres for public (e.g. bridge-repairing) or charitable (e.g. church-building) purposes, but less to private individuals.

There were however no less than three gifts of timber to Anketill Malore, the first on 24th April, 1234, of six oaks to make posts and beams for his house of Tyverinton (Terrington), the second of six oaks for his house at Mulethorpe (Mowthorpe) on 7th April, 1238, and the third of two oaks on 18th July, 1238.

Terrington is 7½ miles west of Malton, and Mowthorpe a mile south of Terrington, in the north-east purlieu of Galtres and just north-west of Bulmer. Terrington is about 19 miles due east of Hutton Conyers. About the time of these gifts, the name Anketill Mallory crops up in the east Midlands in Walbran's records. I know no reason why the Yorkshire Anketill Malore should be so favoured by the King.

In Terrington Church is a board listing the known Rectors since 1234. The second entry shows that on 14 June 1247 in the reign of Henry III, Henry de Schelton was presented to the living by Sir Anketill Malorie. This is the same man who was granted oaks by the King. From Terrington to Mowthorpe runs a ley. Malorie's house at Mowthorpe stood on Mowthorpe Hill, exactly at the point where several leys cross (one from Wheeldrake Howe to Bell Hall south of York, one from Blakey Topping to Sheriff Hutton, one from Coxwold to Kirkham Priory, and others) commanding a tremendous view across the Forest of Galtres.

Under 'Asketil, Anketil' the *Oxford Dictionary of English Christian Names* quotes Camden saying in 1605 that the name 'Anskettell' was 'used much in the ancient house of Mallories'. The Dictionary suggests that the first element derives from an Old Norse original signifying 'god' or 'divinity', but adds that the second probably has nothing to do with 'kettle'. According to Walton, a Sir Anketin Mallory held lands in Rutlandshire in 1383, and another was sheriff of Lincolnshire in 1390. The *Dictionary of*

National Biography says that at least four families named Malory were long connected with the English Midlands.

As strong a case as he can make out for *Morte Darthur* having been written by a Yorkshire Sir Thomas Malory is put by William Matthews, Professor of English at the University of California, Los Angeles, in *The Ill-Framed Knight: A Skeptical Inquiry into the Identity of Sir Thomas Malory* (1966). His scepticism is aimed at Professor G. L. Kittredge's identification of the *Morte Darthur* author as a Warwickshire Sir Thomas Malory whom Matthews shows to have been a robber, freebooter and rapist. Among his many sources Matthews cites Walbran's *Genealogical and Biographical Memoir* and also his 'Yorkshire Genealogies' (MS, York Minster).

Matthews makes it clear that the Yorkshire Mallory family had widespread estates. Notably, one of them was the manor of Hylton Floghen, which Matthews describes as 'in the parish of Brampton and just south of Penrith by Inglewood Forest', and points out that it was Inglewood Forest that was particularly rich in Arthurian legends.

In reality, it appears, Hylton Floghen was much nearer to Appleby than to Penrith, was on the other side of the River Eden from both, and was well outside the very strictly demarcated limits of Inglewood Forest even at the time of its greatest extension. Nevertheless, it was only a few miles from Edenhall, Burrell Green, Haresceugh Castle and Nether Haresceugh; and it was on the ancient non-Roman north–south road. Moreover, the Yorkshire Mallorys were Lancastrians, supporters of Henry VI in the Wars of the Roses. Indeed, as Matthews says, 'At the opening of the 1460s, it seems possible that the oldest of the Malory sons [i.e. the eldest brother of the Malory whom Matthews proposes as the putative *Morte Darthur* author] gave his life at the battle of Towton.'

That was in 1461, the year when Henry VI gave Sir John Pennington the Luck of Muncaster Castle, and the year after the Musgraves' coming to Edenhall. Next year, 1462, the then head of the Yorkshire Mallorys, Sir William, made a quitclaim deed bequeathing half the manor of Hylton Floghen to his son William.

Four years later, the victorious Edward IV issued a general pardon to Lancastrians, with named exceptions. The second exception was 'Thomas Malarie, knight' – Matthews's presumptive author. Incidentally Matthews points to some passages of *Morte Darthur* which probably refer directly or indirectly to the Wars of the Roses.

It is necessary to preserve caution in dealing with all Arthurian theories, including those of Matthews. He dismisses too lightly the evidence of John Bale, the fifteenth–sixteenth-century commentator, and the conclusions drawn by Professor John Rhys in his introduction to the 1893 edition of *Morte Darthur*.

Bale, who was born in 1495, wrote in 1548 (following Leland) in his *Illustrium Maioris Britanniae Scriptorium* that Sir Thomas Malory, the author of *Morte Darthur* (which Caxton had published in 1485), was *Britannus natione*, and also: *Est Mailoria in finibus Cambriae, Devae flumini vicina*, i.e. that Malory was of the British (Welsh) nation, and that there was a Mailoria or Mailory in the Welsh borders near the River Dee. To this, Matthews derides Bale for saying that Sir Thomas Malory was born at Mailoria, which in fact Bale carefully avoided saying. Matthews even adds: 'No one, not even a Welshman [what does he mean by that? After all, Matthews is a Welsh name], has ever located such a place, either on the Dee or anywhere else.'

Bale did not say *on* the Dee, but in the neighbourhood. That perhaps does not matter much. What does matter is that Rhys – a Welshman, even! – wrote that before he knew anything of Bale's statement, he himself had noted that the name of the author of *Morte Darthur* was found written not only Malory or Malorye but also Maleore (refer Walbran's 'Anketill Malore'); and that Malore 'reminded me of *Maylawr*, *Maelawr* or *Maelor*, the name of two districts on the confines of England and Wales: a "Welsh Maelor" is included in the County of Denbigh, and an "English Maelor" in that of Flint'. That is to say, one on either side of the Dee. How was it possible for Matthews to overlook this? For his information, it may be added that Pentre Maelor is a mile east of Wrexham in Denbighshire, between that town and the Dee, Grid reference SJ 367490; and on the opposite bank of the Dee is the small detached part of Flintshire around Overton and Bangor-on-Dee known as Maelor Saesnep ('English Maelor').

Matthews also airily dismisses Professor Eugène Vinaver's argument for Malory's possible connection with Wales. Vinaver had pointed out that Malory departed from his French sources to bring in Welshmen. 'Not everyone who talks about Heaven', says Matthews, 'has been there.' No – nor have they been in southern France. Matthews himself uses an exactly similar argument to suggest that Malory wrote *Morte Darthur* while he was a prisoner of war of Jaques d'Armagnac, later Duc de Nemours, in the south of France. Of the names of places in that area introduced into Malory's book XX, Matthews says: 'There can be little doubt that they are his own additions; and it seems almost certain that they must derive from some special knowledge of southwestern France.' I think he is right; but what is sauce for Matthews is sauce also for Vinaver.

Matthews – perhaps over-eager to show Malory as a Yorkshireman – is cavalier in his dismissal of a Welsh connection. But after all, I myself am an Englyssheman (as Malory spelled it in *Morte Darthur*), a Brigantian, a Yorkshireman, a native of Leeds (which is a Welsh name); and I could also be described as *Britannus natione*. The Malory family owned estates in many parts of Brigantia. The *flumen Deva* is Brigantia's south-western border. Even if Malory the author had no estates there, his family might have sprung from that area or retained family connections there (later descendants of the Yorkshire family moved to the Chester area). The Mallorys also might well have maintained, within that Walton-Walshford pocket near York, a cultural tradition stemming from the Brigantian Celts or indeed from even earlier.

Matthews adduces Walbran's genealogies to show that a Sir Christopher Malory, of Hutton Conyers, married Joan, heiress of Robert Conyers, and died in 1374. His son Sir William died in 1421, succeeded by another William, who married Joan, daughter of Sir William Plumpton of Plumpton near Knaresborough. Their son, another Sir William Malory, married Dionysia Tempest, heiress to Sir William Tempest of Studley. They had no less than eight sons and five daughters (seven sons and six daughters according to Walbran). The third son was named Thomas, and this is the man whom Matthews proposes as the *Morte Darthur* author. His father Sir William died in 1475. Dionysia, according to Walbran, was given as 36 years old on 24 October 1451. At that rate, her third son might be expected to have been about 45 years old in 1485, the year when *Morte Darthur* was completed, or about 26 when 'Thomas Malarie, knight' was excepted from Edward IV's general pardon. A Yorkshire Thomas Mallory was therefore at least available as possible author for the classic.

Thereby hangs a possible clue to the origin of two Caxton books owned by Ripon Cathedral Library.

The library was visited one hot summer afternoon in the time of Dean Waddilove, early in the nineteenth century, by the Rev. Thomas Frognall Dibdin, a nephew of Charles Dibdin the poet and composer, and himself a noted expert on ancient books. Dean Waddilove showed him the library catalogue. In this, Dibdin noted two entries: *English Chronicle, Antw. 1493* and *Boetius Old Engl.*, stated to be in folio. He quickly discovered the first of these, and found as he expected that it was a reprint of Caxton's text by Gerard de Leed of Antwerp.

As for the second, Dibdin did not doubt that it would turn out to be not folio but the quarto poetical version printed at a Tavistock monastery. He and the Dean hunted high and low in the hot and stuffy library, until in desperation Dibdin pulled out 'a melancholy-looking "forrel", or white sheepskin covered folio volume', as Dibdin wrote later in his *Bibliographical Odyssey*. Opening it, he saw that it was Caxton's own prose imprint of the *Boethius* (the fifth-century Roman, last of the Latin writers, translated into Old English by King Alfred the Great). It was 'large, clean, and perfect – save one leaf!'

'Yet the book is unusually thick. I persevere,' Dibdin wrote, 'and find, at the end of it, nothing more or less than a beautiful and perfect copy of Caxton's *Book for Travellers*, of which Lord Spencer's copy had been considered unique. The worthy Dean wonders and smiles, and smiles and wonders again.' Well he might, for Dean Waddilove himself was such an expert in ancient books that it is surprising that he had not discovered the Caxtons himself already.

But what were the Caxtons doing there? The usual answer is that they were included in the books bequeathed to the cathedral by the former Dean Higgin. Anthony Higgin, a native of Manchester, was Dean of Ripon from 1608 until his death in 1624. But in 1583 he became Rector of Kirk Deighton and retained that living – combined with his tenure of the office of Dean – until his death. Kirk Deighton is just north of Wetherby and about equidistant from York and Ripon. It is at the western end of the Walton-Walshford pocket. And it is virtually next door to Ribston Hall, which is just across the fields as one looks from Kirk Deighton churchyard – Ribston Hall, where someone wrote in the *Merlin* MS 'Here begins the book which Sir Thomas Malori translated . . .'.

Higgin's appointment to the living of Kirk Deighton occurred less than 100 years after Caxton had printed *Morte Darthur*. When Higgin was also Dean of Ripon, Sir William Mallory, Kt, of Studley, was mentioned in 1598 as the Archbishop of York's High Steward for the Liberty of Ripon.

The Sir Thomas Malory who wrote *Morte Darthur* was obviously very literature-minded. His book is one of the finest in the English language, as well as being one of the first to be printed. To compile it he had read many (manuscript, not printed) books in various languages, including French, German and Welsh as well as Old English. It is difficult to imagine that he, the author of Caxton's best-seller – which has remained a best-seller for nearly 500 years ever since – would not be interested in the other books that Caxton produced. Indeed, it would not be surprising if Caxton put him on his special complimentary list for free copies.

If so, then copies of Caxton's *Boethius* and *Book for Travellers* would go to Sir Thomas. From Sir Thomas they would go to his descendants. In that way they may have come into the hands of Sir William Mallory the High Steward for the Liberty of Ripon, and perhaps been bought from him by his bibliophile neighbour the Dean of Ripon. Ripon Cathedral's Caxtons, therefore, may well have belonged to the man who wrote down the story of 'King' Arthur, who was one of the very first British printed authors and who went a long way to the formation of the English language in its most beautiful aspect. I like to think so, if only because the Rev. T. F. Dibdin was one of my forebears.

A strange sidelight is cast by Mrs Patricia Crowther, the well known Yorkshire witch (*Witchcraft in Yorkshire*, 1973). She notes that in 1654 William and Mary Wade, of Studley, were accused of bewitching Elizabeth, aged 14, the daughter of Lady Mallory of Studley Hall. Lady Mallory stated in court that the witch Mary Wade confessed, and the child recovered; the witch later withdrew her confession, and Elizabeth resumed the fits which were the manifestation of the witching. The result of the case was not recorded, but Mrs Crowther considers it probable that Mary Wade was acquitted. By that time, indeed, it is true that unless an alleged witch was accused of causing an actual death, the charges were commonly thrown out; and this was especially so in Yorkshire, as will be seen in a later chapter.

As for 'King' Arthur, the last word should lie with Mr Sam Brewster. 'The fascination of Arthurian legend,' he writes, 'is that here meet the primitive, the very ancient, the highly mythological, the pagan, the Celtic, the historical, the Christian, the heroic, the chivalric, the adventurous, the mysterious.'

Certainly the mysterious. A dash of spice is added to the Malory stew in the *Yorkshire Archaeological Journal*, vol. 33, in 'The Honour of Kirkby Malzeard':

> In the sixteenth and seventeenth centuries the Yorkes were staunch Romanists. One of them, Sir John Yorke, is said to have been brought before the Star Chamber, and heavily fined, on account of a masque he held at Gowthwaite, in which Christopher Mallory (a younger brother of Sir John Mallory, of Hutton Conyers) in the guise of the devil carried King James to hell.

A further dash is given by Gerald the Welshman's *Itinerarium Cambriae*, describing a journey which he made through Wales in

1188 (quoted by Professor Gwyn Jones in his Introduction to Professor Charles Dunn's 1963 Everyman edition of Geoffrey of Monmouth's *History of the Kings of Britain*):

> Gerald ... relates of one Meilerius of Caerleon that by reason of the evil spirits whose familiar he had become he could among other things distinguish truth from falsehood and, though he could not read, point out lying passages in a book.... When the Gospel of St. John was laid on his breast, the spirits vanished completely. But when Geoffrey's *Historia* was laid in its place they instantly returned, settling not only on Meilerius but with turbulent relish on the book itself.

The name 'Meilerius' obviously could mean 'man of Maelor'. It is perhaps a good thing that he was consulting his spirits centuries before *Morte Darthur* could be placed on his breast.

The origin of the Malory name, however, is one of the most mysterious questions in all Britain. Just south of Aberystwyth is a very striking conical hill. It is called Dinas Faelawr (Mailor's Castle). This Mailor is described in legend as a giant of the race which inhabited Britain before the coming of the Celts.

Were the Malorys of pre-Celtic descent? Were they therefore favoured, as against both Saxons and Celts, by Norman and Plantagenet kings? Is this why so many Malory families existed in the Midlands where Mr D. Elliston Allen finds the remains of Britain's Neolithic stock?

7

MOST ACCURSED KIRKS

My uncle Arthur Grimshaw, eldest son of Atkinson Grimshaw the Leeds Victorian artist, was a composer. With Frank Kidson, he was one of the founders of the revival of folk music, and published a considerable number of old folk songs. One was a straightforward Irish lullaby, called 'Shoheen, Sholo' and with a refrain based on that phrase. In late 1972 the same phrase occurred in a BBC Third Programme item as the refrain of the lullaby with a murderous edge from County Cork, mentioned earlier. The producer of the programme, Mr A. L. Lloyd, kindly gave me details.

The story was that shortly after her marriage, a woman disappeared and was presumed dead. Just a year later, a neighbour recognised her sitting on a fairy mound. She was rocking her fairy baby, and singing what appeared to be a lullaby. The refrain was that of a lullaby, all right, but the rest, in Irish Gaelic, gave instructions on how her non-fairy husband could rescue her by coming with a wax candle in the palm of his hand, and a black-handled knife, and striking 'the first horse going through the gap' into the hillock and plucking the herb that was 'in the doorway of the fairy fort'. If he failed, she must 'stay and be queen over these women'.

As Mr Lloyd points out, the story could have affinities with the Scots ballad of *Tam Lin*. There is also, however, a link with the fairy mound feature of a great deal of legend and folklore not only in Brigantia, not only in Britain, and not only among the Celts – a reflection of it, indeed, may lie in the Egyptian Pyramids (as Alfred Watkins pointed out).

When the probably Brigantian Malory in the fifteenth century wrote his *Morte Darthur*, he avowedly used 'certain French books' as a large part of his sources. Some of his material, however, he obtained from the alliterative poem called *Morte Arthur*, the author of which was probably a native of Yorkshire, Cheshire or south Lancashire. It was probably also he who wrote a poem, one of the greatest in English literature, called *Sir Gawain and the Green Knight* which dates from about 1386. This is not only written in 'Brigantian' English (complete with 'nobbut', for example) but shows every sign of being cast in Brigantia, in the Pennines – tentatively placed in the area of the Congleton Bride Stones and the 'firbolg' people of Biddulph Moor. On the other hand I am indebted to Lord Inglewood for the information that Professor Tolkien had at one time suggested that the Green Knight's Castle of Hautdesert might have been the forerunner of Lord Inglewood's own residence, the mansion of Hutton-in-the-Forest near Penrith in the Forest of Inglewood.

Oddly enough, built into the courtyard wall of Hutton-in-the-Forest, and immediately above an ancient well, is a stone bearing a pagan carving of a man-like figure emerging from a bough in a sort of metamorphosis. This seems to be clearly a representation of the Celtic forest-god known as the Green Man, one later form of whom was the Green Knight. Sir F. Madden, who first edited *Sir Gawain and the Green Knight* (1839), thought that the forest into which Sir Gawain rode after leaving the Wirral was Inglewood – which is certainly also the scene of *The Marriage of Sir Gawain*.

In *Sir Gawain and the Green Knight* Gawain is represented not in the Malory mould of a black-hearted, vindictive, jealous semi-villain, but as a chaste paragon superior to Sir Lancelot.

The poet has Sir Gawain setting out from Arthur's Camelot first of all 'through all the length of Logres' (i.e. England), then far into north Wales; then, leaving Anglesey on his left, he comes to Holy Head – apparently not the Anglesey Holyhead, but Holywell in

Flintshire. From there he crosses the Dee estuary into the Wirral Peninsula, after which no clear indication is given of his direction except that he comes to mountainous country. Gawain was known alternatively as Wawain, and in the poem either form is used according to the alliteration. An earlier form is 'Walwein'. It should be noted that close to Holywell, at the spot where Gawain would probably have started to cross the estuary whether by ford or boat, is a village called Walwen.

Let us make confusion utterly confounded. For the year 1344 the *Chronicle of Lanercost* (the priory in north-west Brigantia, on the Scottish border) records: 'The truce in Britanny having been concluded, several nobles of England assembled at Carlisle under my lord Bohun Earl of Northampton, in order to fortify Lochmaben.' But the translator, Sir Herbert Maxwell, in a footnote adds that Bohun was 'Wowen in MS'. The year concerned was forty-two years before *Sir Gawain and the Green Knight* was written.

Before Gawain's journey, however, the poem starts with Arthur's court celebrating New Year. The King himself will not sit at table until the feasting is, as it were, keyed by some adventure. Apart from him, the chief man there seems to be Gawain, who sits beside Queen Guinevere. He thus takes the place accorded in Malory to Sir Lancelot – who is nevertheless mentioned with his brother Sir Lionel as being present, but is in no way picked out as prominent. But whereas Malory's Sir Lancelot is a guilty lover of the Queen, the Gawain of this poem is specifically described as devoted to the Queen but a clean, guiltless, innocent knight – in fact, that is the whole point of the narrative. If there had been a Holy Grail around, it is this Gawain who would have 'achieved' it.

A gigantic Green Knight, carrying a huge axe in his right hand and a sprig of holly in his left, proudly rides his horse into the court and up to the high table – calculated bad manners like those of Culhwch in the *mabinogi* of *Culhwch and Olwen*. There he issues a challenge: any knight to give him a single unopposed blow with the axe, on condition that at the next New Year the same knight shall present himself at the Green Knight's place to suffer similarly an unopposed blow. Gawain offers himself for the challenge in the place of Arthur. The Green Knight dismounts, and Gawain cuts off his head with one stroke. The Green Knight thereupon picks up his head, mounts his horse and holds the head up to face the high table. The head tells Gawain that in a year's time he must appear at the Green Chapel, and with that the Green Knight rides off with his head tucked underneath his arm like any Gothic ghost.

This beheading-by-request theme is in direct line with pagan Celtic and perhaps pre-Celtic cult. In the *mabinogi* of *Branwen Daughter of Llyr* (i.e., as Shakespeare would have it, Cordelia daughter of Lear), one of the four ancient 'branches' of the *Mabinogion*, the semi-divine hero-giant Bendigeidfran (i.e. Bran the Blessed – 'bran' means literally 'raven') commands his companions to cut off his head. They are ordered to take it to the White Mount in London (the Tower, where Welsh ravens are still kept – and where traitors' heads used to be displayed) and bury it there with its face towards France to prevent any harm coming to Britain from across the sea as long as the head was hidden there undisturbed.

In the English romance of *Sir Gawain and the Carl of Carlisle* (later than *Sir Gawain and the Green Knight*), the gigantic Carl asks Gawain to behead him to free him from a spell and restore him to the shape of an ordinary knight. In another later version he is a dwarf, who becomes a full-size knight when Gawain at his request beheads him. The Introduction by Professor Norman Davis to the 1967 revised Tolkien–Gordon edition of *Sir Gawain and the Green Knight* sees these versions as 'a special development of the beheading theme, in which the notion of an apparently desperate return blow as a test of courage and honour has been replaced by that of a mere technique of disenchantment'. Surely, however, the mere technique of disenchantment appears to be a far older explanation than a mere test of honour and courage which could have arisen only in terms of romantic chivalry? Meanwhile, there can be no mistake: the raven motif, Sir Gawain, and the beheading theme, wherever they began, all have versions located in north-west Brigantia.

To continue with *Sir Gawain and the Green Knight*, towards the end of the year Gawain sets off to seek the Green Chapel. After the long journey described above, he meets a hospitable baron who puts him up over Christmas at his castle. Two ladies are there, one old and extremely ugly but highly honoured and surrounded with attendants. Her complexion is yellow, her cheeks are rough and wrinkled, she wears a neckerchief which hides her neck, while chalk-white veils cover her black chin, and her forehead and face are hung with silk and ornaments so that only her black brows, her eyes, nose and sour and withered lips are to be seen.

> Hir body was schort and thik
> Hir buttockes balwe [swollen] and brode [broad].

This specimen of the Loathly Lady seems afflicted with the Hottentot trait of steatopygia like the Mesolithic people shown in Spanish caves. By the hand, however, she leads a young woman whom Gawain thinks more beautiful than Guinevere. Her kerchiefs, scattered with many bright pearls, leave her breast (apparently meaning her chest) and throat bare and brighter than snow; and she looks attentively on Gawain. On New Year's morning the host goes off hunting while Gawain is still asleep, and the damsel sneaks into his room, raises the bed-curtain and sits on the side of the bed. When he raises his eyelids she jokes about binding him in bed and says they are alone in the building and the door is bolted.

> Ye are welcome to my cors [body]
> Do as you like,
> It is for me to be
> Your servant, and so I shall.

Gawain pretends that he is not the renowned knight she thinks him to be, but she does all she can to tempt him. He kisses her once.

Next morning, New Year's Day, after an even more vigorous but fruitless tempting, she gives him a magic green 'lovelace' to wear in her honour, and he puts it on over his armour. He is given an escort to guide him to the Green Chapel, and sets out.

> They went by banks where the boughs were bare,
> They climbed by cliffs where clung the frost,
> The heavens were high, but ugly under was the sky,
> Mist swirled on the moor, melted on the mounts,
> But each hill had a hat, a huge mist-plume.

On the summit of a high hill, covered with snow, the escort refuses to go any farther, shows Gawain the way and departs. The knight rides down a bank to a stream. He can see no chapel, but high, steep banks on either side, with rough, knobbly cliffs and splintered rocks and crags that seem to graze the clouds. Then in a glade he sees what looks like a mound, a broad barrow beside a channel of the stream, which boils and bubbles past. Gawain dismounts, fastens his horse and walks round the barrow, which has a hole at one end and on either side. It is overgrown with grass, and hollow within:

> Nobbut an old cave
> Or a crevisse of an olde cragge. . . .

Is this the Green Chapel, he wonders, 'this chapel of mischance, the most accursed kirk that I was ever in'. He shouts a challenge. The Green Knight answers from the top of the bank, and makes his way down behind a crag and emerges from a hole at the bottom, carrying his huge axe. Not without a flinch, Gawain receives a blow, which only nicks his neck because of the green lovelace's protection.

The Green Knight then reveals that he was Gawain's Christmas host; that he sent his wife to tempt him; and that the whole test was contrived by the old lady, who is Morgan le Fay – 'Morgan the goddess' – Arthur's half-sister, Gawain's aunt.

This magnificent poem is accepted as being cast in Brigantia. It also has many points in common with the ballad *The Marriage of Sir Gawain* which stems from Celtic myth as well as Arthurian legend. This ballad centres on Tarn Wadling. Its source is a fragmentary manuscript which was in the possession of Bishop Percy. He reproduced it in his *Reliques of Ancient English Poetry* (first published in 1765), and considered that it was older than Chaucer and was the source of Chaucer's 'Wife of Bath's Tale', which would make it older than *Sir Gawain and the Green Knight*.

Tarn Wadling was a lake – drained in 1858 by Lord Lonsdale – on the eastern side of the Carlisle–Penrith road at the village of High Hesket. Immediately north-east of the 100-acre site of the lake, and just south-east of the village of Aiketgate, is a hill (OS Grid reference 486463) on which it is still possible to see the remains of foundations said to be those of Castle Hewen. This is believed to have been the citadel of King Urien of Rheged and his son Owain/Ewan/Hewen. *The Marriage of Sir Gawain*, however, refers to it only as the Castle of Tarn Wadling, and makes no mention of Urien or Owain.

As in *Sir Gawain and the Green Knight*, so in *The Marriage of Sir Gawain*, King Arthur, Queen Guinevere and the court are celebrating Christmas, but in this case specifically in Carlisle ('Carleile'). Beside Arthur, Guinevere and Gawain, others listed quite incidentally as present are Lancelot, Steven, Kay, Banier, Bors, Gareth and Tristram. Those listed in *Sir Gawain and the Green Knight* are Arthur, Guinevere, Gawain, Agravaine, Bishop Baldwin, and Owain; the omission of the last from *The Marriage* is perhaps significant; perhaps there the giant himself may be seen as Owain, or the narrative should be seen as pre-dating Rheged.

In *The Marriage*, as filled out by Bishop Percy to accord with other sources, Arthur is sworn by a distressed maiden to take up a challenge from the giant-knight of Tarn Wadling. Arthur receives the giant's demand, which is to answer the riddle:

> What thing it is
> That a woman most desire.

Arthur returns dejected to Carlisle, and explains to Gawain that at Tarn Wadling he found

> a bold barron
> With a great club on his back
> Standing stiffe and strong.

He did not fight the baron because

> me thought it was not meet
> For he was stiffe and strong with all
> He strokes were nothing sweete.

I.e. discretion was the better part of valour; so the baron gave him the riddle to answer in a week, on New Year's Day.

When the week is nearly up Arthur sets off for his appointment; riding over the moor, he sees a woman 'cladd in red scarlett', sitting between an oak and a green holly — this situation has magical significance. One of her eyes is where her mouth should be, the other is high in her forehead. Her nose is crooked and turned outward, her mouth is foul and wry. She offers to solve his problem, and in return he agrees that she shall marry Gawain. At Tarn Wadling he tells the baron that the woman

> Says that a woman will have her will
> And this is all her cheef desire.

The baron swears vengeance on 'my sister, a misshappen hore', by burning her on a fire.

Arthur's knights go to the moor and find the ugly woman, again sitting between the oak and the green holly. Kay, rude as usual, sneers at her, but Gawain marries her. That night she changes into a beauty. She says she can be a beauty for half the twenty-four hours but must be a hag the other half, and asks him to choose. He replies:

> Because thou art my owne lady
> Thou shalt have all thy will.

He thus breaks the spell entirely so that she will be beautiful at all times. And here she tells him something of importance:

> My father was an old knight
> And yett it chanced soe

> That he marryed a younge lady
> That brought me to this woe.
> Shee witched me being a faire young lady
> To the greene forrest to dwell
> And there I must walke in womans likenesse
> Most like a feeind of hell. . . .
>
> [About nine stanzas missing.]
>
> That looked so foule and that was wont
> On the wild more [moor] to goe. . . .

This bears distinctly on Malory's fifteenth-century *Morte Darthur*. There Owain is always described as son of King Urien, but his relationship to Morgan le Fay is mostly left vague; Morgan, on the other hand, is described as Urien's wife. Only in the dramatic scene where Owain seizes the sword from Morgan as she is about to murder the sleeping Urien is she named as Owain's mother, and Owain there does complain that 'an earthly devil bare me', while Morgan begs for mercy from 'fair son Owain'. But it has been suggested that Urien was married twice, and this would accord with the proposition that the baron of Tarn Wadling and the ugly maiden – and Owain – were the children of Urien's first wife and the stepchild of Morgan.

The description of the ugly maiden in *The Marriage of Sir Gawain* is noticeably similar to that of a messenger-maiden in the *mabinogi* of *Peredur Son of Evrawc* (Efrawg):

> They [including both Gawain/Gwalchmai and Owain] saw a black curly-headed maiden enter, riding upon a yellow mule, with rough thongs in her hand to urge it on; and she had a rough and hideous aspect. Her face and hands were blacker than the blackest iron that has been dipped in pitch. Her complexion was not more ugly than her form. She had high cheeks, and the flesh of her face was hanging and baggy, and she had a snub nose with distended nostrils. And one eye was of a most piercing mottled grey-green, and the other was jet-black and sunk deep in her head. Her long yellow teeth

were yellower than the broom-flower. Her belly swelled up from the breastbone higher than her chin. Her backbone was in the shape of a crook, and her hips were wide and bony.

Snubbing Peredur, she addresses herself to Arthur, and the adventure she presents is taken up in the first place by Gawain (Gwalchmai). He fades unaccountably out of the story, and the narrative switches to Peredur, who fights first a black man of Ysbidinongyl and then another black man who rises from beneath a cromlech (a stone slab in one translation). Not only are there the similarities between the ugly maidens, the black men (the baron of Tarn Wadling is 'black') and the arrival of one of them from beneath the rock (as it were the hole in the cliff at the Green Chapel), but Ysbidinongyl is a name which suggests a Hospice of Ongyl/Ingle, and it is in the Forest of Inglewood that both Castle Hewen/Tarn Wadling and the Giant's Cave lie (it will also be recalled that it has been suggested that the Inglewood mansion of Hutton-in-the-Forest is on the site of the Green Knight's Castle of Hautdesert). Moreover, according to the *mabinogi*, Ysbidinongyl is within reach of the Castle of Wonders, of which an earlier chapter has treated.

A mile or two south-east of Castle Hewen, just east of Ewan Close Farm, is a cave called Giant's Chambers. A little farther up the River Eden is St Michael's Well, and it was St Michael above all others whom the early Christian church called in to combat the power of paganism. On the opposite bank of the river, below the Main Farm, is Morgan's Well. Immediately opposite St Michael's Well, however, separated by *Kirk* Bank from Tib Wood (Tib was a name for a spirit), is the site of an ancient St Michael's Church, which had a Roman chancel-arch like that of Escomb, but which was abandoned in 1360 after having been mysteriously 'polluted by bloodshed'. And on the opposite bank of the Glassonby Beck from the site of St Michael's Church is the site of a tumulus. Perhaps the tumulus could have been the Green Chapel – which was 'not two myle' from the castle where Gawain was entertained. Is this the Most Accursed Kirk? Or was it the kirk that was polluted by blood only about twenty-five years before *Sir Gawain and the*

Green Knight was written? Both Castle Hewen and Hutton-in-the-Forest are 5 miles away.

There are a number of other candidates in Brigantia for the position of the Green Chapel. The limestone areas of the Craven district of west Yorkshire and the Cresswell district of north Derbyshire would provide many places where such a chapel could look like 'nobbut an old cave, or a crevisse of an olde cragge', with holes in the end and sides and where the Green Knight could drop down a pothole and emerge at the foot of the cliffs. But while the geology of those areas conforms with the story, the legend seems to swing farther to the north-west – and there are possible places in that area too.

Not only are there the Giant's Chambers near Ewan Close and the Giant's Cave near Edenhall. Half a mile from Caldbeck in Cumberland, on the western edge of Inglewood and only ten miles from Castle Hewen, is a series of waterfalls on the Howk Stream, where a natural bridge of rock forms two caves called the 'Fairies' Kettle' and, more significantly, the 'Fairies' Kirk'. A mile south-east of this is Castle Hill, on which is a large round cavity cut out of the rock, 16 yards in diameter and with an entrance only 3 feet wide; it could have been roofed – not far from here there was an ancient Christian chapel built of wattle which until the seventeenth century was roofed with bracken thatch. In many parts of this area of Cumberland the distressed damsel might well have thought, as she said of the giant baron's castle, that there was 'some spell of magic hereabouts'.

It is commonly assumed that 'kirk' and similar words in a place-name indicate the existence from more or less ancient times of a Christian church. Such words may sometimes indicate the opposite. 'Priest' and 'prest', similarly, are perhaps too lightly assumed always to refer to a Christian priest; for instance, Priest's Tarn high on the moors behind Great Whernside is an unlikely spot for a Christian priest to be found, but it is not far from the pagan shrine of Vinotonus.

A presumptive old trackway goes above the northern bank of the Haweswater Beck in the Lake District, to a prehistoric henge called Tow Top Kirk. There never was any Christian kirk here. If one asks locally for an explanation of the name, the answer is: 'Probably they had some sort of religious ceremonies here in prehistoric times.' Within the outer earthen circle is a smaller one, and inside that are one or two groups of stones where a near-by farmer has found what appears to be a hearth, or at any rate a place where something was burnt. Probably indeed this was a sacred site of some kind, but not a Christian one. There is, however, no mound. From it goes an unmapped track (a ley) to the summit of High Street.

The kind of erection described in the poem corresponds more to a 'long barrow' or chambered tomb, though even that would have only one entrance. The poem's description would better fit at least two places both only a mile or so from Tow Top Kirk. One is the Giant's Graves on the flat ground at the foot of Haweswater. The other is on the flat top of Knipe Scar, where just beside a stone circle is a very obvious-looking 'fairy mound'. Equally near is the artificial hill called Castlesteads beside the River Lowther just north of Askham village; and there is another similar Castlesteads on the opposite bank of the river.

Such great sepulchres as the long barrows were certainly used as religious centres – but they were not the only such centres. The flat henges without mounds, the saucer-like hill-tops with a standing stone in the cup, and the great and small stone circles, were also cult sites, recognised as such by one people after another; and some of them bear the name of 'kirk'. Sometimes no sign can any longer be traced except an unexplained name such as 'Kirkbride Hill'.

One stone circle on the southern side of Ilkley Moor, alongside the old track that crosses the moor by Bradup from north to south, is known by two names: Brass Castle, or Kirkstones. It is said to be haunted. High on Denton Moor, on the opposite side of Wharfedale north east of Ilkley, is a farm called Dunkirk ('Kirk Hill'), and one of the stone semi-circles on this moor, too, is called Kirkstones. Mr E. T. Cowling, in *Rombalds Way* (1946), has pointed out in reference to these sites that 'kirk' often pointed to a pre-Christian religious centre. The same may apply to 'chapel' in its various forms, 'capple', 'copple', 'keppel' and so on. This term often appears where a road or trackway crosses a stream – and frequently at that point there is a legend of some evil spirit to waylay the traveller. Another word that appears in more or less corrupted form is 'temple', used where there is no more sign of a temple ever having existed than Gawain could see of a chapel. Timble, just beyond Dunkirk farm on the north-east side of Denton Moor, is such a place; and Timble with the valley around it will figure much in these pages – complete with pagan religious ceremonies as late as the seventeenth century.

Church bells tolling from underground or from beneath the waters of a lake – this is a theme of legend attached to a number of places, and it may be wondered whether it is a kind of inversion of the Green Chapel motif. At Fisherty Brow, near Kirkby Lonsdale, south Westmorland, and at Kirksanton, near Millom, west Cumberland, there is no lake, but in each case there is a hollow – believed to be natural – in the ground, where the tradition is that a church stood there long ago, until the earth suddenly opened and swallowed it up, congregation and parson and all. If one puts an ear to the ground on Sunday morning, the church bells can be heard ringing far below. So can they be heard like a ghost-peal coming from under the waves of Semmerwater in Wensleydale, and the gloomy Gormire Lake at the foot of Sutton Bank below Hambleton Street.

Similar tales are told in Scotland, Wales and Cornwall. In Wales the Castle of Arianrod near Clynnog in Caernarvonshire was swallowed up by the sea. So was the Welsh kingdom of the Cantref y Gwaelod, near Harlech. And so was the land around the Scilly Isles, where indeed the remains of ancient dwellings are explored under the shallow sea by divers.

The *Life of St Kentigern* mentions Morken or Morcant, a wicked king of Strathclyde, who had King Urien of Rheged treacherously murdered during a joint expedition against Deodric the son of the Saxon King Ida of Northumbria. Morken's capital was said to be at Mockerkin, between Cockermouth and Whitehaven in north-west Cumberland. The town and its king were so wicked that God sent storms and earthquakes which engulfed the capital and covered it with the present Mockerkin Tarn. (This recalls the Malory story of how Urien's wife Morgan le Fay – Morken? –

sought to kill him. One may wonder whether there is in these legends a confusion of Morgan le Fay with the British arch-heretic Pelagius/Morgan.) The same fate befell a village in the Furness district of southern Lakeland which is now covered by Urswick Tarn. And again at the beautiful Talkin Tarn, near Brampton, east of Carlisle, an old man was refused shelter and help by the villagers, and he asked God to punish them. A deluge fell, the earth opened and the village vanished; and although the Tarn is bottomless, from the middle of the lake one can look down and see the roofs of the houses.

These legends are a mirror of the very ancient myth — not confined to the Celts — of the Otherworld under the water: the converse of the story of Tarn Walding.

It has been mentioned that the early Christian Church often invoked St Michael the Archangel in particularly pagan areas. The land alongside the Eden where the 'polluted' St Michael's Church stood is a case in point. Not only were there the pagan centres clearly located at the Giant's Caves, the fairy Wells of Edenhall, Burrell Green and Nether Haresceugh, and Long Meg and the former great stone circle of Grey Yauds, but also a number of other wells which the church never successfully canonised, such as Morgan's Well (how extremely strong the tradition must have been to retain that name to the present day!). The re-dedication of the Edenhall well to St Cuthbert never thoroughly established itself.

At Kirkoswald, Col. Fetherstonhaugh relates a tradition that when St Aidan and King Oswald came, they found the people worshipping a stream of water which flowed from a well at the base of the hill. 'They converted the villagers and covered their pagan shrine by building a church on its site and over the stream. We have our church built over a stream of water now, and St Oswald is our patron saint.'

But the pagan influence was very strong hereabouts. Col. Fetherstonhaugh wrote of a well in his own garden which 'is still [1925] believed in by some as a cure for sore eyes' — and indeed his garden was so beautiful that the cliché could well have been applied to it. A Helly (i.e. Holy, but not Christian) Well is on the

Raven Beck beside Nether Haresceugh, where the Nether Haresceugh Luck was supposed to have come from.

Ancient churches dedicated to Michael exist at Arthuret, where a battle allegedly between two lots of Celtic Christians took place in the sixth century (there is a suspicion that the Holy Grail was involved – and perhaps Morgan/Pelagians as well); at Bowness-on-Solway, with a mound called Knock Cross near the church; at Kirkby Thore, where there may have been a shrine to the Scandinavian god Thor; and among many other places at both Lowther and Shap, where these two villages sit surrounded by tumuli, mounds, monoliths, Thunder Stones and stone circles.

8

THE VERVAIN PATH

❖

Brigantia's ancient culture revolved around religious centres of two kinds: the natural and the 'artificial'. The second category comprised gods who were unattached, or only tenuously attached, to any particular phenomenon of Nature. Some of them had developed from 'natural' deities linked to natural objects – as, indeed, it is said that 'Jehovah' was originally a single holy rock in Palestine, or as the One God of the Pharaoh Akhenaten (Ikhnaton) derived from the sun. Such godly genealogies have little or nothing to do with the more developed philosophical concepts of divinity, and may be said only to illustrate the obvious fact that to explore the abstract, man must start from the concrete.

The kingdom of Brigantia, like other Celtic lands, had its few 'general' deities who were accessible more or less anywhere and at any time for the pleader; and some of them have continued to receive pleas right up to at least the nineteenth century and perhaps still do. Among these figures was Epona, the Great Mother (in Welsh legend Modron – 'Mother'), who was envisaged as riding a goose across the sky. She is probably the origin of the pantomime figure of Mother Goose, but she also has more respectable and dignified affinities with divine mothers in almost every major religion. Another, likewise common to many faiths, is her son, who in the Celtic contexts becomes Mapon (Mabon, Maben, etc.) the Son of the Mother, and needs no other identification. A somewhat special case is Brigantia, the goddess of the nation (and there were presumably lesser divinities of each sub-nation).

Next came deities who ruled over wide and not clearly delineated realms, just as Rome's Neptune ruled over the sea wherever it was (to the British his place was later taken by the Welsh Davy Jones), or as Greece's goddess Ge was the personification of the Earth. Almost of this order was the Celtic god Cernunnos, whose realm was Nature and particularly the Forest.

It appears that there may have been a single goddess who was responsible for wells. In central and eastern Brigantia nearly all holy wells were re-dedicated by the Christian Church to St Helen. In western Brigantia, on the other hand, the commonest dedication is to St Bride; and it may be that the pagan Bride was originally the goddess of the St Helen's wells; those that were re-dedicated to St Mungo/Kentigern may originally have been sacred not to a goddess but to a pagan god. Ross and other authorities have pointed out how important wells were in the cultural-religious life, as they were in the day-to-day existence of human communities; and how the Celts in particular, and probably the pre-Celts or 'proto-Celts', expressed their veneration of wells by throwing valuable articles into them.

Meanwhile, as industry and urban civilisation develop in England, the use of water resources increases enormously and as a result the underground water table drops. Wells are drying up. In any case they are being either neglected and allowed to become overgrown, or capped off, or explored for the possibility of boreholes. A heritage of incalculable potential value is being thoughtlessly, hastily and perhaps irremediably ruined.

'In every system of religious beliefs, places in which the rites are performed must be in evidence,' says Ross (*Pagan Celtic Britain*, 1967) in her introduction to the section on sacred wells.

> Some sort of focus for the sacred rites, in which or near which the inevitable insignia of cult are housed, is to be presupposed. These may vary from richly adorned, sculp-

tured images of the gods, to crude stones thought to be imbued with the divine afflatus.

In 1972 it was reported in all seriousness that Tewit Well, on the South Stray, Harrogate, was to be 'taken down' and 're-erected' somewhere else. But how can a well be moved? In reality, of course, the proposal was to re-erect merely the superstructure – which in fact at one time stood over a different well in Harrogate Valley Gardens. Tewit Well itself would simply be capped off. That would end a chapter, for this iron-water spring was the first spa-well to make Harrogate famous; it was discovered in 1571 by Mr William Slingsby who until then had been an enthusiastic patron of continental spas.

Tewit Well, then, is not one of the very ancient wells which are scattered all over Brigantia. Many of those have received far less care than Tewit Well. Some are utterly neglected, some have even been destroyed for trivial or specious reasons. But these wells are among the most ancient and important monuments of the land and should be rescued before it is too late.

Not for nothing has the Church of England a Bishop of Bath and Wells – a significant combination of title. The city of Bath owes its existence to a well which was a very sacred shrine to the Celtic divinity Sulis, long before the Romans came to Britain and turned this well into one of the major centres of the Imperial civilisation. Nobody would dare to suggest wiping out – or 'moving' – the Roman establishment.

Or would they? Between Ripon and Bedale, 3 miles east of Masham in the middle of Brigantia, is a place with a name as significant as that episcopal title: the village of Well. According to the Ordnance Survey map, here is a 'Roman building (site of)'. It lies on Holly Hill, which may be a corruption of Holy Hill. But one would be hard put to it nowadays to find the well. That spring was a religious shrine in Roman times, and it is virtually certain that the divinity worshipped there was the centre of a pre-Roman cult. Until only a short time ago, in historical terms, it was a 'decorated' well.

The importance of such water-shrines for archaeology has been vividly shown by, for instance, the discoveries made at Wookey Hole, in Somerset (very close to Wells and not far from Bath), which included fourteen human skulls. Even more informative has been the examination of two wells at Carrawburgh, Northumberland, in Brigantia, at the remains of a temple dedicated to the Celtic goddess Coventina. Among the large number of objects found in the main well were votive heads made of bronze. Heads – real human skulls or artefacts of metal or stone – are clearly associated with many sacrificial wells although relatively few such sites have so far been properly investigated.

When the Romans came to Britain, many of the existing Celtic divinities whom they found being worshipped here were equated with members of the Roman Pantheon. Sulis, for example, was treated as a local manifestation of Minerva. Then in the fourth century AD the Roman Empire became Christian. It suddenly became necessary for any important religious sites to be rededicated. This is part of the explanation for the fact that in some areas, especially Cornwall, churches are dedicated to saints whose existence is referred to nowhere else. They are simply the old gods and goddesses converted into saints.

The Empire was Christianised as a result of the favour shown to Christianity by Constantine the Great, who was first proclaimed at York and whose mother, as explained earlier, is believed by many to have been a Brigantian Celtic Christian princess called Helen. It was her influence which above all made the Empire Christian. Not surprisingly, therefore, most of the pagan holy wells in east Brigantia were now dedicated to her. There are St Helen's Wells all over the area. Examples are one beside the River Wharfe between Wetherby and Tadcaster, one between Skipton and Bolton Priory and one near Eshton, north of Skipton.

At Linton-in-Craven, near Grassington, beside the River Wharfe, is a formerly well known spring called Lady Well. This dedication – in effect, to the Virgin Mary – would seem to date much later than the canonisation of the St Helen's Wells. St Helen was regarded as so very Celtic, so closely associated with the ancient Celtic Church. The Virgin Mary would become a proper figure for such a dedication only after the Celtic Church had been absorbed into the Roman Church in the seventh century. This might mean that until about that time the well at Linton was still essentially a pagan cult-centre. After all, only a short distance down the same river, at Burnsall, is a Holy Well which to this day bears a pagan name.

William Howson (*An Illustrated Guide to the Curiosities of Craven*, 1850) discusses Burnsall. 'Near the extremity of this village', he says, 'is a copious spring, remarkable for having preserved its original dedicatory name Thruskell, i.e., the fountain of Thor.' He was echoing the misconception of the famous Dr Whitaker's *History of the Deanery of Craven*. In reality this name has even more venerable origins than the Norse god. Thrush Keld means Fairy Well, and it is not long since this Thruskell ceased to be periodically decorated. (A similarly 'uncanonised' source, of course, is Morgan's Well on the bank of the River Eden in Cumbria.) There is another Thruskell Well a mile and a half to the north of the Hebden Beck.

Often names have become confused like this. One example is probably a hill overlooking Meanwood, a suburb of Leeds, with a spring near the top of it. The hill is known both as Miles Hill ('Miles' pronounced as in the measure of distance) and Sugarwell Hill. Sugarwell refers to the spring, which gives very clear water and – in the stock phrase – has never in memory been known to run dry. The well is just beside one rounded summit; another summit, of the same height and joined to the first by a short stretch of ground only slightly lower, used to be crowned by a small but dramatic grove of trees which have now almost vanished.

Some people refer to the one summit as Sugarwell Hill and to the tree-topped one as Miles Hill. It is explained that beneath the trees is the grave of a Roman soldier (*miles*). There is no such grave. I suspect that Miles here is none other than *mil-es* – Celtic for Honey-Water: that is, Sugarwell. Fifty years ago I heard it said that in the childhood of the adults around me the bushes near the Sugarwell used to be decorated with bits of cloth and rag in the classic folklore way.

St Mungo's Well at Staveley, near Knaresborough and Ripon,

was famous as a healing well (the word 'healing' is cognate with 'holy'). There are records in the seventeenth century of its being visited from places as far away as Fewston, Blubberhouses and Thrushcross for the sake of its curative waters – especially to treat ailments of the eyes. Eye-trouble (commonly trachoma) was a much more deadly and feared matter in former days than now. Most of the healing wells were particularly reputed to be 'good for the eyes'.

Giggleswick, near Settle, has a number of wells which not long ago were regarded as healing. Of one of them, I was assured in 1972 by an educated and sophisticated man that its water would cure sore eyes. For all I know it will. Giggleswick Church stands in the middle of the group of wells. Inside the church, as a corbel to an arch, is a carved stone Celtic head far older than the church itself. Built into the wall on the outside is another, probably about 1,700 years old or more. The Church's dedication of 'St Alkeld' is the Saxon for 'Holy Well'.

Over the hill at Kirkby Malham, the church has two well known Celtic stone heads built into one wall in the nave. There is a third in the porch, which came to light for the first time when I was discussing the other two heads with the vicar while we were sitting in the porch and I noticed the third just over the vicar's left shoulder. Two hundred yards away up the dell is a 'spa well' reputed to be sulphurous and healing.

I was told of a stone head built into the gable-end of a barn at Coniston Cold, north of Skipton. I found it – apparently an early example – and idly wondered whether there was a well anywhere near it. 'Why, yes,' I was informed, 'there used to be one just on the other side of the road, not ten yards away, and there were two others in the village.'

Coniston Cold: 'Cold' is clearly enough 'Keld' ('well'). Professor Smith (*Place-Names of the West Riding*) says that Coniston is called Cold because of its exposed situation. He cannot have visited the sheltered, lush little place. The three wells there, meanwhile, are now scarcely a memory. The St Helen's Well between Skipton and Bolton Priory is rarely visited and proposals for water-boring near by might have dried it up altogether. The one on the lower Wharfe, just beside a ford which the Romans used, is now abandoned on the edge of a sewage farm. Only the one at Eshton still seems safe. Surrounded by a low stone kerb, it lies in a peaceful little grove of trees, fenced off from desecration. From the near-by river come the rather eerie croaks of herons — there is a heronry not far away. Bend double beside the pool, and feel the big stones that stand under water at the junctions of the kerbstones, and you will find that they are carved stone heads.

2 *Stone head in the church porch at Kirkby Malham*

High over the moor called Hunter Bark an ancient green road runs from Long Preston to Settle. At dawn and at dusk from this lane one may sometimes look down on to a huge sea of mist that hides the entire Ribble valley. At such times it is as if Settle and Giggleswick have been overtaken by the same fate as the legendary town lost beneath the waves of Semmerwater, from which the bell of the *Cathédrale engloutie* can be heard tolling. Up on the moor, one may also faintly hear the pealing of church bells and the chiming of a civic clock from the hidden valley below. But although Settle and Giggleswick are real enough when one descends from the moor, a mystery lies thickly over them.

There are faint clues. For a start, why are there so many stone heads in the Giggleswick-Settle area? They are constantly turning up. Some sceptics consider that the very number of these strange objects casts doubt on their 'authenticity' and their presumed 'Celtic' origin. It is not only their number that might arouse doubts. Some of these stone heads have features so sharply chiselled that it seems incredible that they could have been carved in Romano-Celtic times 1,500 to 1,900 years ago. Others, by contrast,

3   St Helen's Well, Eshton

are so rough and crude in execution that they might be thought to come from some village carver of the Middle Ages – or even of a few decades ago. Neither of these points of view is fully logical, although in each case the guess might be correct.

For instance, there was that third stone head in the porch at Kirkby Malham. I sent photographs of it to Dr Ross, with the suggestion that it looked reminiscent of a crude carving found at Carrawburgh. She agreed. It also strongly recalls some Gaulish Celtic carvings. But no one can say much more than that. Oddly enough, if some of these heads could be proved to have been carved not more than fifty years ago, many specialists on 'Celtic heads' would be delighted; for the astonishing thing is no longer the existence of relics of Celtic pagan culture in Brigantia, or of the prevalence of the head-cult in Celtic society – these things are far beyond doubt – but the continuity of that tradition down almost to modern times.

The head in the porch at Kirkby Malham forms a corbel at one end of an arch. The other end is uncarved, though made of a block of similar stone. The stone head in the church at Giggleswick is also at one end of an arch; the other end has no carving. The stone head outside the same church is at one end of a rain-moulding; there is no carving at the other end. This curious feature may be repeated at dozens of churches throughout Brigantia. Usually, but not quite always, the head is at the left-hand end of the arch when it is viewed from the most normal position. (The Giggleswick head now used as a chancel-corbel, however, was formerly built into the church's interior wall in a much more accessible and noticeable position; I do not know if it was then at the end of an arch.)

The St Alkeld to whom the Giggleswick church is dedicated is otherwise known only from the church at Middleham, in Wensleydale, which likewise is associated with a holy well. The 'saint' is supposed to have been a Saxon Christian princess who was strangled by heathen Danish women. There may really have been such a martyr.

Meanwhile her story is reminiscent of the ritual annual unroofing and re-roofing of a temple by the women of an island community at Sena Island, Brittany, near the mouth of the Loire, quoted by Ross. 'The woman who dropped her load in the roofing operation was torn to pieces by the other women and the remains carried round the temple in honour of the god.' As for the 'Danish' women at Giggleswick, Ross mentions that in the mythology of the Celts of Ireland the Mother of the Gods was Danu, and her people were the Tuatha De Danann. In Welsh she was Don. It may be wondered whether a version of these names may have become 'Danish'.

Giggleswick's St Alkeld's Church is traditionally associated with the Ebbing and Flowing Well, which stands beside the modern main road north of the village on the way to Buckhaw Brow. It is commonly but erroneously said that the well has ceased to exhibit its peculiar syphon action or indeed to flow at all. It is also, I believe erroneously, said that this well has not had a long existence. There is no doubt that until this century it was the object of 'sacrifices', which possibly indicates great antiquity. A stained glass window of 1903 in the church portrays in one panel 'St Alkelda' being martyred by the 'Danish women' (the Christian tradition), but another panel shows sacrifices being made to the Ebbing and Flowing Well, thus clearly linking 'Alkelda', the well, and pagan traditions.

That spring, however, is probably not the one most closely associated with the church. A hundred yards or so to the north-west of the building was a particularly venerated stream called the Holy Well, now covered by part of the buildings of Giggleswick School. Perhaps the two stone heads incorporated in the fabric of the church are relics of a pagan shrine at the Holy Well. The head above the chancel appears to be emerging from waves. It is at least possible that the first Giggleswick Church was built precisely on the position of a heathen Celtic temple. That is believed to have happened, for instance, at Goodmanham, near Market Weighton, in east Brigantia, when the Saxon king became Christian and his High Priest Coifi desecrated his own idols and altars. If something like this occurred at Giggleswick, then the Celtic goddess of the waters perhaps stands pretty well where she stood before ever Christianity came to Britain.

Even this is only part of the story. Ross visualises Brigantia the realm as 'a strong hegemony of tribes, their territory covering at least the geographical area of the modern six northern countries of England ... deriving its name and seemingly achieving its ultimate unity under the protection of a powerful goddess'. But a modern suspicion is that Brigantia the goddess may originally have been not a Celtic divinity but a mother-goddess of the Iberians.

A number of place-names in territorial Brigantia do not seem to fit Anglo-Saxon or Celtic languages, but they may be cognate with words in the language of the Basques of the western Pyrenees, regarded as the last unified European representatives of the Iberians. A silver cauldron found in Jutland (the famous 'Gundestrup Cauldron') is eastern Celtic, probably from the Danube, but its ornamentation includes many human figures who are all wearing Basque berets. One figure – either a god, or a priest performing a human sacrifice – wears a hat like the spiked beret still worn by the Portuguese dockers and porters of Funchal, Madeira. These headdresses may be eastern Celtic, but the Celts might have adopted them from Iberian predecessors.

This is where we come to the deepest mystery of Ribblesdale. In the privately owned Pig Yard Museum at Settle is a small, flat figurine made of lead, which at the end of last century was found in Bankwell, another spring close to Giggleswick Church. The figurine was described at that time as a child's doll of Elizabethan days – apparently because of the shape of the skirt. Only recently were a number of features noticed that caused it to be reinterpreted as a fertility goddess and probably a sacrificial offering to the well.

There are some highly curious features about it, first in the central front panel of the skirt. The hatched decoration of the four main triangles corresponds in precisely the same order with that of the four principal sections of one of the three triskeles on a well known bronze shield found in a hoard at Tal-y-Llyn, Merioneth. That coincidence alone is unlikely to the extent of great odds to one. Taking the next outer panel of the skirt, the hatching here corresponds to the adjoining strip of ornamentation on the shield. The outermost zigzags of the skirt correspond with the edge of the shield.

Second, the strange-shaped pendant-like object on the figurine's chest recalls the ornament depicted by Powell

4   *The Bankwell (Giggleswick) figurine*

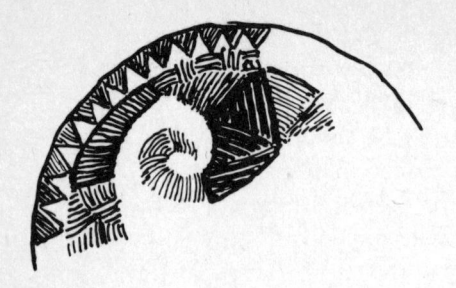

5   Part of the hatching on the shield from Tal-y-Llyn, the relevant sections lined heavily

(*Prehistoric Art*, 1966) on the chest of a pottery figurine from Cîrna, Rumania. The arms-akimbo position of this figurine is the same as that of Bankwell.

The Tal-y-Llyn shield is of the La Tène period of early Celtic art. The Cîrna statuette dates from the Bronze Age between about 900–1,000 BC and about 700 BC. It was in this late Bronze Age that bronze came to be produced by alloying copper not with tin as previously, but with lead. As was mentioned in Chapter 1, this change in technique occurred somewhat later in Brigantia, in spite of the fact that Brigantia had plenty of lead, but not tin. But the Bankwell figurine, after all, is made not of bronze at all, but of cast lead. Its date of production is therefore plunged back in the mists of mystery. Is it Brigantia herself? Was Giggleswick a sanctuary of the goddess? Was there a temple to her at Giggleswick, served by priestesses who killed one of their number when she followed Coifi's example and became a Christian?

A well is a source. From it flows a stream, which may grow into a major river. Rivers themselves were sacred objects to the Celts and to their predecessors (for many rivers bear pre-Celtic names). Ross has pointed out the examples from Gaul of a temple being placed at the source of a river, in particular the Seine. 'In Britain,' she adds, 'positive archaeological evidence for temples situated at the source of rivers is lacking; but something in the nature of those attested for Gaul, but in a less sophisticated style, can no doubt be inferred.' As apparent goddess-rivers she mentions the Wharfe, as well as the Dee (the Brigantian one which flows into the sea alongside the Wirral Peninsula), the Clyde, the Severn, and the

Braint of Anglesey and the Brent of Middlesex (both of which may be derived from the goddess-name Brigantia).

An ironic comment on all this is provided by the source of the River Eden, where it comes down from the eastern side of the Mallerstang valley through the spectacular Hell Gill. The Rev. W. Nicholls (*The History and Traditions of Mallerstang Forest and Pendragon Castle*, 1883), says that in the middle of the nineteenth century Mr William Mounsey, of Carlisle, returned home after travels in Egypt and other countries of the East. At that time the source of the Nile was a problem of great attention. There is nothing to show whether Mr Mounsey was aware of any tradition, in the East or anywhere else, of shrines at the sources of rivers. Even so, what he did bespeaks wide knowledge.

He traced his native River Eden from its mouth to its source, and had an elaborate inscription cut on a monument made of Dent marble. This was carried up the steep and rough hillside of Mallerstang Edge and erected near the river's source.

One section of the inscription was in Greek, beginning with a sentence from Homer's *Iliad*: 'Let us flee with our ships to our dear native land' – which is what Mr Mounsey had done. After this came a passage which Mr Nicholls says was quoted by Coleridge from the sayings of the Persian mystic Zarathustra: 'Seek the channel of the soul – whence, or by what means, after being the slave of the body, thou shalt raise the soul again to the position from which thou wert derived, uniting thy deed to the holy Word.'

After this is another Greek quotation, reading: 'We have a country from which we come and our father is there.' Last comes some Latin, which in translation records: 'Having begun his journey at the mouth and finished it at the source, William Mounsey, the wandering hermit, fulfilled his vow to the Genius and nymphs of the Eden on 15th March in the year of Christ 1850.'

Mr Mounsey knew heathen languages, and he sported a fine, flowing beard, so he was naturally known in Mallerstang as 'the Jew', and his monument was 'the Jew Stone'. When the Settle-Carlisle railway was being built through Mallerstang, some workmen spent one Sunday afternoon on the fell, and came across the marble monument. Since it was inscribed in something other than the Queen's English, they realised that the safest and proper thing to do was to break it into three pieces, which still lie there on the desolate moor.

A curious feature of the holy wells that were canonised in the early days of Christianity is that they, in particular, are often accompanied by a malevolent and dangerous 'boggle'. The St Helen's Well at the northern end of the ford where the Rudgate crosses the River Wharfe near Boston Spa has a strong tradition of this sort. Edmund Bogg (*Lower Wharfedale*, 1900) recounts how a Walton sexton named Smith told him of the legends of 'padfoots and barguests, and "that grim foul beast with clanking chain" which on dark nights kept its vigil by the Rudgate'. Clanking chains are a frequent feature of not only ghost-stories but malevolent spirits in general. An example is Herne the Hunter in Shakespeare's *Merry Wives of Windsor*. Ross dealt with the subject in 'Chain Symbolism in Pagan Celtic Religion' (*Speculum, 34*, 1959).

The sacred character of the Wharfe is illustrated by comments made in the seventeenth century by William Fairfax, of Newhall, Fewston, near Otley, the eldest son of Edward Fairfax the poet who will be a special study in later pages. William Grainge, of Harrogate, who paid much attention to Edward Fairfax's life and work says in his edition of Fairfax's extraordinary *Discourse of Witchcraft* (1621), published by Grainge under the title *Daemonologia*:

The fifth eclogue of Edward Fairfax commences thus:

> Upon Verbeia's willow-wattled brim,
> As Maspas drest the wands and wickers trim. . . .

On this his son (William) has this note: 'Verbeia I take to be the ancient name of the Wharfe which watereth the native country of our family, and I am in this confirmed by an altar so inscribed, which altar is observed by my father some years before Sir Robert Cotton and Mr. Camden came to this same monument where it stood at the town of Ilkley' (Woodford in Ward's MS). 'It seemeth probable to me that Verbeia was the supposed nymph of the river, for the altar was erected to her *in water* [Italics in original], and there stood, as late as the memory of the parents of such as live yet in the house. In the steeple (of Ilkley church) is a bas-relief, which Dr. Stukeley calls a figure of Hercules strangling the serpents, but the tradition of the place makes it a statue of the Goddess Verbeia anciently placed on her altar.' Gough's Camden, III, p. 289, ed. of 1806.

As for the St Helen's Well at the Rudgate, the *Dalesman* magazine in October 1971 published a letter from Mrs Dorothy Tate along with a photograph of herself as a little girl tying a piece of rag on to the bushes beside the well. The photograph, she says, was taken in about 1908. According to the traditions, however, she had gone the wrong way about 'decorating' the well, which should be done in secret.

Bogg took Dr Frederic Arnold Lees, the botanist, and Robert Baines down St Helen's Lane to the well on the bank of the Wharfe. Near it, alongside the path, they found a number of hallucinogenic and nervine herbs which were part of the stock-in-trade of witchcraft: bryony, wild hop and vervain (which does not normally grow wild in Britain). Bogg says that Leland mentioned a chapel of St Helen at the well – as there also was at the St Helen's Well at Eshton, near Skipton. Lees and Baines described the decorations such as the future Mrs Tate tied on as being 'what West-Yorkmen call mèmaws – trifles of a personal character, yet each meaning much'. It seems that this word may be derived from 'memoir' in the sense of something to be remembered by.

Lees and Baines wrote in the *Temple Magazine* of January 1900:

There are veritably hundreds of these bedizenings affixed and removed surreptitiously (probably before sunrise), according to an unwritten law, for none are ever caught in the act. And yet during the summer months a careful observer may detect almost weekly evidence of a shy communicant with the ghostly genius of someone – country maid or her dumb, shy swain. What murmured litany (if any) had to be said is lost; most likely nothing more was necessary than the unspoken wish. But now, with the schoolmaster so very much 'abroad', and fetich lore in dire discredit, it is among the most difficult of things to get any trustworthy information. Pieced together and codified, fact and hearsay testify as follows:

The visitor to the grove, before rise of sun, has to face the tree [a wych-elm overhanging the well] to detach from his or her own person some piece of garment, to dip it in the well, and having knotted or whilst hanging the fragment to any convenient twig of the witch-elm, is to breathe a 'wish' telling no one what that wish may be; these conditions strictly observed, what is desired shall come to pass.

Gipsies, village crones, and land-hands bent double with age profess to know little [Lees and Baines concluded] yet somebody transmits to the younger generation what they have received from their forebears. There remains the fact that the custom is kept up still.

In reality, secrecy appears to be an inherent part of the cult as will be seen in connection with the Howgill Black Horse and dobbie; and it is believed that the Druids, though literate, would allow nothing of their cult to be committed to writing. One may recall the 1970 five-cent piece found in 1972 in the Fairy Well at Edenhall. The secrecy, which I have termed an 'avoidance feature', is exhibited both by the local people and sometimes, apparently, by the object itself.

9
GIANTESSES IN BROAD BONNETS

❖

As permanent as rivers, and as stimulating to the imagination, are the strange rock-formations that stand on many hill-tops and moors in Brigantia. They must have been cult-figures from the earliest times of man's habitation; and to this day they exert an influence. The most famous of these weird groups is that of Brimham Rocks, near Pateley Bridge in Nidderdale. Walbran in *A Guide to Ripon* (1851) said of Brimham Rocks that their 'grim and hideous forms defy all definition'. Walbran was orientated towards medieval ecclesiastical architecture rather than towards natural forms, and would probably have been one of those who at that time found the Lake District mountains 'hideous'. He might also be suspected of laying it on a bit thick – for people in Victorian times were as eager to be terrified as they are now – except for the facts than in general he wrote with great restraint, and that he was a man of noted integrity.

In another sentence, Walbran hit the nail right on the head. 'When standing among the rocks', he said, 'our uncontrollable impression continues to be of perplexity and astonishment.' That states the truth exactly.

Some years later the Rev. William Smith (*Old Yorkshire*, 1881) said: 'Brimham is celebrated for its rocks in singular and grotesque shapes', a description so sober as to occasion cause to wonder whether he had ever been there. He makes up for it, however, by adding: 'Near Brimham is the place called Graffa Plain – i.e. the plain of the graves. Graff, O.E., a ditch or moat, a grave. . . .' He leaves it to anybody with more interest than perhaps he had himself, to find out just where, 'near Brimham', this Graffa Plain might be. The *British Gazetteer* does not help much – it says: 'Graffa Plains: near Harrogate.' Plain or plains, they are near Harrogate only if, say, Ripon or Boroughbridge might be located by the same phrase.

Graffa Plains in fact are a fine sweep of heather lying on Brimham Moor between the Rocks and Brimham Beacon, immediately to the south of the Rocks; and the 'graves' consist of a number of grass-grown tumuli or barrows. 'Graffa Plains' – this is an authentic name, perfectly in accord with the huge and eerie rocks alongside – rocks that might be thought of in sombre moments as the tombstones of Titans. It is a name far more appropriate than those attached to the 'Dancing Bear', the 'Turtle Rock', the 'Yoke of Oxen' and the 'Lovers' Leap' which may be pointed out to the visitor at the rocks themselves. Some of the other rocks bear names of a different kind: the Druid's Altar, Druids' Cave, Druids' Circle, and the Idol Rock itself. A booklet by John Palmer and Max Pemberton says that such names stem from the suggestion by eighteenth-century antiquaries that this was a pagan temple administered by a Druid priesthood. The same authors go on to show that the strange shapes were formed not by Druids but by natural forces not yet fully explained. Indeed, such references to ancient pagan ceremonies at Brimham Rocks have for many years been ridiculed as naïve romanticism. Ideas, however, are changing.

Brimham Rocks are probably the most impressive group of natural rocks in Britain. On the moor rise high, contorted, sometimes ludicrous, often terible pillars like gigantic stalagmites without the cave to contain them. Look at one of them, then go round to look at it from the other side, and it will be unrecognisable. Walk about, and a rock that looks interesting and even inviting turns into a forbidding and austere or a ferociously aggressive figure. You have to walk about. It is virtually impossible to remain in one place. Between the dark rock pillars

6 *At Brimham Rocks*

are deep, narrow chasms carpeted with green grass, brown heather and yellow sand, and you are drawn through these clefts as if by hidden magnets from one startling vista to another. There are even big tunnels through the rocks which it takes some effort to resist – and which have magical traditions attached to them akin to those of the wishing-wells.

'Our uncontrollable impression is of perplexity and astonishment', said Walbran. On second thoughts, it is an understatement. The rock fantasies of Brimham are as tangible as they are sometimes terrible. Primitive man could not conceivably have avoided feeling himself here in some kind of divine presence. So perhaps the antiquaries' names of Idol Rock and Druids' Altar were not so very far off the mark after all, though this place may have been hallowed long before the Druids. It does not very much matter. It does not matter, in the end, whether early man practised a primitive cult here or not. It is enough that at this present time one cannot look at these unforgettable rocks unmoved.

Bogg said that local people still believed that there was a spirit which inhabited Brimham Rocks. Unlike so many manifestations, this one does not seem to have been regarded as malevolent to man. It was not spoken of lightly, but it was known as the Son of the Rocks. The account recalls Mapon.

The sources of the Nidd and its upper tributaries lie in one of the wildest, least known and most inaccessible parts of Brigantia. The Nidd itself rises on the eastern side of Great Whernside and is enclosed at the mountain's foot in two large reservoirs, one below the other – Angram and Scar House. Until 1975 there was no public road. They could be reached only by an extremely rough track from Middlesmoor over Rain Stang, or by an even more arduous path from Park Rash, over Little Whernside and into Coverdale by Dead Man's Hill.

This last-named is one of those path-summits which by tradition were the scene long ago of the murder of a pedlar – a crime of which, as a rule, no official record exists and which may in reality memorialise some prehistoric human sacrifice. This instance is of greater significance than most.

Harry Speight (*Nidderdale from Nun Monkton to Whernside*, 1906), says that Dead Man's Hill

is probably the Nidderhow of Mowbray's charter (1250) defining the boundaries of the Byland Abbey lands in Nidderdale. It received its present appellation from the horrible circumstance of three human (headless) bodies having been discovered here in 1728 buried in the peat. They were supposed to be the remains of three Scotch pedlars, who, after disposing of their goods, came to a foul end while traversing the lonely road out of Nidderdale into Coverdale. Yet some say they were murdered at one of the lonely farms in the dale, and that their heads were severed from the bodies to prevent identification.

Though the circumstances of the murder are but a lingering tradition in the dale, the fact of the finding of the murdered men 'without heads' is duly recorded in the old township books of Middlesmoor, under date May 30th 1728. The following are the hitherto unprinted particulars:

'May 30th, 1728. Three murder'd Bodies were found burrd. on Lodge Edge without heads.

	£.	s.	d.
Expenses at the time to the Coroner	0.	13.	4.
For sending warrants into Coverdale	0.	0.	8.
For carrying the Biers	0.	0.	6.
To Sexton for making the graves	0.	1.	6.
To Antho. Hanley for conveying the murder'd bodies away when found	0.	1.	0.

'When the crime was committed is not known, neither were the Murderers ever brought to justice.'

Nor, probably, were they ever likely to be. It looks as if in Middlesmoor Churchyard are buried not one but three prehistoric human sacrifices, whose heads were ceremonially removed and put somewhere else – perhaps in Priest's Tarn beyond Great Whernside, or perhaps at the Vinotonus Shrine.

There is another Dead Man's Hill not many miles away, on the Kettlewell-Kilnsey road in Wharfedale, between Kettlewell and the bridge over the river Skirfare, at a point where the road south turns suddenly up and to the right over a knoll. And – again not many miles away, but in the opposite direction where the ancient road down Coverdale goes between West Witton and Wensley to an old ford over the River Ure – is Dead Man's Dub ('dub' means 'pool'), which Watkins would have expected to be a sighting 'flash': Watkins would see 'Dead Man' as a corruption of 'Dodman', meaning a (prehistoric) road surveyor; but the finding of the three bodies at the head of Nidderdale – as also of human remains in tumuli which are sighting-points – may argue against this reading.

Once down to Middlesmoor, the traveller is on a metalled road and in civilisation – understood as a ribbon along that road through Lofthouse and Ramsgill to Pateley Bridge. It is a narrow ribbon. To either side, but especially to the right (west), extend great areas without roads, houses or signs of human life except the occasional shooting-lodge. It is possible to set off from near Lofthouse, up the How Stean ravine and onwards up on to the high moors by the Great Stean Gate which is a track that is difficult to distinguish even in fine weather; to walk by the crest of Acoras Scar and the scarcely noticeable mountain called Meugher; and – miles farther on – to emerge at Yarnbury farm, with a two-mile metalled road leading down to Grassington. The walker is wise if he picks a good day for it and makes proper preparations.

Meugher is a shy hill. It can be seen 6 miles away – just, and only on a clear day – from one point at Fancarl on the main road from Pateley Bridge to Skipton. From relatively near, it stands across the huge wilderness as one walks over Rain Stang above Middlesmoor; and from there, just below the flat top of Meugher, can be seen the purple gash in the moors which is Acoras Scar. To reach the point on the Great Stean Gate along the crest of Acoras Scar takes over an hour from How Stean village by Land Rover.

That is the measure of these moors – not so much in miles as in wildness.

The meaning and origin both of 'Meugher' and of 'Acoras' are unknown. Etymologists make a Saxon guess at Meugher. Acoras they leave almost unmentioned and unillumined. Meugher is locally pronounced 'Mewfer' or 'Mewver', or sometimes 'Mew-ha' or 'Mew-gha', although visitors often call it 'Mew-ger' with a hard 'g'. The earliest known written record of it, in 1120, gives it as 'Magare', followed in 1307 by 'Mukowe'. The nearest similar place-name is Mughaire, on the Spanish side of the Pyrenees in the Basque country.

Two or three miles away, on the moors to the west of Ramsgill in Nidderdale, is a splendid millstone grit group called the Wig Stones. More or less facing them, on the opposite side of the valley high about Ramsgill, stand two astonishing objects: Jenny Twigg and her Daughter Tib. Close behind these great stone stacks are a string of smaller but also strangely shaped rocks which would be notable but for the two magnificent giants nearby. This ridge is called Sypeland Crags on Fountains Earth. The two groups – the Wig Stones to the west of Nidderdale, and Jenny Twigg and her Daughter Tib to the east of it – are key-points, and their names are key-names.

Of the few people who see the Wig Stones, some naturally imagine the name to indicate rocks which look like bewigged heads; and one at least of them in fact does, from one angle, look very much like that. But on the same moors, only two miles to the south-west above Grimwith, there is another group of rocks called Wig Stones, which cannot be said to have such a resemblance. Smith (*Place-Names of the West Riding*), discussing the Ramsgill Wig Stones, considers that the name means 'moving stones, logan stones' – literally, perhaps, wiggling stones – from the Saxon *wigga*. It could be so. None of these stones seems to be movable, but they do look decidedly wiggly.

On the other hand it might be a Saxon adaptation of an earlier name. For instance, the Gaelic Celtic *uig* means 'a retired or solitary den', and the Wig Stones (either group) could indeed bear such a reference. It could also be that the Celts in their time had

7   *The Wig Stones, Raygill*

similarly adopted and adapted a name from predecessors. There is another line of possible origin; or, rather, a double line which might have a single common beginning. If the stones were 'moving', 'rocking' stones, they would be 'wick' or 'quick' in Old English and in modern dialect. On various parts of the moors of this part of Brigantia occur variants on this word.

Smith gives no explanation of Wicking Crag or Weecher Flat and Weecher Brow, all on Ilkley Moor above Eldwick, or Wicken Tree Crag on the other side of the same moor above Ilkley. But he does derive Wicken Hill (near Barkisland) and Wicken Clough (at Heptonstall), neither of them very far from Ilkley Moor as the crow flies, from Saxon *cwicen*, 'mountain ash' (rowan). It is a very reasonable derivation. Not much less reasonable, however, would be to see the origin in *wicca*, the Saxon for 'wizard', or *wicce*, 'witch'. Smith does not mention this possibility. As it happens, however, the mountain-ash etymology leads in the same direction — although, again, Smith does not mention it.

There is no rowan (or any other tree) now at Wicken Tree Crag, or on Wicking Crag, or anywhere near either of them. There may once have been. Perhaps it matters little. Most people are aware that the rowan is supposed to ward off any attacks, or even visitations, by witches, fairies or other magic-wielding beings. What is less often realised is that this supposed power resides in the rowan's character as a pagan holy tree. It may indeed be that it was supposed to confer immunity from witches because it indicated that the person concerned was a sympathiser of the witches. Or it may represent one of rival witch-groups.

The rowan is itself magical, a witch-tree. It is used to this day in certain parts of west Yorkshire, Lancashire and other areas of Brigantia as a charm for the classical purpose of getting rid of warts. The 'needfire' which was used as a cure or preventative against cattle-disease, and earlier for many other magical purposes, had to be ignited by rubbing two pieces of rowan-wood together until the friction produced smouldering. Johnston's *Botany* (1853) says: 'The mountain ash is a sacred tree in Cheshire as elsewhere. . . . I have noticed an objection on the part of Cheshire labourers to cut one down.' It thus appears that if the Wicking Crag does not mean a witch-crag directly, it means a crag notable for a sacred witch-tree or trees.

'Weecher' seems more difficult to reconcile with the tree-reference, though not with a direct reference to witches. Weecher Brow is an escarpment of rocks facing back on to the moor — on to Weecher Flat, in fact — and providing concealment from the road and the valley below. The Wig Stones, in any case, do not appear to have any tree-meaning. Even Smith's derivation from a word one meaning of which is 'moving' leaves other interpretations quite open, especially since this idea of 'wick' or 'quick' is associated with the concept of *wicca*-wizard or *wicce*-witch.

An obsolete Scottish word 'Wiggie', according to Wright's *English Dialect Dictonary*, is a name for the Devil, i.e. for the chief divinity of any surviving pre-Christian religion; and 'wight' is a dialect word, used in Brigantia, meaning 'strong, mighty, powerful'. But E. E. Wardale (*Old English Grammar*, 1923) quotes a Northumbrian word *wih*, meaning 'idol'. It is when one stands in front of the Wig Stones that one appreciates how closely the names of 'Witch Stones' or 'Idol Stones' fit them, were it not for the fact that the phrase 'witch-stones' is also used for small stones with a natural perforation which were (and are) used to protect a building from entry of a witch.

At this point it is time to climb aboard the broomstick and fly straight across Nidderdale to Fountains Earth (it was an appurtenance of Fountains Abbey, near Ripon) and the eerie rocks called Jenny Twigg and her Daughter Tib. They stand to one side of the distorted, twisted, squashed and torn Sypeland Crags, which they dominate even though they stand lower. One of these rocks which looks like a mixture between an altar and an anvil stands on the skyline; yet by comparison with the two huge objects below, it becomes insignificant.

William Grainge (*Nidderdale*) said that on Fountains Moor

> is a large group of naked rocks, some of them of enormous bulk, called Sypeland Crags; they are of the coarse millstone grit, like those of Brimham, the grotesque grandeur of which they imitate, though on a smaller scale. Two of them a short distance from the main group are tall upright pillars and at a distance have the appearance of giantesses in broad bonnets, from which resemblance they have received the names of Jenny Twigg and her Daughter Tib.

The remarkable fact is that this passage, apart from passing references in walkers' handbooks and the like, is the only mention in literature of these exceedingly strange objects. They are ignored as completely as the Wig Stones. No author comes as near as Grainge to explaining the names of the 'giantesses'. Smith, incredibly, does not mention them at all. One might suspect a conspiracy of silence like that surrounding the decorated wells or the Howgill 'Black Horse'. Jenny Twigg and her Daughter Tib are given these names on the Ordnance Survey maps; but the Survey's original authority for the names was lost in a disastrous fire during the Second World War. No local people seem to have any firm idea of the origin other than that 'there must have been someone called that living hereabouts at one time'.

It seems possible (though unlikely) that Jenny Twigg might at one time have been something like Janet Wig. Alternatively, the Wig Stones might once have been called Twig Stones, the initial 'T' becoming misinterpreted as the dialectal contraction of 'the' to a glottal stop. *Tuig* in Gaelic means 'to be wise', which might be appropriate. There are 'Jenny' features all over Brigantia. Most (but not all) seem associated with millstone grit rocks, and with 'fairy' beings. Of the Yorkshire ones, none is mentioned by Smith. 'Jenny Plain' was a field-name at Harrogate. At Malham there is a waterfall hidden away in a ravine, and with a cave entrance beside a pool below the fall; it is called Jenny's (or Janet's) Foss, and in this instance Jenny is insistently stated to have been 'Queen of the fairies of the whole district'.

'Jenny' is a significant and puzzling word. A derivation from Welsh names such as Guinevere or Gwen is often quoted, but seems to have no serious basis. In all kinds of ways 'Jenny' is attached to objects and concepts that have to do with the magical, supernatural and pagan divine. 'Jenny-green-teeth' is the unprepossessing name for an unfriendly spirit haunting wells and ponds, and also for the lesser duckweed ('witches manna') growing on the pond's surface – there is a pool thickly covered with it immediately in front of the Wig Stones. The wren, that most sacred of all birds in Europe, is commonly called Jenny Wren. The *English Dialect Dictionary* mentions that in Leicestershire 'it is thought sacrilegious to kill a robin or a wren,

8 *Jenny Twigg and her Daughter Tib*

and even to take their eggs is a profanity certain to bring ill-luck'.

About one in four of all the witches or alleged witches mentioned in the great and horrible witch-hunt trials of early seventeenth-century England and Scotland was called Jenny or, more formally, Janet or Jannit (or sometimes Jane). Nearly another quarter was divided equally between Isobel and Margaret. The latter name, in the forms of Meg and Peg, is also a common reference to a *genius loci* in some parts of Brigantia.

The persistence of the name 'Jenny' was borne in on me when I was making enquiries about Jenny Dibb, a witch of the Washburn Valley of the seventeenth century. It transpired that Mr Albert Dibb, of Folly Hall (on the eastern side of the Washburn, opposite Timble Gill), was a direct descendant of that Jenny. On being told of the idea that there might be a connection between the frequency of the name 'Jenny' as applied to witches, and the name of Jenny Dibb, he exclaimed: 'That's funny. The women in our family are still called Jenny. My sister was Jenny, and my own daughter is another Jenny.' Miss Dibb turned out to be a modern, sensible young lady who evinced a healthy disapproval of witchcraft.

At the summit of Dead Man's Hill between Middlesmoor and Kettlewell, where the three headless bodies were found, is a point at which three tracks diverge into Nidderdale, Coverdale and Wharfedale, and three walls almost meet here. The opening is served by a simple gate of peculiar structure giving way to each of the three tracks. It is known as Jenny's Gate.

There is no Jenny or anything like it in the nomenclature of known Celtic divinities. Some of the fundamental principles of witchcraft appear to be directly opposed to the principles of pagan Celtic religion. As we have seen, the rowan and the mistletoe, which were sacred to the Celts, are regarded as hostile to witchcraft. May it not be that witchcraft – the origin of which is lost, but is certainly of great age – is the remnant of the religion of those who were here before the Celts?

After an article of mine on these matters had been published in the *Yorkshire Post*, Mrs G. E. Taylor, of Scawby, Lincolnshire, sent me the following information:

I was particularly interested in your suggestions about the name 'Jenny', especially the possibility of her being a goddess of the Iberian or pre-Celtic people, as here in Lincolnshire a certain sharp bend in the River Trent between Wildsworth and East Ferry (on the east side of the river) is known as 'Jean Yonde' or locally as Jenny Hurn, and appears on the map as Jenny Hurn and Jenny Hurn Drain. [Hurn might be identical with Windsor Forest's Herne the Hunter.] In *Lincolnshire Folk-lore* by Mrs. E. H. Rudkin (1936), pp. 34–6, she refers to local superstitions of a Boggard (Jenny Hurn) who haunted this particular point of the river, and was described as 'pygmy, man-like, with long hair and the face of a seal', which crosses the river in a small rowing boat 'shaped like a large pie-dish' and browses in the fields on the bank. Old keelmen also avoided that bend of the river after dark because of 'bumps on the side of their boats'.

I have always felt the inhabitants (native) of the Isle of Axholme were quite different from the Anglo-Saxon and Danish type of most of us in north-west Lincolnshire, and imagined they were descendants of a pocket of Celts left there in the marshes untouched by invaders – but now I wonder if they could be from a still earlier people. I also wonder if a 'pie-dish craft' might not be a coracle; and there is a local saying: 'At one time the Islonians all had long hair.'

In *Early Days in North West Lincolnshire* (1949) Harold Dudley, who was Curator of Scunthorpe Museum and Librarian for many years, on p. 158 quotes from Abraham de la Pryme's Diary (Sept 1697), p. 147 as follows (describing Castle Hill, a Roman camp or 'city' between Scawby and Hibaldstow): 'I then asked if there were any springs hard by, and they answered that there were two: the one called Castle Hill Spring, and the other Jenny-Stenny Well.'

Encyclopaedias attribute the peculiarities of the people of the Isle of Axholme area to descent from Dutchmen brought in during Stuart times. Those, however, would not be particularly unusual in physical characteristics.

So much for Jenny. Who, then was Tib? Incidentally, research has failed to establish which of the two rocks in upper Nidderdale is Jenny and which is Tib. Pundits assert that Tib as a dialectal name stands for Tobias. In this context, that is nonsense. Who has never heard an old woman call her cat 'Tibby'? The *English Dialect Dictionary* refers to a Yorkshire phrase 'tib-cat' as meaning a female cat. The cat was the commonest form assumed by a witch's 'familiar' or 'spirit'.

One should be on guard against assuming too readily that the familiar was called Tib because it was in the shape of a cat. The reverse may be true. It may be that cats were called Tib because they were in the shape of a divinity or semi-divinity known by that name. 'Tib' after all, might be seen as cognate with Div (and the Saxons' Tiw) and thus with Deus, Zeus and the very word 'divinity' itself. The notion of the divine cat – or catlike god – goes back very much farther than the Celts (who in fact did not make very much of the cat) to Pasht and Bubastis of the Nile and the Euphrates. As Ross points out, apart from certain objects and folklore motifs 'the evidence for the cat as an important cult animal in Celtic mythology is slight'. In witch-lore, on the other hand, it is vital.

A huge boulder close to the Plumpton-Spofforth road, near Knaresborough, has a large hole through it, and half-way through the hole is a basin 2 feet deep and 4 feet across. The rock is called the Hell-Hole (i.e. Holy Hole). Natural holes through rocks seem to have been regarded as potently magical, perhaps more powerfully so than similar holes through smaller talismanic stones. The existence of the large tunnels through some of the Brimham Rocks may suggest stronger evidence for that site's ceremonial significance. At Kirkby Lonsdale, in the bed of the River Lune near the Devil's Bridge, is a rock with a large hole through it, which is pointed out as the Devil's Rock. The Hell-Hole at Plumpton is 900 yards from a venerated St Helen's Well.

The magical properties of the holes through the walls in the crypts of Ripon and Hexham Cathedrals, through which people were expected to crawl, may indicate substitutes. So may the hole through the stone slab called the Low Cross at Appleton-le-Moors, north of York: agreements were made binding with a handshake through the hole.

Many more outcrops than those mentioned are marked on the 1-inch Ordnance maps; many more still are on the 2½-inch and 6-inch editions; and many, many more are not marked on any maps at all. Even where they are marked, there is little indication of the strange features that may be found there.

On the opposite side of Nidderdale from Brimham Rocks is Guisecliffe, a long escarpment of grit; on the moors behind it nothing short of the 2½-inch Ordnance will show Old Wife Ridge. Here are many rocks of shapes so fantastic that they might have inspired Mussorgsky's *Night on the Bare Mountain*. They have no recorded names. One of them seems about to take wing. Two are passionately kissing. Another is transfixed in a whirling dance. A pair are hopping over the moor like gigantic poultry. Another stands, huge and ponderous, on a silly little pedestal, like a circus elephant.

Many of them look off-balance. This heightens the effect of motion and tension, and may have given rise to the idea that they are 'rocking stones'. All over the map of central Brigantia the grit outcrops are spattered with the term 'rocking stones'. Some sceptics have toured the area, trying to rock each stone so marked and failing completely. Both Harry Speight and E. Hargrove, however, in their scrupulous books describe how between 1830 and 1910 they themselves rocked some of these stones at Brimham and elsewhere.

There is a suspicion that 'rocking stone' may in some instances be a corrupt interpretation. Between Bolton Priory in Wharfedale and West End hamlet in the Washburn valley is a shooting-lodge consisting of two buildings – one for the guns, the other for the beaters. Between these buildings is a large balanced boulder. On the maps this boulder is named 'rocking stone', the shooting lodge is described as 'Rocking Stone Hall' and the moor 'Rocking Stone Moor'. Some maps, however, mark 'Rocking Hall' and 'Rocking Moor'. The local people call them 'Roggan Hall' and 'Roggan Moor'. I failed to rock the boulder. To call the moor 'Rocking Stone Moor' from this boulder is ridiculous in view of the fact that this moor and all the moors around are littered – on the maps – with 'rocking stones'. If they all really did rock, the mathematical probabilities would make the mind boggle.

To judge from the indices of their journals, neither the Yorkshire Archaeological Society nor the Yorkshire Dialect Society, nor the Yorkshire Philosophical Society, seem ever to have considered the millstone grit and its extraordinary manifestations. From the foundations of these organisations up to recent times, one may look in vain for anything under the headings of Jenny (except one passing reference to the Harrogate 'Jenny Plain'), Tib, Wig, Meugher, Acoras, Rocks or Millstone Grit; very little under Place-names, and only one mention of a Widow Twigg who owed some rent in the sixteenth century near Rotherham.

At once less, and more, mysterious than the forces which shaped the natural rock-monsters were the forces that carved the 'cup-and-ring' stones of Brigantia. These artificial monuments are found not at the heads of the valleys but farther down, especially in mid-Wharfedale. Some, such as the highly sophisticated Swastika Stone, are stated to be the product of a later people than others; indeed, the Swastika Stone has been ascribed to the Celtic Iron Age. Such tentative datings can be founded only on the most tenuous stylistic arguments. No methods comparable with the radio-carbon technique have been devised to apply to these carvings. But if the Swastika Stone had been Celtic, a Celtic name for it would probably have survived in some form; and most of these carvings are utterly out of sympathy with all that we know of Celtic culture.

Many of the carvings are well known – on some of them, in fact, hundreds of picnic parties eat their hard-boiled eggs every weekend from Easter to October – and have been much described. Lengthy studies were carried out by E. T. Cowling, author of *Rombalds Way*, the monograph on the prehistoric trans-Pennine route which passes along Rombalds Moor, Otley Chevin and by Adel Crag through the area where the cup-and-ring stones lie thickest on the ground.

Central to this route between Flamborough and the Ribble

mouth is the Chevin, and it dominates the whole area around it. Philologists have derived its name from an old Celtic form with the meaning of 'Under the Ridge'. Suggestions have arisen, however, that its origin is pre-Celtic: for one thing, the Chevin is the ridge itself, not the town beneath. It has a brooding, secret look, and its very name is an enigma. Nevertheless, the Celts did indeed leave their stamp on it. Or was it the Celts?

Around the north-west end of the West Chevin is a low but distinctive wood-crowned hillock with the odd name of Whale Jaw Hill. Nobody recalls any whale's jaw hereabouts. The name is probably a corruption of the Saxon terms 'Welsh Shaw'. 'Shaw' means 'wood'; 'Welsh' means 'alien', not necessarily 'Celtic'. Along the top of the Chevin runs a road which until recently was narrow, rough and little used, but is now becoming very popular for weekend outings from Leeds. This is Yorkgate, or what Cowling calls Rombalds Way.

The existing metalled road runs closer to the lip of the hill edge than the Roman road which ran from York by Tadcaster over the Chevin to Ilkley and Skipton, and then down the Ribble to Ribchester. The road was realigned many years ago because of an alteration of local government boundaries. The Roman road has now almost vanished under the plough. But in any case, it did not coincide with the road that existed before the coming of the Romans and that was nearer to the present highway. All these parallel roads make the Yorkgate.

The excellent little museum at Otley, below the Chevin, was founded by Cowling. Among its exhibits are two carved stone figures, male and female, which many years ago were found close to Yorkgate. They are presumably Celtic. Certainly older than the Celts, however, is the solitary monument called the Bull Stone, on the West Chevin. It stands in a field close to the point at which an ancient bridle path (a ley) crosses the Yorkgate. There is another Brigantian Bull Stone at the extreme tip of the Duddon estuary in west Cumbria.

Otley's millstone grit monolith is about 6 feet high and $2\frac{1}{2}$ feet thick, roughly square in section but undoubtedly sculptured. It is reminiscent of the much larger Devil's Arrows at Boroughbridge and the Rudstone in east Yorkshire and may well be of much the same date. It also strongly recalls the tilted High Cross at Appleton-le-Moors.

But whereas the Arrows are simply splendid pillars, the Bull Stone has a shape which suggests a fertility significance. It is also covered by scores of 'cups'. Cowling thinks it likely that there may have been a stone circle associated with the Bull Stone for religious ceremonies.

Close by Yorkgate, at the highest point of the West Chevin, is a long scar of impressive rocks which can be seen on the skyline from many miles away. At one end of them is a small house, where in summer refreshments are dispensed. The building's real name is Beacon House, but it is generally known as Jenny's House. The rocks are Jenny's Crags. For a long time I regarded these as further examples of the use of this name to refer to some ancient magical being, until I met Mr Cowling. 'Her name was Jenny Veall,' he told me, 'and she lived in the house and sold tea and cakes.'

9 *The Bull Stone, Otley Chevin*

Never mind – the prehistoric track here aligned on a ley passes Jenny Veall's front door step – and exactly at the point where the ancient beacon used to be lit. There are a number of cup-and-ring stones on the Chevin but they are most frequent and most highly developed farther north, on Ilkley Moor. This moor seems to have been of very great importance, for prehistoric monuments are spread all over it, well away from the Yorkgate (which in fact drops down to the settlement of Olicana by the River Wharfe). Round the north-western side of the moor, overlooking Airedale, there are not only whole clusters of 'tumuli' and 'ancient dykes' but also some dramatic natural rock formations. The best known of these are the Doubler Stones, which the place-name authorities suggest simply means 'duplicate' (there are two major stacks close together). Nobody local, however, pronounces the name as 'dubbler' but always 'doobler', even though the same speaker pronounces 'double' as 'dubble'. The authorities are apparently unaware that in Brigantia a doubler is a large, shallow dish, bowl or plate. The Doubler Stones of Ilkley Moor, which are just that shape, are among the few dominant natural rocks that bear cup-and-ring carvings.

Over the Wharfedale side of the moor, just north of the upper stretch of Hebers Gill above Ilkley, is the Swastika Stone. It is not the dominant rock of its group. It is in fact quite a small one, about a yard long and nearly as much the other way, making a more or less flat surface raised only a few inches above the surrounding rough moorland grass. Immediately beyond it is a much larger rock which, seen from the side, forms a bold scar jutting out over Wharfedale. Standing facing the Swastika carving, one faces also out over the valley and up into the Pennines, as noble a view as any in Britain. But it is the enigmatic carving that holds the attention.

Nobody could mistake it for anything other than a religious symbol. Within that limit, various interpretations have been put upon it – fire, or the sun, are favourites – but nobody knows. The figure's tail is especially baffling while at the same time it gives the whole an added validity. If this design represented either fire or the sun, then it represented either object only as a projection, a sort of metaphysical shorthand, for a greater complex of apprehension. The motif is not primitive, but full of power.

It is perhaps sufficient to regard this mysterious sign, like a hymn in a forgotten tongue echoing down the ages, as one of many evidences of a deeply felt religious experience and conviction

10 The Swastika Stone, Ilkley Moor

among the people who dwelled in Britain thousands of years ago; perhaps the people who expended untold labours and great ingenuity to set up not only the great monuments of Stonehenge and Avebury but also the impressive pillars of the Devil's Arrows at Boroughbridge and the Rudstone in east Yorkshire, the great circles of Long Meg and her Daughters and of Castlerigg, both in Cumberland, and the tremendous networks of leys.

It was perhaps they, too, who constructed the strange round earthen platforms that stand in line north of Ripon, the similar platforms near Penrith at a junction of important ancient roads, and the one which stands commandingly at one side of the settlement described hilariously on the maps as the 'Druid's Temples' on Burn Moor, between Wasdale and Eskdale on a shoulder of Sca Fell. From that last platform a guard could easily watch all routes over the moor without himself being seen, and flocks could be gathered in from surrounding pastures long before an intruder could get near; but the platforms themselves obviously have a much greater significance than that of mere look-out posts.

The people who lived in these settlements, high up on the hills of the West Coast or of the Pennines, had no known system of writing; but it would be a stupid mistake to regard them as mere savages. It was from their concepts of the world and of spirit that, in part, our own concepts derive.

The Swastika and the cup-and-ring markings of Ilkley Moor and Otley Chevin are not inscribed on the rock monsters, but nevertheless the huge contorted natural masses are all round. It is these great rocks, perhaps, that make the sacred setting, comparable with the great pillars and vaulting of York Minster where the Altar itself is a relatively small object on which attention is concentrated. The Minster is less grand than Wharfedale seen from the millstone grit outcrops above Ilkley; and the High Altar is perhaps no more demanding or productive of sober apprehension than the Swastika Stone.

These carven stones are not graven images; that is, they probably never were worshipped in themselves, just as the Minster Altar is not. They are no more than a setting for human wonder and acknowledgment. Standing beside the Swastika Stone or beside Jenny Twigg, the sense of this can scarcely be avoided.

Some authorities have interpreted the various kinds of cup-and-ring markings as diagrams of a sort. Up in the north-west of Brigantia, Long Meg, the megalith standing outside the stone circle of her Daughters, bears on her south-eastern flank – protected by her maternal bulk from the prevailing west wind – such a carving, in the form of concentric rings with a single line running up to the left in about the 'ten o'clock position'. It is very similar to the design of the carving on the Knotties Stone on Otley Chevin, to some of the figures on a stone at Eira Dos Mouros at Pontivindra in Spain, and to one at Auchanbruaich in Scotland. Most of these carvings, however, it is very difficult to envisage as diagrams; and the one on Long Meg is only part of a less distinct but very similar sophisticated decoration.

Other stones have designs which are as puzzling and evocative as the Swastika. Not more than two or three miles from the Swastika as the crow flies, but on the opposite side of Wharfedale, on Snowden Carr, is a rock bearing a carving known as the Tree of Life. Of this stone Cowling says that it 'is one of the few known to local inhabitants, and marks the site of many May Day religious

11   The Tree of Life Stone, Snowden Carr

services'. To this it may be added that not all the local inhabitants readily tell inquirers about it.

The Tree of Life stone is no diagram. It fits more easily into the context of Yggdrasil the Scandinavian ash tree whose roots held the earth together, of the tree in which the divine Llew Llaw Giffes in the shape of an eagle perched according to the Welsh legend, of the sacred oaks of Celtic mythology and of the king-trees and queen-trees which stood in each forest – sometimes known by those terms, like the King and Queen Oaks of the New Forest. It is of the family of the Blubberhouses Oak of the Forest of Knaresborough, the Skyr-Ack or Shire Oak of Headingley near Leeds, the huge oak which formerly stretched out an arm almost to the Church of St Michael at Cowthorpe in the Walton-Walshford pocket, or the great oak of Inglewood Forest north of High Hesket in Cumberland where the hermit Robert of Corbridge sheltered. Not so long ago ceremonies took place at the Tree of Life on May Day – if indeed they have yet ceased, for it is a valley where things do not cease readily nor outsiders easily learn of them. The queen-tree is a theme that we shall meet again.

10
MAGIC RAVENS

Some of the great rocks of Brigantia are in the line of tradition that touches upon very ancient myths of bird-gods and bird-demons, the last traces of which have scarcely yet vanished.

About three miles west of the Ramsgill Wig Stones, at the foot of Meugher and in the heart of the wilderness, is an escarpment called Hen Stone Band and a group of rocks called the Hen Stones. Roughly the same distance due south of the Ramsgill Wig Stones there is another group of Hen Stones (and also a second cluster of Wig Stones). Still farther south, on the moors south and south-east of the splendid crag called Simon's Seat, are yet two more groups of Hen Stones. Nobody seems so far to have noticed or commented on the sequence.

'Hen' in this context does not refer to farmyard poultry. Like the Irish *en* or the Scottish Gaelic *eun*, it simply means 'bird', in the same way as the English 'moor-hen' means 'moor bird' – of either sex ('moorcock' is a later word). The Hen Stones could be farmyard cocks and hens, or doves and linnets, or evil and menacing ravens – even eagles. Caesar in his *Gallic Wars* said that the *gallus* (by which he appears to have meant the farmyard cock), the goose and the hare were sacred to the Britons. 'The Celts', says Ross, 'believed the world to be haunted not only by sweet-singing, pain-dispelling otherworld birds, but by malevolent bird-flocks in the service of hostile gods. . . . In more recent traditions, death is thought of as coming in the form of a bird, sometimes a great black screaming night bird.'

After climbing up the steep track from Howgill to the crest of Barden Fell at Simon's Seat, one should look straight across the moor. It falls away in the foreground, across a small watershed, and then rises again to a ridge. All along that ridge is a row of rocks which, even from this distance (about half a mile) look quite different from the solid mass of Simon's Seat. They lean in all directions, climb precariously on top of each other, and open colossal maws like those of dinosaurs from a science-fiction film. This is the most important of the groups called Hen Stones. If these are to be thought of as birds, then they are not farmyard poultry but the savage flock of the Celtic raven-goddess the *Mórrígan*. Any people who lived on these hills and were in regular contact with the rock outcrops were bound to be intensely affected by such an environment. Rocks of this sort must be propitiated.

A mile to the east is a separate group of Hen Stones, quiet and recumbent. These are not the warrior-birds of the *Mórrígan*, but much more Rhiannon's singing birds who have sung themselves to sleep for seven years in the Welsh legend. It was Rhiannon's birds who sang to the heroes as they bore the magical head of Bendigeidfran, the Sacred Raven.

But the magical and divine significance of the bird-rocks of Brigantia may go back beyond the Celts. Of the *Mórrígan* herself, Ross says that such a raven-goddess may have 'a European ancestry older and more general in distribution than the Celts themselves'. Dealing specifically with the raven as an important Celtic cult-bird, Ross adds: 'It likewise figures as a solar bird in the mythology of late Bronze Age Europe.' The solar association was indicated by the symbol of the wheel; and the conjunction of raven and wheel can be startlingly and mysteriously found in Brigantia in the context of the seventeenth century AD — as for instance in the carved stone doorhead at Langcliffe Hall, near Settle.

Ross points out that 'in later folklore traditions the raven became a favourite familiar of witches'. The seventeenth century was a time of intense persecution of witches, and the Brigantian area was fully involved in this and in the resistance to it. But the appearance of the ancient raven-and-wheel motif publicly blazoned at Langcliffe in that very period does not seem to have been noted.

A raven-cult may indeed have existed and long persisted in north-west Brigantia, in the Rheged area. It was of Rheged that Owain was Prince. One of the stories of the old Welsh *Mabinogion* called *The Dream of Rhonabwy* related how Arthur asks Owain to play a game of chess (or, rather, a chess-like game called *gwyddbwyll*). As they play, messengers come one after another to tell Owain that Arthur's men are attacking Owain's ravens. Instead of calling his men off, Arthur bids Owain to get on with the game. When most of the ravens have been slain and the rest are too hurt to lift their wings, Owain at last gives the order for his standard to be raised. Thereupon his ravens are revived and hurl themselves on Arthur's men, swooping down, carrying them up into the air and tearing them to pieces, until Arthur crushes the golden *gwyddbwyll* pieces to dust and begs Owain to call his ravens off. The standard is lowered and peace is restored.

The episode is represented as taking place during a joint campaign, including other Celtic chiefs under the general leadership of Arthur, against the Saxons. It could well be an allegory of a period of uneasy and untrusting treaty between Arthur and Rheged during which each side kept up guerrilla attacks on the other. It has been pointed out that the Welsh word for 'raven', *bran*, is often used as meaning 'warrior'; but the story pointedly avoids confusion by referring to Owain's ravens' wings and feathers. These are magical warrior-birds, which in the *mabinogi* of *Iarlles y Ffynawn* are said to have been bequeathed to Owain by his paternal grandfather, Cynfarch (Kynverch) – by-passing his son Urien, Owain's father.

Two miles or so south of Haresceugh Castle in Rheged – the farm with which was associated the lost Luck of a silver-rimmed wooden bowl – the ancient Carlisle-Appleby road, the *Strata Regia* (King's Road), passes the village of Melmerby. A 1677 account of Melmerby Church by the then rector, Richard Singleton, mentioned one coat of arms of 'the Highmoores of Onse brig' with a crossbow between 'three black cocks'; and another coat of arms bearing 'things' which Singleton hesitantly called 'eaglets' in four rows – six, three, two and one. In both these cases it might be possible to see a memory of Owain's ravens.

Just beyond Haresceugh Castle is the village of Renwick, which is a corruption of Ravenwick (a Danish name which may be a translation of an earlier Celtic one). The stream that flows down from Renwick Fell through Renwick to Kirkoswald, with Nether Haresceugh and its Holy Well on the northern bank, is the Raven Beck. The next parallel beck up-river along the Eden is the Hazelrigg Beck, but its valley is inexplicably called Daleraven. It is at that beck's debouchment into the Eden that the St Michael's Chapel was sited which was 'polluted by blood' in the fourteenth century, and this beck has its source on an offshoot of Cross Fell called Fiend's Fell. At Renwick, when the old church was being pulled down in about 1590 – so legend says – the workmen were frightened away by a monster described either as a huge black 'bat' or as a cockatrice (a deadly creature with the head, wings and legs of a cock and the tail of a serpent), which was slain by a man called Tallentire to win the manor for himself.

Over this whole area the hostility between the Christian Church and paganism seems to have been bitter and prolonged. It is the home ground of Owain, who from Castle Hewen could reach it immediately by a crossing over the Eden at Armathwaite.

How many places-names including the word 'raven' are there in the Cross Fell area and in the Lake District? One would expect scores of them.

In reality – judging by the 1-inch Ordnance Survey – there are only a few; and they form something that looks remarkably as if it might be a boundary line of Rheged: Raven Seat Moor (OS Grid reference 855045) on the north side of upper Swaledale; Raven Thorn on West Baugh Fell; Ravenstonedale Common (it is not known where any Ravenstone may have stood); Crosby Ravensworth; Raven Howe on the High Street range; Raven's Edge and Raven Crag, standing respectively just east and just west above the summit of Kirkstone Pass; and Raven's Barrow on Cartmel Fell overlooking the Leven Estuary.

From here there is a big gap until Raven Crag overlooking the top end of Eskdale, and Ravenglass at the bottom end; but

Ravenglass is stated to be a corruption of Celtic *afon-glas* meaning 'grey river' (the Roman name was *Glennaventa*). In the north there are Raven Crag above Mungrisdale at the eastern end of the Skiddaw-Blencathra massif, and Ravenstone at the western end on the shore of Bassenthwaite Lake. On the opposite shore of that lake, just beside Bridekirk, is a village bearing the same name as that of the man who rid Renwick of the cockatrice: Tallentire.

Within the huge, mountainous area described by these twelve 'raven' points, an area including the whole of the Lake District, so far as I can see the 1-inch OS map shows not a single raven place-name — and little indication of a possible reference to a Celtic *bran*, 'raven'. That makes a coincidence which it is not possible to ignore.

But what about Caesar's cocks and geese? The very powerful Celtic goddess Epona (who was Romanised as Minerva) was represented as riding across the sky like a witch, but mounted on a goose, not a broomstick. She is the origin of the pantomime Mother Goose, who plucked the feathers from her steed to make a snowstorm.

Back at Kirkoswald in Raven-land, Col. Fetherstonhaugh tells a less kindly story. He says that on Shrove Tuesday — when the Christian Church shut its eyes to pagan devilries — 'it was the custom to bury a cock in the ground with just its head showing, and to pelt it to death'. It may here be remarked that Malory's manor of Hylton Floghen was only a few miles away; was it Flog-Hen? Tullie House archives, Carlisle, have no record of this manor.

The Shrove Tuesday custom was more explicit a little farther south. Joe Steel, a well known mason poet, described the 'hen hunt' to Dr Thomas Gibson of Orton *(Legends and Historical Notes of North Westmoreland*, 1887). About twelve men were blindfolded, the hen was put into a pit and they tried to hit it. Dr Gibson says that an annotator of Tusser (who wrote in 1620) stated that the hen was hung on a man's back, along with some horse-bells, and the others chased him. The hen, when dead, was boiled with bacon, and pancakes and fritters were made.

Tusser said that a hen which had not laid eggs before Shrove Tuesday was threshed with a flail, and the man who killed it won it. 'In other places', Dr Gibson added, 'a hen was thrown down and maltreated by the blinded ruffians, and the legends sayd the hen spoke' – a fairly clear memory of ornithomancy.

Nobody knows when Christianity came to Britain. It is suggested that it arrived even before the Romans, and established its first wattle church at Glastonbury in Somerset – perhaps even at first as a joint undertaking with the pagan Druids, with whom the site was probably of great sanctity. The well known legend is that the Glastonbury church was set up by Joseph of Arimathea; a school of thought considers that it might have been established not by him directly but by his associates and on his instigation. At any rate, the first church in Britain, or one of the two first (the other was at St Pancras in London), was at Glastonbury. Another chapel, traditionally stated to have been of wattle, thatched with bracken, was at Raughton Head in the Forest of Inglewood, north-west Brigantia; nobody knows how old it was. In 1667, when it was ruinous, it was rebuilt, and again in about 1760 – this time as a substantial and handsome building. Formerly a chapel of ease for Castle Sowerby, it is now an independent living.

The Roman Empire on the whole was remarkably tolerant of all faiths so long as at least lip-service was paid to the official Roman gods and particularly to the divine nature of the Emperors. It was not when Constantine the Great put the monogram of Christ on his standards, but after the Western Empire had collapsed, that the Roman Church abandoned such tolerance and not only anathematised 'heretical' Christian leaders, but also began to insist on the abandonment of non-Christian religions. From this period begins the long process of the supplanting of more ancient faiths by the new Gospel, which would share its authority with nobody else. But there was no sudden end to the old. There was no end at all. The old cult in Britain, under the pressure of official Christianity, divided into three main streams; and all three, if they are sought, may still be found to this day, especially in Brigantia.

Every vicar is familiar enough with the relics of pagan ritual incorporated into Christian custom. From the 'ritual cannibalism' of the Communion service to the kiss given by the best man to the bride, the whole field has been raked over *ad nauseam*. Curiously, these vestiges of pagan custom have little reference in particular to Celtic religion. The reference is usually to features common to paganism over a very wide area, even world-wide, but of a social stage earlier than that of the Celts in Roman or immediately pre-Roman times.

Virtually every old church in Brigantia seems to be built on what was formerly a pagan cult-site. Many relatively modern churches have succeeded earlier churches built on the same places. Probably there is no church still existing that was the actual edifice to replace a pagan shrine. But it appears that wherever there was formerly a pagan cult-centre attached to a settlement or a village, there a church was built in its place (if the original structure was not simply re-consecrated). Where a pagan centre was not attached to a settlement – as, for instance, at a crossroads or at a sacred well on a route between two settlements – there a Christian hermitage or chapel might be established. Not many villages, it seems, have no reference to a pre-existing pagan centre.

Very commonly, a village church is built on a mound, which is often round (that at Kirk Hammerton, near York, is a good example). Generally, somewhere near will be a well which until recently was annually 'decorated', which was the subject of votive offerings in the form of bent pins or coins, and which was dedicated to a saint – commonly Bride, Helen or Mungo/Kentigern. And remarkably often, somewhere in the fabric of the church will be found a carved stone head from a pre-Christian Celtic cult – or perhaps a later imitation.

Sometimes a carving will be found which does not represent a head but which is even more specifically pagan. Such, for instance, is the Devil Stone – so named – in the church at Copgrove, near Ripon. Formerly inside the chancel, in restoration last century it was banished to the outside wall exposed to the elements. The church is, as might be expected, dedicated to St Michael. Another such carving is the eerie 'Eye of God' stone built into the tower of Newchurch (the building is sixteenth century, but the tower is much older), near Pendle Hill in western Brigantia; which god?

The church of Long Preston, near Settle, was erected in the early fifteenth century on part of what has been described as a Roman fort. Over the porch is an object which has been termed a trefoil Celtic cross. There does not appear to be any possibility of seeing it as a cross of any kind. A small piece has been broken off the top. If the mind's eye replaces that piece, the object looks like an oak leaf, recalling for instance the carved oak nymph of Coventina from the well at the pagan shrine at Carrawburgh in northern Brigantia. The Long Preston object is extremely reminiscent of an oak leaf which appears on the chest beneath a carved male stone head with typically Celtic flowing moustache and 'imperial' beard found at Heaton, Bradford, now at Cartwright Hall Museum, Bradford, and illustrated in *Celtic and Other Stone Heads: First Series* (1973), written and published by Mr Sidney Jackson of Shipley, Bradford. The church at Long Preston replaced a Chapel of St Michael.

There would be nothing at all unusual in the inclusion of such a pagan symbol in a Christian fabric. It happened so frequently as to indicate a definite policy. The early Tudor church of 'St Alkeld' at Giggleswick, dedicated to a holy well, has a carved Celtic head inside and another outside. In the churchyard is an unexplained stone pillar, on which it is not difficult to envisage a cult-head in the classical Celtic manner. These pre-Reformation churches nearly always have a pillar in the churchyard, sometimes adapted as a sundial.

Kirkby Malham's church – again St Michael's – was restored in the nineteenth century by Walter Morrison, MP, and as a result of his advice two very good Celtic stone heads were built into the wall of the nave. Presumably they had been located on the premises. Morrison also provided the church with a porch; and in this is the third Celtic head of an earlier and ruder type.

This church's historical brochure – like almost all others in similar circumstances – mentions everything except the stone heads; the brochure's photographs of the interior even avoid showing them, except by chance the head in the porch the existence of which was unknown until I happened to notice it. The brochure of St Alkeld's does just mention the interior head, merely as being 'sometimes described as the oldest stone in the church', but says nothing of the exterior head or the churchyard pillar. One might be forgiven for thinking that such churches' authorities were embarrassed by or even downright ashamed of such possessions instead of proud of them.

Oswald went round his realm with Paulinus 'canonising' pagan springs, many of which are now marked with a Church of St Oswald. One such is at Kirkoswald in Cumberland. Mr John Hayes Segger, of Lazonby, informs me that inside the church porch the entrance arch has a carved stone head at each end. One of them is scarcely distinguishable. The other, at the left-hand end, has decidedly Celtic-type features, but is carved on the stringcourse around the arch as part of the springers. The wall is twelfth- or early thirteenth-century workmanship. The head is therefore very much an example of the survival of a tradition.

Another St Oswald's, on top of a mound, at Farnham near Knaresborough, is highly instructive. Inside are carved stone heads of the crowned St Oswald, and his Queen who persuaded him to become Christian. On the outside of the north wall is a rain-moulding with a carved head of quite another style. At the foot of the church tower is a window with an arched moulding which at the right-hand end comes down to a Celtic-style head, while the left-hand end is adorned by a tricephalos – a single head with three faces. It is especially noteworthy, however, for the way in which four eyes are made to do duty for the three faces. The style of the work is similar to that of the single-faced head in the porch at Kirkby Malham.

There is another but medieval tricephalos in Brigantia in Cartmel Priory in Furness. Instead of ears, it has two smaller heads growing out of its temples; and the central head is giving a prodigious wink.

The church at Rudstone in east Yorkshire stands at the crossing of several leys. In the churchyard is the famous Rudstone, more than 25 feet high. Near by are many prehistoric remains. These and the monolith attract much attention. Nobody seems to have noticed that within the church entrance is an arch, the left-hand end of which rests on a stone head which is placed on its side. I know of no similar instance. The features have been somewhat defaced.

Walbran (*Guide to Ripon*, 1851), in dealing with Bolton Priory, says of the roof: 'The cornice is painted in panels, with flowers and heads much faded; and three sculptured bosses of similar design adorn the centre beam. One of these is sagely conjectured, by the country people, to represent the devil.' None of this, perhaps, was as surprising as a feature that Walbran noticed at the end of the chancel of Fountains Abbey, where there was a Lady Chapel. He describes some key-stones here which were installed by Abbot Darnton (1478–94). One of these 'displays a head entwined with snakes – a symbol of the Evil principle, or more particularly of Pride; and in the interior, the figure of an angel, holding a scroll inscribed "Anno Domini 1483".'

12 *The Green Man at Fountains Abbey*

This head is the Green Man, a survival from the Celtic gods, in particular of Cernunnos the god of Nature. His head is entwined not with snakes but with boughs which issue from his mouth. At Fountains Abbey it is improper not merely because it belongs to the heart of paganism, but because this was a Cistercian establishment where even statues of angels were supposed to be prohibited. No wonder there was a St Michael's Chapel up How Hill above the abbey. Indeed, E. Hargrove (*History of Knaresborough*, 1832) calls this hill Michael-How-Hill (other writers name it Mickle-How-Hill) and explains: 'Upon the summit of this hill was a chapel, called St Michael's de Monte.' That is equivalent to the 'St Michael's Mount' island off Cornwall's south coast, and the corresponding Mont St Michel off the coast of Brittany where Arthur slew the baby-eating giant. Why did Abbot Darnton put that head in the abbey? And why did no one apparently protest? On the same side of the River Skell, about a mile farther downstream, is a place named on the OS 2½-inch map as Green Man Gate.

Cernunnos had either horns or, more characteristically, the antlers of a stag. Typical of him was Herne the Hunter, of Windsor Forest, the legendary figure referred to by Shakespeare in *The Merry Wives of Windsor*, Act IV, Scene 4:

> There is an old tale goes that Herne the Hunter,
> Sometimes a keeper here in Windsor Forest,
> Doth all the winter-time at still midnight,
> Walk round about an oak, with great ragg'd horns;
> And there he blasts the tree, and takes the cattle,
> And makes milch-kine yield blood, and shakes a chain
> In a most hideous and dreadful manner. . . .
> Falstaff at that oak shall meet with us,
> Disguis'd, like Herne, with huge horns on his head.

Herne's Oak in Windsor Forest was huge and ancient. In the Forest of Galtres, north of York, there was a Herne-figure known as *Le Gros Veneur* (the Great Hunter), and in 1283 Anthony Bek, Bishop-elect of Durham, met him while hunting in the forest (reported by G. M. Cowling, *History of Easingwold and the Forest of Galtres*).

Geoffrey of Monmouth (Thorpe edition), among the remarkable series of prophecies allegedly uttered by Merlin, describes one which undoubtedly contains a great deal of obscure pagan folklore about a damsel who will work healing by leech-craft and work various wonders:

> He that will kill her shall be a stag of ten tines, four of which will bear golden coronets, but the other six will be turned into the horns of oxen and these horns will rouse the three islands of Britain with their accursed bellowing.

Stone heads do not bellow, but some heads in Brigantia have a macabre liveliness. Up to the modern day, there have been many instances of skulls which behaved in an independent fashion very much like the severed heads of Celtic folk-tale and legend, and they come from all parts of Brigantia. There are certain old houses in Brigantia which still keep such assertive and active skulls, locked up in cupboards or behind screens in the skulls' favourite hiding-places, and the owners are reluctant publicly to admit their existence.

The best-known – indeed, it is sometimes described as notorious – example consists of the skulls of Calgarth Hall, on the eastern shore at the northern end of Windermere. These were alleged to be the heads of a man and his wife whose piece of land was coveted by the lord of Calgarth Hall. They refused to part with the land, and he had them falsely convicted of theft and executed – but at the moment of execution the man threatened that their heads would haunt the Hall for ever.

Traditionally the skulls were kept in a niche at the Hall. They could not be kept away. All sorts of means were used to get rid of them. They were buried on the mountains, burned, calcined, ground to powder and dispersed by the wind, all in vain. Most significantly, they were several times sunk in the well or thrown into the lake – like the skulls of Wookey Hole in Somerset or of Coventina's Well at Carrawburgh in Northumberland – but they always turned up again at the Hall. All the same, they are said not to be there now.

Their story is typical. Dr Gibson of Orton mentions a skull that used to be at the foot of a stair at Heyfell and, when taken away by people who were moving, always returned (the same thing was told of some crockery at a house at Kickersgill).

Clarence Daniel (*Twelve Headless Men and Other Derbyshire Ghost Stories*, 1973), refers to three such skulls. One is kept at Flagg Hall, Derbyshire, and refuses to be moved. A second was kept on a window-sill at Dunscar Farm, near Castleton. The third, which might be described as a very strong personality, was called Dickey o' Tunstead. In spite of its name, it was a woman's skull, which was kept in a staircase window at Tunstead Farm (staircase windows and niches seem to have been favourite habitats for skulls). If it was taken away from the farm, disaster followed disaster until it was brought back.

The skull was hurled into Coombes Reservoir (a modern adaptation of the sacrificial well motif) – 'but the fish died'! It was thrown into the river, but was hastily pulled out again. Consecrated ground was no better – the skull was twice buried in the churchyard of Chapel-en-le-Frith, but had to be dug up again. With all this, it responded generously to kind and respectful treatment, often giving warning of misfortune, guarding against accident, or helping in other ways.

Another place blessed with a skull was Brougham Hall, just south of Penrith. Gerald Findler (*Legends of the Lake Counties*, 1970) says:

> Whatever was done with it, whether buried on land or in the sea, it had to be restored. Unless it was kept in the hall, the inmates were never allowed to rest by reason of diabolical disturbances and unearthly noises throughout the night.

The same author relates the story of Threlkeld Place, east of Keswick. A new tenant there found a skull in a small, dark room which the previous tenant had not used. He accordingly buried it, with due reverence. Immediately afterwards his wife went to clean out the little room – but found the skull was already back there, in the niche where her husband had found it. He took it to St Bees Head and threw it into the sea. When he got back home there was the skull in its usual place. Various other attempts were made to dispose of it, all in vain. Very closely similar instances are recorded from Browsholme Hall (in Bowland) and Burton Agnes Hall (near Bridlington). The Burton Agnes skull was later bricked up in a wall, but that at Browsholme is kept in a cupboard. In both cases chapter and verse are given for the associated phenomena.

Kathleen Eyre (*Lancashire Legends*, 1972), describes a headless statue standing beside a spring near the river at Waddow Hall, in Ribblesdale. Traditionally it is the figure of St Margaret, but her name has been reduced to Peg o' th' Well – which is about as witchcraft-laden a name as could be devised. The statue is said to claim a human sacrifice every seven years, and this sounds a much more pagan attribute than one of a Christian saint.

On one occasion Peg had nearly drowned a visiting clergyman (again, an un-Christian thing to do), and the angry lady of the house chopped off the statue's head with an axe. The head was put in a lumber room in the attic. A cheerful, matter-of-fact servant found it there, cleaned it up and put it in the pantry. She was asked: 'Does she never plague you now?' The servant replied: 'There is not a better girl in the parish. I fear she was much slandered.'

At Wardley Hall, Worsley, in south-east Lancashire, a skull was preserved which was supposed to be that of Roger Downes, a libertine of the court of Charles II. The skull was kept in an embrasure between the hall and the staircase. A maidservant, says Miss Eyre, thought it was an animal's skull and threw it into the moat, but there was a sudden terrifying storm until it was restored to its niche. Disasters occurred every subsequent time it was disturbed.

Miss Eyre also describes two damaged skulls, male and female (the sexes are in fact not easy to distinguish), which about 1750 were pulled out of Bradshaw Brook and put on a mantelpiece at Timberbottoms Farm at Turton, in mid-Lancashire. Whenever the skulls were moved therafter, the family was plagued by rattlings, knockings and ghostly forms. The skulls were even thrown back into the river from which they came, but in vain. In 1840 the farmer had them buried in Bradshaw Churchyard, but they had to be dug up again and put back in their place at Timberbottoms. Later the skulls stood for many years on the family Bible in the study at Bradshaw Hall, and nowadays they are on view at Turton Tower. Miss Eyre does not say whether they still give trouble.

A notable feature is that several of these skulls are supposed to have been found in a river or a well, but that they refuse to be put back there. On the other hand the skulls seem to have no objection to being incorporated in the fabric of the building to which they are attached. Dickey o' Tunstead is believed to be now built into a wall of the farmhouse. The Brougham Hall skull was bricked into the wall and has been quiet ever since. The same solution was found for the skull of Threlkeld Place – but the farmer made doubly sure and moved with his wife to another farm. The building-in theme recalls the frequent occurrence of stone heads – Celtic or later – incorporated into buildings, especially barns, in Brigantia. The heads are regarded as 'lucky', as indeed in a sense they are.

So was the head of Bendigeidfran in the *mabinogi* of *Branwen Daughter of Llyr* – the head which was taken to the White Mount in London to guard against invasion. It cannot be coincidence that under 1282 the *Chronicle of Lanercost* records that Llewellyn ap Gruffudd, Prince of Wales, in battle against the English 'was beheaded incontinently. . . . The head of Llewellyn, who had been slain by the treachery of his own people, was sent to the King [Edward I] although he would not have approved of this being done. However, it was taken to the Tower of London [i.e. the White Mount] and fixed upon a stake. . . .' David, Llewellyn's betrayer who was also treacherous to Edward, was quartered, and 'the villain's head was bound with iron, lest it should fall into pieces from putrefaction, and set conspicuously upon a long spear-shaft for the mockery of London'. This, of course, was the traditional use to which the 'Traitors' Gate' was put.

Another of Miss Eyre's examples comes back to the grimmer traditions which seem to lie behind the cult of the skull and head. It concerns Mowbreck Manor at Wesham, near Kirkham, in the Fylde. During the reign of Elizabeth I the owner of Mowbreck Manor, John Westby, gave shelter to Vivian Haydock, a Roman Catholic who became a priest late in life and who had a son, George, also a priest. While Vivian was about to celebrate midnight Mass in the private chapel at Mowbreck Manor, George was being arrested in London. The father saw the severed, bloodstained head of his son hovering above the altar and whispering: *Tristitia vestra vertetur in gaudium* ('May your sorrow be turned to praise'). The father died of shock. Many other people are said to have seen the 'Gory Head' in later years. The story has obvious affinities with that of the Green Knight's head – and with the many tales of ghosts whose heads chatter away while tucked underneath the arm of the 'body'.

Attila the Hun drank from the skull of his enemy. So did the Mongol Jenghis Khan, Emperor of All Men, whose skull-cup was plated with silver; and on his tremendous ride from Rome to the Mongols' tented capital of Karakorum in the Gobi Desert John of Plano Carpini, the monk-ambassador of the Pope, passed along a route marked by cairns that were built not of stones, but of human heads, the symbols of the Pax Mongolica. One man told Clarence Daniel that as a youth he used the skull of Dickey o' Tunstead for drinking water.

A strange story of 1973 has reference to the 'Devil's Head' in the roof of Bolton Priory. Under the heading of ' "Curse" ends tomb search', the following report appeared on the front page of the *Yorkshire Post* of 3 March 1973:

> Amateur archaeologists have called off their search for the burial place of a notorious Yorkshireman. One has spoken of a curse, another has said his wife was confronted by a man in medieval costume, and a third has spoken of a vision of something 'very black and very evil' at the mouth of a tomb they had been excavating. The tomb is in the priory ruins at Bolton Abbey [correctly, Priory] in Upper Wharfedale.
>
> The team were looking for the family vaults of the Clifford family, medieval lords of nearby Skipton and owners of vast estates in that part of Yorkshire. They had hoped to find the bones of John de Clifford – 'the butcher' – killed in the Wars of the Roses in 1461. He was said to have killed in cold blood the young Earl of Rutland in 1460.
>
> One of the team went home after working on the excavation to find his wife crying. All the house doors were locked. She told him she had been lying on the couch in their living room and on looking up had seen a man. He was about 5ft 6in. tall and looked very strong. He was in his thirties, wearing a jerkin open to his chest and a puff-sleeved shirt. He had shoulder-length dark hair. 'He just stood and stared and I stared back,' said the wife who did not want to be named. 'What she described was a man in late 14th century or early 15th century costume,' said Mr. David Clough, a member of

the team who is a deputy headmaster at Barnoldswick, near Skipton [did he mean late 15th or early 16th?].

The following Saturday Mr. Clough called on two other members of the team, Mr. and Mrs. Louis Hodgkiss, of Hawkswick, Littondale. 'Louis said he was having no more to do with the tomb and said we could not use his tools', said Mr. Clough. 'He had been ill with 'flu and believed his illness was due to the digging. He told me: "I have had the curse of the Cliffords on me this last week".'

Mr. Hodgkiss's wife, Dr. Winifred Haward, an historian, told Mr. Clough that while her husband was ill she had a vision of something 'very black and very evil' at the mouth of the tomb they had been working on. Dr Haward, an agnostic, also told him that while she had been at the Priory she had been drawn into the church to pray for the souls of the people they were searching for.

Mr. Clough said in a grave they excavated in the south transept of the ruins they found a woman's skeleton. After resealing the tomb the strange experience had ceased. At one time during the excavation he had entered the church alone but had to get out because he felt something 'very strong and very frightening'.

Let it be clear at once that I had nothing whatever to do with that report. Before it appeared, however, I was aware of the circumstances described and, indeed, of others. Some of the persons involved no doubt were embarrassed by the publicity and by their involvement in so strange a tale of the occult. They need not so have felt. By a curious coincidence, a few days before the report appeared I had come to know of some other relevant matters which cast a new light on the whole incident.

I had been pursuing the remarkably thorough researches of John Richard Walbran, the nineteenth-century Ripon archaeologist and author of the erudite *Guide to Ripon, Harrogate, Fountains Abbey, Bolton Priory and Several Places of Interest in their Vicinity*, already repeatedly cited in abbreviated title. The fifth edition of that work, published in 1851, describes how at the east end of the nave of Bolton Priory are eight large rough stones laid side by side and raised 20 inches above the floor. 'These cover the Vault of the Claphams, of Beamsley,' says Walbran, 'who, according to tradition, were interred there upright.'

The same vault is described by Whitaker in the *History and Antiquities of the Deanery of Craven* (third edition, 1878), who says:

> Bolton was the burial-place of such of the Cliffords as died in Yorkshire: for those who ended their days in Westmorland would probably be interred at Shap. . . . As there is now remaining a slab of grey marble, in the wall of an outhouse at Bolton, with a groove for the Garter; and as John Lord Clifford, slain at Meaux (East Yorkshire) 10th Henry V, was the only one of his family who had that honour before the first earl, I conclude that his body was brought home for interment (I have now ascertained this fact from the *Chronicon de Kirkstall*).

Later Whitaker says that William de la Moore, of Otterburne, who held 'Bethmesley' (Beamsley) through his wife Thomasine, had an only daughter and heiress named Elizabeth. She, marrying Thomas Clapham, brought the manor of Beamsley into that family.

> The oldest son of this match was John Clapham, a 'famous esquire' in wars between the houses of York and Lancaster, who is said to have *beheaded* [emphasis added] with his own hands the Earl of Pembroke, in the church porch of Banbury. He was a vehement partisan of the house of Lancaster, in whom the spirit of his chieftains, the Cliffords, seemed to survive.

At this point there arises some confusion between Cliffords and Claphams, and uncertainty whether the 'Butcher' John was a Clifford or a Clapham and whether his victim was Earl of Rutland or Pembroke. The year of the killing was the same — 1460, that year to which we seem to keep on returning — in each case, and in each case the killer was killed in 1461. Cyril Harrington, in the *Dalesman* magazine of December 1951, refers to Sir John Clapham, 'a staunch Lancastrian', who voluntarily acted as executioner to despatch some prominent Yorkists. Himself then captured by his vengeful enemies, he was executed by being 'impaled' – as if he had been a prisoner of a Celtic chieftain, or of Queen Boudicca.

Whitaker also says that the Clapham family 'sprang from Clapdale Castle'. Clearly never having been to it himself, he quotes Roger Dodsworth, who toured the Craven churches in 1620, as saying:

> John Clapham, ye last of Clapdale, past yet to William Clapham, of Beamsley, father of George, that sold it to Ingleby about 40 years ago. But I think it was built by Adam de Staveley, or o'e of his ancestors, who sold the chace of Ingleburrow to Roger Mowbray in the reign of King John.

Of Bolton Priory, Whitaker says that

> at the east end of the north aisle of the church is a chantry belonging to Bethmesley Hall, and a vault, where, according to tradition, the Claphams were interred upright. I have looked into it through an aperture in the pavement, but could discover no remains of coffins, except one of the Morley family (who later owned Clapdale). Perhaps this unnatural position of the bodies had caused them and their coffins to collapse.

At any rate, it had not caused the collapse of Whitaker, who was able to distinguish all this 'through an aperture in the pavement' – what did he use to light up the interior?

Here I began to recall something I had heard three years before the excavations at Bolton Priory. Mr Michael Wooding, of Settle, thereupon confirmed what he had told me previously.

Mr Wooding is the well known cave diver. When Mr Sid Perou was making the film *The Lost River of Gaping Gill*, which

BBC Television repeatedly broadcast, Mr Wooding was the 'star'. He and Mr Perou were temporarily living at the vacant Clapdale Farm or Castle. They heard a tradition that some knights of the Clapham family were buried upright, in full armour, in a crevice in the limestone rock beneath the floor of the 'castle'. Mr Perou had seen that floor searched with a metal detector, which reacted distinctly on one section. He did not tell Mr Wooding which section it was, but challenged him to find it with metal divining rods.

Mr Wooding did so, and had no difficulty in locating the same long, narrow section. He was suddenly seized, however, with an extreme dread of an evil presence. He ran out of the house, out of the yard, up the hill and out of sight of the building before he could drop to the grass for his breath. He did return to Clapdale, but was never in it again alone and never without a feeling of unease and oppression. His description is reminiscent of some of the experiences of the Bolton Priory excavators. Moreover, there are a number of other people – potholers, cavers, and local residents – who are afraid of Clapdale Castle, to my knowledge.

It may be wondered why any of the Claphams should be buried under the house-floor instead of in the churchyard down the valley. Indeed, it is far from certain that anybody is buried there at all – just as it is uncertain that there are any skeletons in the Priory tomb. It has been stated that the crevice was in fact formerly used as a cesspit. But Mr Wooding at the time of his experience had never heard of any Claphams being buried at Bolton Priory, upright or in any other position.

Nor did he know, and apparently the Priory excavators did not know, about the fact contained in the earlier editions of Walbran's *Guide*: the fact that in the roof of the Priory was the sculptured boss 'sagely conjectured by the country people to represent the devil'. That roof was installed by the last Prior, Richard Moon, before he had to surrender the building to Henry VIII. It is under this boss that not only some of the excavators, but other responsible persons whom they did not mention (perhaps they did not know), say they have seen and that they often see a black-clad figure like the Augustinian canons who ruled the Priory. That sculptured boss stands over the area of the excavations. In 1973 a very sober-minded editor told me he had wondered whether Prior Moon himself was the Devil. No, the excavators were not alone in their fears.

But there was also that other head that Walbran noticed, the Green Man at Fountains Abbey. There they both were in the fifth edition of the *Guide*. The twelfth edition in 1875 was a posthumous one, a memorial to Walbran, edited by his friend Canon Raine. In this version the reference to the Fountains carving stops short at the description of 'entwined with snakes', omitting the phrases about the Evil principle and Pride; and in this same edition the whole of the reference to the sculptured boss is suppressed. Astonishingly, the 1972 guide to Fountains Abbey, published by the Ministry of the Environment, refers to the Green Man only in a hurried, fleeting phrase as 'a head'. Yet it is by far the most arresting and significant stone in the whole vast ruin. These heads were unmentionable.

11

VIEW FROM
THE ROWAN TREE

❋

When I was a boy, school assembly each morning included the Prayer of St Chrysostom. It was led by the headmaster, who was a Canon of the Church of England, a sincere, kindly and wise man. One phrase in the prayer appeared to me to be: 'And there is no help for us.' It was not until years after I had left school that I discovered the words were in fact: 'And there is no health in us.' To the schoolboy that would have made no sort of sense anyway. The prayer, quite a beautiful one, had reduced itself to mumbo-jumbo.

Conversely, it is unsafe to dismiss the ritual and incantations of witchcraft, now or at any time, as all a mere mumbo-jumbo without any real meaning and without any purpose except to mystify and impress the credulous. There may be more in it than that, just as there was in the Prayer of St Chrysostom. Cynicism may be too easy. A 'rigmarole', before it had been thus reduced, originally meant a Papal Bull. The very phrase 'mumbo-jumbo' refers to a kind of priest in a Sudanese village who wards off evil spirits, which could be said to have been St Chrysostom's job.

It is too facile to dismiss (as many do) the witchcraft described in the horrific witch-trials of the seventeenth century and earlier periods as nothing but over-heated fancies both of the hunters and of the alleged witches themselves. It was not for mere fancies that a medieval Pope ordered the destruction of Avebury Ring and similar prehistoric monuments in Britain on the grounds that they were being used for pagan ceremonies; and it was not for nothing that the Avebury surgeon-barber was neatly crushed by one of those giant monoliths as it was felled, and thus lay hidden for centuries – a final human sacrifice. Perhaps it was his disappearance that prevented the destruction of Stonehenge. The Pope's writ, and the King's, was not always as strong as older law.

Nobody knows how intensively the pagan rites were observed before the Pope's decree or afterwards. But the *Chronicle of Lanercost* says that about AD 1282 in Easter week

> the parish priest of Inverkeithing [near Dunfermline, at the northern end of the modern Forth Road Bridge], named John, revived the profane rites of Priapus, collecting young girls from the villages, and compelling them to dance in circles to [the honour of] Father Bacchus. When he had these females in a troop, out of sheer wantonness, he led the dance, carrying in front on a pole a representation of the human organs of reproduction, and singing and dancing himself like a mime, he viewed them all and stirred them to lust by filthy language.

Curiously enough, Inverkeithing Church stands exactly on the Belinus Line referred to earlier in this book.

Official media and authorities had to take the attitude that such practices did not exist. But part of the evidence for the continuation of pagan beliefs lies in the continuation of the Church's efforts to adopt and adapt pagan legends, holy places and hero-divinities to Christian concepts. Even Robin Hood, the enemy of the abbots – and himself perhaps a manifestation of the Green Man – is presented as a Christian liege of the King. Mrs Patricia Crowther has described the translation of Cernunnos the antlered pagan god into Santa Claus with his reindeer.

Despite all the efforts of Church and State, the ancient practices did survive, even if in distorted and only partly understood form.

Even the bloody persecution under James I failed to stamp them out. The manifestations of witchcraft, in the form of accusations and trials, were strongly in evidence in Brigantia. In other forms, they still are.

A period of only about sixty-five years covers the principal time of persecution of alleged witches in Brigantia; and it was also a time of remarkable resistance to that persecution, a resistance which blazed up and met defeat in some areas and outright victory in others. Three principal areas of Brigantia are concerned: the Pendle district of Lancashire; the Washburn valley of Yorkshire; and, in a smaller way, the Skell valley west of Ripon in Yorkshire, in the witchcraft accusations by Lady Mallory. All three are linked together by threads which have not hitherto received notice.

The sequence may be said to start in 1590, when Henry Robinson of Old Laund Booth, Pendle, bought Swinsty Hall (or more probably foreclosed a mortage on it), on the western bank of the Washburn valley opposite the village of Fewston and close to a gully called Timble Gill.

William Grainge tells a curious story about Robinson's acquisition of the hall. Starting with a description which to this day cannot be bettered, he writes:

> Swinsty Hall yet stands, the best, most substantial and majestic of the old halls which grace the valley of the Washburn. It stands with its clustered chimneys and many gables, grey and grand in lonely solitude, a pile of mystery surrounded by legends. There is no road, not even a paved trackway for packhorses leading to it from any quarter. There is no stone quarry near from which it has been hewn, and yet it has been piled up stone by stone at a great cost of time and labour.
>
> Tradition states that the stones of which it was built were brought on packhorses from the opposite side of the Washburn valley. We might almost be tempted to think that some mighty magician had moved it by his art from some other locality and placed it here in this lonely situation as the place of concealment for some enchanted beauty.

The popular mind, sorely puzzled to account for its existence, invented the legend of the poor weaver, the plague, and the waggon-load of gold, which is something to the following effect: The builder of the hall was a man of the name of Robinson [it was in fact built by a man named Wood, from whose descendant Robinson acquired it] who in his youth was a poor weaver, and resided in a humble cottage near where the hall now stands; he left his humble home, and travelled to London at a time when the plague was raging in that city, when death had left many houses totally uninhabited and desolate, wherein no survivors were left to bury the dead, and no heirs to claim their wealth.

Our northcountry adventurer seeing this state of things, not forgetting himself amid the general mourning and confusion, took possession of the gold thus left without an owner to such an extent that he loaded a waggon and team of horses with the wealth thus acquired, with which he returned homeward, and in due time reached the place of his birth.

But the story of the plague had reached the place as soon as himself and gold, and none of his former neighbours would admit him into their dwellings for fear of contagion. He washed his gold in the Greenwell Spring, near the Hall, and with the wealth thus acquired, purchased the estate and built Swinsty Hall.

Shades of Neuchâtel, Wookey Hole, Coventina's Well and other Celtic pagan treasure-pools! This tradition suggests that the Greenwell may once have been a votive spring into which valuables were ceremonially cast (on the Continent these Celtic sites contained so much submerged treasure that the Roman conquerors put them up for auction). The story also conveys a possible explanation for certain sites (there is one beside Giggleswick Station, near Settle) which are officially described as 'either a holy well or a plague-stone where money was washed in inter-village trade during periods of plague': a holy well may indeed have been regarded as not only a balm for sore eyes but a disinfectant for tainted money. The Greenwell Spring of the Swinsty legend lies behind the village of Timble. It is now a boggy mess, but there is a tumbled ruin of worked masonry which seems to have been a chapel.

Four years after the real Henry Robinson — who, coming from Pendle, may indeed have sprung from a weaving family — acquired Swinsty Hall, in 1594 was published John Darrel's *The Strange and Grievous Vexation by the Devil of Seven Persons in Lancashire*. It was a foretaste of horrors to come, and it appears that it may have been read by Edward Fairfax, Robinson's neighbour.

King James VI of Scotland in 1597 published his book *Demonology*, an obsessive account of how to recognise a witch and of the appropriate methods of destroying her (or him). Three years later a volume was printed in England entitled *Godfrey of Boulogne or the Recoverie of Jerusalem done into English Heroicall verse by Edward Fairfax Gent*. This book, dedicated to Queen Elizabeth I, was a translation — in such very good English verse as to stand as a classic in its own right — of *La Gerusalemme Liberata*, the famous poem of the great Italian poet Torquato Tasso (who had died five years before Fairfax's translation appeared). Tasso and Fairfax concern themselves in quite a special way with witchcraft, and they reveal a deep knowledge of witch-lore, some of which goes back thousands of years. Up to the present, the poem's connection with the then current witchcraft turmoil in general, and with witchcraft in the Washburn valley in particular, does not seem to have been noted.

By 1604 King James had become James I of England, and had promptly enacted his notorious Acte Against Witchcraft to put into legal effect the principles of his *Demonology*. It helped to take people's minds off the passage of the English Throne to a Scottish King. Two years later Shakespeare staged *Macbeth*, linking an ancient usurpation of the Scottish Throne with the three witches.

In 1612 the first and major trial of Pendle witches took place. It has been much described. Thomas Potts, the Clerk of the Court, kept records on the basis of which next year he published a book, *The Wonderful Discoverie of Witches in the County of Lancashire*. The classic novel *The Lancashire Witches* by Harrison Ainsworth, written from the Roman Catholic and Jacobite viewpoint, is nevertheless first-rate reading for anybody and reflects deep insight. Excellent treatment of the subject is also provided by Robert Neill's *Mist Over Pendle* and *Witchbane*.

In the Pendle case, two old hags known as Chattox and Demdike, each of whom cultivated the reputation of being a powerful and vindictive witch, were rivals. Their hatred of each other went to such lengths that when they were being questioned by the magistrate, and later at the Assizes in Lancaster, each – with her group of supporters – accused the other and implicated as many as possible of the other's friends and relatives as well. Strangely enough, these accusations were not altogether unwelcome to the accused side, as they increased that side's fearsome reputation. Confessions formed much of the evidence (although, of course, they were largely obtained by torture). The defendants thus played into the hands of the prosecution. Old Demdike died in prison. A number of others were executed for murder by witchcraft. Two of the people alleged to have been killed by Demdike's daughter Elizabeth were named Robinson, John and James; no other Robinsons are mentioned. The trial did nothing to stop witchcraft, but it did increase the authority of the survivors.

The 1612 executions of the Pendle witches were accompanied by the execution of Jennet (Jenny) Preston of Gisburn, which is just in Yorkshire over the border from Pendle, so that she had to be dealt with at the assize in York instead of Lancaster. At York, she had been acquitted the previous Lent of murdering a child named Dodgson. Four days after that acquittal, it was alleged at the trial of the Pendle group, Jennet Preston attended a conference (apparently a sort of annual convention) of the Lancashire witches on Good Friday – a favourite date for such events – at Malkin Tower, the house of Old Demdike or her daughter Elizabeth. This building was long ago pulled down and it is noteworthy that its very site is now alleged to be unknown (in reality ashlar remains of it can be seen at Grid SD 865425).

At that conference, it was alleged, Jennet Preston asked the other witches for their help in murdering Thomas Lister of Westby (ancestor of the Lords of Ribblesdale), because he had prosecuted her at the York Assize at Lent. He did in fact die. After this evidence had been given against her, she was again tried at York, charged with bewitching Lister to death, and this time she was found guilty and executed.

She herself was said to have undertaken, at the Malkin Tower conference, to be hostess at the feast to be held on the Good Friday of the following year; but it was agreed that 'if they had occasion to meet again in the meantime, they should all meet on "Romleyes Moor"' – Romillies or Rombalds Moor between Skipton and Ilkley. Such a rendezvous would not have been convenient for the Pendle witches, but would have been decidedly so for Jennet Preston (had she not been executed in June). But Rombalds Moor was also not much more than on the opposite side of Wharfedale for the witches of Washburn.

'My little niece came to stay last year, and her fingers were covered in warts,' a middle-aged Washburn valley lady told me. 'We have a rowan tree at the bottom of the garden – there, see? I took her down to it and told her to walk three times round it anti-clockwise and then touch the trunk with both hands. Next morning the warts were distinctly smaller. In a week, before she went home, there was no trace of them left.'

Her anecdote was one of the examples – I know of others – of the survival of practices and traditions from the days of widespread witchcraft and probably farther back still. But three centuries ago the Washburn valley was the centre of a witchcraft sensation and of a mystery that has never been solved.

Henry Robinson's Swinsty Hall still stands, within sight of the rowan tree. Less than a mile north-westward from Swinsty Hall was Newhall, Fewston, the site of which now lies under Swinsty Reservoir. At Newhall lived Edward Fairfax, of the great family that came from the Walton-Walshford 'pocket' and that provided two illustrious generals of the Civil War, while he himself was a major poet and the translator of Tasso.

Fairfax went on record explicitly saying that he and Robinson were in dispute over some matter not described. He wrote this in his extraordinary book *A Discourse of Witchcraft as it was enacted in the family of Mr. Edward Fairfax, of Fuystone, coun. Ebor*, 1621, edited and published by William Grainge of Harrogate under the title of *Daemonologia*.

Judging by Fairfax's account, Robinson's wife was mentally disturbed in some way and there was a suggestion that she threatened or tried to kill herself or someone else. Her physical health seems to have been poor. 'She is of good estate, and is a very good and honest woman', Fairfax wrote. Robinson, however, was a 'great favourite' of the local women whom Fairfax accused of witchcraft, 'yet he hath little cause to do so, for besides the trouble of this wife, he had a former wife bewitched to death by the witches of Lancashire, as in the book of those witches and executions you may read'. In fact, however, the only known record of the trial is that of Potts; and, as we have seen, the only Robinsons named therein as having been murdered by the witches were men.

Fairfax accused seven women, the chief of whom was Jenny Dibb, or Jennit Dibble, of bewitching his daughters Helen and Elizabeth. He gives much detail about each of the seven, and describes Jenny Dibb as 'a very old widow, reputed a witch for many years; and constant report confirmeth that her mother, two aunts, two sisters, her husband and some of her children, have all been long esteemed witches, for that it seemeth hereditary to her family'. Her 'familiar' was a great black cat called Gibbe, 'which hath attended her now above 40 years'.

It is striking that Fairfax never mentions what he must have known: that Jenny Dibb was employed by Robinson as a servant at Swinsty Hall. In February 1607 she was married (in Fewston Church!) to Richard Jeffray, but stuck to her maiden name. All the seven women apparently were church-goers; and Fairfax covertly insinuates that they were favoured by the Vicar, the Rev. Nicholas Smithson – who held the living for no less than forty-one years from 1591 to 1632.

Of one of the women Fairfax says she 'has so powerful hand over the wealthiest neighbours around here that none of them refused to do anything she required; yea, unbesought they provided her with fire and meat from their own tables; and did what else they thought would please her.'

In the parish of Fewston, Fairfax said, there were so many witches that 'the inhabitants complain much of great loss sustained in their goods, especially in their kine'. They therefore sought the help of the 'wiseman' who was as much a magician as the women. 'These wizards teach them to burn young calves alive and the like; whereof I know that experiments have been made by the best of my neighbours, and thereby they have found help, as they reported. So little is the truth of the Christian religion known in these wild places and among this rude people.'

In the early stages, it appears from Fairfax's account, an attempt was made to recruit the children to witchcraft. Jenny Dibb's daughter, Margaret Thorpe, told Helen Fairfax that she knew forty witches, seven of whom belonged to the same 'company' as herself. Helen told her (according to Fairfax): 'I think thy sister at Timble is as evil as thou art, for she speaketh with black things at Timble Gill.'

On Thursday 21 March 1621, according to the *Discourse* one of the seven women appeared to Helen, who was in a trance – she is constantly reported as being in that state. The woman told Helen that she had been at the bedside of Robinson's wife (at Swinsty Hall) that night, and that Robinson's wife 'would either kill herself or some other, and then they would have her, as she had none to read to her or instruct her, and that she would never think ill of Bess Foster' (one of the alleged witches).

Early in April came the first York Assizes trial of the seven women accused by Fairfax. His charge was thrown out. The witches, according to his *Discourse*, held a great celebration. On Thursday 10 April – the eve of Good Friday – they had a feast in Timble Gill, quite near Swinsty Hall. 'At the upper end of the table', says Fairfax, 'sat their master, viz., the devil, at the lower end Dibb's wife, who provided for the feast and was the cook: and therefore that she could not come to the children that day . . . but the next day, being Good Friday, they saw her.'

A highly dramatic event took place on Thursday 30 May – and it is not easy to see how this could have been due solely to Fairfax's imagination, however fevered. On that day, he says, Helen was carried away by one of the witches and her black cat over the water above Rowton Bridge, and over Ralph Holme's ground, then over the moor, and so through the field gates across Braime Lane, above Cryer's house, then over the great hill there, and so across the fields on the north side of Slater's house, and to the high moor on that side upon a hill.

There she saw many women together, amongst whom was Dibb's wife and the strange woman, who had a great fire there. At that instant it chanced that Maud Jeffray [a friend of Helen's] came to her and marvelled to see her there in that state. Her brother came also, when his sister told him that she saw Thorp's wife and the black cat, one on one side and the other on the other side, bring her. Whereupon he went and took hold of her, and led her towards his father's house, which was not far distant.

The cat left her and went to the company, but Thorp's wife followed them to the house, where both the wenches fell in trance. . . . Then Henry Jeffray came with all speed running to advertise me at my house of the accident; and found me and others in much care, seeking the woods and waters for her, least she someway perished, and sorrowing for her loss. . . .

I took some with me, and went to Jeffray's house, where the children were both in trance; in which Thorp's wife told Maud Jeffray of the manner how she had carried my daughter away. . . . Then brought I her home, and by the way she shewed me the way she had passed; which was over hedges and difficult places, for the space of more than a mile. The time was also so short betwixt her taking out of the house and her being found on the moor, that it was not possible she should go thither in so short a space.

Two points arise. First, the bonfires seems to have been a general social event, organised by the witches but open to anybody. Second, it might be suspected that Helen had been taken to the bonfire by a forgotten ley, but I have failed to identify any corresponding alignment.

The witch-feast on the moor was of great significance. Only the previous month Fairfax's prosecution of the women at York had failed and they had all been acquitted. By this time, however, they knew that they were to be put on trial again at the August Assizes, again accused by Helen's father. Their action, therefore, was an open defiance of him and a vivid proclamation of their power. Grainge in his edition of the *Discourse* considers, I believe correctly, that the hill concerned was Bank Slack, an Iron Age hill-fort on the moor above Fewston. A fire on Bank Slack (I have seen one when the farmer ignited the gorse bushes there) could be seen for many miles around up and down the valley. It was a sign of the witches' law.

A little over three weeks later, the realisation seems to have spread among the women that they were shortly again to stand trial for their lives. Thorp's wife told Helen on Saturday 29 June, according to Fairfax, that until the Assizes she would 'do the worst she could, for she would not be hanged for nothing'. She said that they (the accused women) would accuse others in the parish who would also hang (had one of them been reading the report of the Pendle trial?). She said that her mother (Jenny) was a witch and her sister was also a witch 'for her mother would not let her be quiet until she yielded to be a witch'.

Some of the women, however, were seeking to save their lives. Thorp's wife told Helen on that same Saturday that Elizabeth Fletcher had been a witch ever since her mother died, 'but now she had given over, and prayed heartily to God . . . and that therefore she would not be hanged. Also she said that Margaret Wait the younger had likewise left off to be a witch.'

Grainge in his edition of the *Discourse* points out of Helen's trances: 'In these fits she had perfect symptoms of the disease called "the mother". . . .' Grainge says that Culpepper gave a cure for this malady as Motherwort, and quotes Sir Kenelm Digby (*Discourse of the Power of Sympathy*):

> I have known a very melancholy woman, which was subject to the disease called the Mother and while she continued in that mood she thought herself possessed, and did strange

things, which among these that knew not the cause passed for supernatural effects, and of one possessed by the ill spirit; she was a person of quality, and this happened through the deep resentment she had for the death of her husband. She had attending her, four or five young gentlewomen. All these came to be possessed as she was, and did prodigious actions.

It may be wondered whether this disease harks back to 'possession' by Modron the Celtic All-Mother. It is certainly a form of hysteria. In the same category are hypnotic phenomena corresponding exactly to symptoms shown by Helen as described by Fairfax.

Many of the details of the bewitching given by Fairfax are highly reminiscent of Potts's account of the Pendle witchcraft case, which Fairfax presumably had read. Other details recall very different sources, as we shall see. Nevertheless, many passages in the *Discourse* show that not only Fairfax, but the women themselves, considered that they really were witches.

At the second Assize Fairfax's charges were again thrown out, on the Judge's direction. Fairfax in his *Discourse* (which he began writing immediately) made some painfully hypocritical remarks about not desiring the death of these women, but went on to show fury at the court's decision and did not hesitate to suggest corruption. 'And upon myself', he concludes, 'was put an aspersion not of dishonesty, but of simplicity.'

James Crossley, editor of the 1845 Chetham Society reprint of Potts's *Discoverie of Witches*, is very scathing about Fairfax:

Never was a more unequal contest. On the one side was a relentless antagonist, armed with wealth, influence, learning and accomplishments, and whose family connections gave him unlimited power in the county; and on the other, six helpless persons, whose sex, age and poverty were almost sufficient for their condemnation, without any evidence at all. Yet, owing to the magnanimous firmness of the judge, whose name, deserving of immortal honour, I regret has not been preserved, these efforts were frustrated, and the women accused delivered from the gulph which yawned before them.

One might here quote Addison's remark in the *Spectator* in 1711: 'When an old woman begins to doat and grow chargeable to a Parish, she is generally turned into a witch.'

Crossley described a manuscript of Fairfax's *Discourse* which included 'a series of ninety-three most extraordinary and spirited sketches made with the pen, of the witches, devils, monsters and apparitions referred to in the narrative'. I have seen some of these drawings. Their modern descendants are the creatures in Walt Disney's film *Fantasia* who come trooping out of the hill-top in the section 'Night on the Bare Mountain'. Perhaps more important, they are in complete accord with the demons and imps in Tasso's and Fairfax's *Jerusalem Delivered*.

Crossley's condemnation of Fairfax is not fair. The *Discourse* gives a much more straightforward account than is usually conceded. There can be no serious doubt that these women regarded themselves as witches, were so regarded by their neighbours, and did all they could to advertise their status as witches. They were in fact professional sibyls.

Grainge quotes Canon Raine (the same man who deleted from the posthumous edition of Walbran's *History of Ripon* all reference to the 'Devil's Head' boss at Bolton Priory, and to the carved keystone at Fountains as the 'Evil principle') in the preface to Raine's *Depositions from York Castle*:

> I am happy to say that in no instance have I discovered the record of the conviction of a reputed witch [not even, apparently, Jennet Preston]. All honour to the northern juries for discrediting these absurd tales. And yet some of these weak and silly women had only themselves to thank for the position they were placed in.
>
> They made a trade of their evil reputation. They were the wise-women of the day. They professed some knowledge of medicine, and could recover stolen property. People gave them money for their services. Their very threats brought

silver into their coffers. It was to their interest to gain the ill name for which they suffered. They were certainly uniformly acquitted at the Assizes, but no judge, or jury, or minister could make the people generally believe that they were innocent. The superstition was too deeply rooted to be easily eradicated.

It might be asked whether the regular acquittals at York, unlike elsewhere, reflected the great good sense of Yorkshire juries or their lively apprehension of the ill-luck that might follow a verdict of 'guilty'. In any case, it is clear that the witches were operating on a large scale what might nowadays be called a protection racket. Regular tribute gave immunity from their malignant spells. If a client suffered a theft, the witch need only give out that the thief fell under her curse, and the property would be returned. This kind of protection racket by cursing has by no means died out yet. The point to note is that within their own realm the witches in fact did preserve law and order – their own law and their own order.

And who was it that was 'weak and silly'? Who won in the end, in the battle of ideologies in the Washburn valley? The acquittal of the women can only have made Fairfax look a fool, or a vindictive meddler, or both, or worse. The witches, by contrast, appeared even more powerful than they had claimed – and more powerful than their sisters in Lancashire.

Nowhere does Fairfax make the slightest suggestion of any action being taken against the witches by ministers of the Church. Yet what Canon Raine justly describes these women as doing is precisely what priestesses of pagan divinities have always done; and not only they, but priests of Christianity as well – for there are still ministers who seek to scare congregations out of their wits with threats of hell-fire and brimstone, and then pass the collection plate around: I have seen precisely this happen, for instance, in a church in the Scottish Highlands. But those same ministers may also offer very real comfort to persons in affliction. So may the witches have done. So may they still do. Even from Fairfax's hostile and prejudiced account, there seems to be a suggestion that these women were in fact, at least on some occasions, trying to befriend and help his epileptic daughters.

Grainge was so impressed by the story of the witches' feast in Timble Gill that he made a special expedition to explore the little valley. So — before knowing of his account — did I. He writes lyrically:

> A pleasant walk it was, the brook making music below and the birds pouring out much louder music above; around were flowers, woods and hills all alike pleasing; we could hardly conceive a scene more unfitted for the purpose by which it is said to have been desecrated.

I, too, found it a pleasant walk; but it was not at all difficult to imagine it as a witches' meeting-place. In fact, as I entered the hollow that was presumably the actual scene, a hare (of all animals!) started up from almost under my feet, and had a good look at me before — in no great hurry — loping off. Hardly had it gone when a pewit appeared and began circling me, screaming angrily as if it were the alleged 'familiar' of one of the seven women.

Jenny Dibb did not live long after the events described by Fairfax. He wrote that on 8 March (before the Assizes) Jenny told the children that she would not be hanged

> but live yet a year longer, which time is now expired, this being the 8th of March, 1622, and the woman in this hour (as the report came to me this instant) lieth ready to die in a fearful sort, talking to her cat, and chiding it from her. The congregation prayed for her on the last sabbath [!].

Both Fairfax and Jenny were wrong. It was more than a year later still, on 1 June 1623, that she was buried — at Fewston Church.

The parish register is missing from 1631 to 1637 — that is, from the year before the death of the Vicar, the Rev. Nicholas Smithson. There is therefore no entry for Fairfax's own death in 1635; and if there ever was any memorial to him in the church, it was destroyed when the building was burnt down in 1696. Thus, ironically, it is Jenny Dibb whom the church records, not Edward Fairfax, Gent.

The family names of all the characters mentioned in Fairfax's story, except his own, are still common in the Washburn valley. And not the names alone.

When I was exploring the ground, a farmer brought in the subject of cup-and-ring stones. He took me to his front door, not more than 300 yards from the rowan tree where the lady cured the child's warts, and pointed across the Washburn valley (the Bride Cross was not far away) to the high rim of Snowden Carr on the western side, where I could make out a lonely tree.

'That's a holly,' said the farmer. 'Underneath it you will find a very fine carved rock.'

I did. It was the Tree of Life Stone.

12
DRAGON'S BLOOD

❖

The acquittal of the Washburn women did not entirely end matters for Edward Fairfax, as Crossley suggests. Two years later he published a second edition of his Tasso translation *Jerusalem Delivered*, which had first appeared in 1600. This second edition was printed by the King's printer, John Bull; and Roberto Weiss, in his introduction to the 1962 re-edition, says that the 1624 issue was apparently printed by command of James I. It was dedicated, however, not to him but to the Prince of Wales, the future Charles I (James died in 1625).

'King James I, who was certainly a shrewd judge of literature,' says Weiss, 'was reputed to have valued Fairfax's *Jerusalem Delivered* above all other English poetry, and it is known that Charles I drew solace from it during his imprisonment.'

This would hardly be a recommendation to a member of the Parliamentarians' illustrious military family. It is also a curious circumstance in another respect. It was Charles I who so distrusted the accusations, verdicts and sentences in the second trial of Pendle 'witches' in 1633 that he himself examined their accuser, the boy Edmund Robinson – who eventually confessed that his evidence was false and had been put into his mouth by his father. King Charles cancelled the death sentence on the seventeen prisoners. It was the very next year, presumably with Charles's approval, that a comedy pouring scorn on the Pendle witch-hunt was performed, with considerable success.

Jerusalem Delivered, while it is indeed very beautiful poetry, is full of descriptions of witchcraft in many ways similar to Fairfax's accusations against the women. The main difference is that in the *Discourse* the chief witch was a hideous old woman, whereas in *Jerusalem Delivered* she is a wonderful beauty.

Tasso himself takes us with a bump back to Morgan le Fay — Latinised as Fata Morgana — and Morgan's three daughters including Nivetta (Merlin's *femme fatale* Nimue). Besides these, in remarkable pagan passages he weaves most of the action of his poem around the passionate witch Armida, a fascinating character who loses nothing in translation to Fairfax's beautiful English and who closely recalls the sexually insatiable goddesses of the Celts.

Tasso and Fairfax (like Milton) let themselves go on the demons, who are described very much like Fairfax's *Discourse* pen drawings. Enchantments include the casting of a magic mist around a chariot (a favourite device, used for instance in *Sir Gawain and the Carl of Carlisle*). But the most interesting feature of the whole poem is the recurrent theme of the enchanted wood, the grove and its great tree. In each case a hero — first Tancred, then Rinaldo — hacks the tree with the sword. It bleeds and cries.

Tasso, and perhaps Fairfax, might have known of the tree *Calamus draco* and other oriental species of Calamus which exude a dark-red substance called 'dragon's blood'. It is also obtained from the dragon-tree *Dracaena draco* which grows in the Canary Isles.

It may be objected that the bleeding tree comes from an Italian's poem about Jerusalem, and has nothing to do with Brigantia. The truth is otherwise. The time has come to draw together the threads of the cat's cradle where they stretch into modern times.

The bleeding and groaning trees were described by an Italian poet whose work did not long precede Fairfax's translation. But trees were only one of many objects of Celtic and probably pre-Celtic cult which are reflected in the folklore of Italy and other European countries. Ross says:

> As with many other peoples, certain trees and groves of trees were sacred to the Celts and treated with veneration. . . . Maximus of Tyre remarks that the Celts venerated the oak as

a symbol of Zeus, and the tree was seemingly used by the Druids in their rites. . . . The Welsh Lleu . . . is described in the *mabinogi* of Math as taking on eagle form and perching in the upper branches of a marvellous oak. . . . The oak . . . is represented . . . as situated on a plain, a common site for trees of cult importance.

H. J. Elwes (*The Trees of Great Britain and Ireland*, Elwes and Henry, 1906, vol. 2.) writes of Kyre House, Worcestershire:

There is also in the deer park a circle with a diameter of fifty yards formed by ten (formerly twelve) oaks of great age and very spreading in habit, and a very ancient oak nearby, called the Gibbet Oak, on which tradition says that criminals were formerly hung in chains.

Such an arrangement recalls the stone circles with an attendant exterior megalith such as Long Meg and her Daughters. 'Gibbet' trees, especially oaks, are a common feature of leys.

The yew and the ash are also frequently named as sacred trees in Celtic tradition. In 1972 I found that my ancestors' grave-slabs in a remote Welsh churchyard each bore a recently made cross, roughly fashioned of boughs of ash; there was no ash tree anywhere near.

Reference has been made at times in this book to the great Skyr-Ack or Shire Oak of Headingley, Leeds, the last remains of which were removed in the 1930s. Across the main road from where it stood is a fine Victorian church with the un-Victorian dedication to St Michael and All Angels. At Cowthorpe, east of Leeds and within the Walton-Walshford 'pocket' (and only 8 miles from the Brigantian capital of Isurium), until a few years ago a famous and enormous oak was still alive. The huge remains can still be seen. It was traditionally said to be 1,000 or even 2,000 years old, but more sober estimates put it at about 600. Within 3 feet of the ground the trunk had a girth of 16 yards and close to the ground it was 25 yards. In a description reminiscent of both the Welsh *mabinogi* of the *Lady of the Fountain* and of the Tasso-Fairfax verses, it was claimed that the branches of the Cowthorpe Oak at maturity covered more than half an acre; and (a rather sinister detail) one enormous branch reached far out, stretching almost to touch the Cowthorpe church – of St Michael and All Angels.

It was recounted that an angler beside the near-by River Nidd heard organ music and found an old Italian with a box-organ inside the oak's hollow trunk. He explained: 'Me thought I would play the old tune in the old tree.' Why? And what was the old tune? It is not reported. But it is said that once a party of seventy-two people held a dance in (perhaps it should be 'under') the tree, to pipe-music provided by a gamekeeper of the late Sir Henry Goodricke, Bt. Again, unanswerable questions arise.

The last relic of each of the various medieval and pre-medieval forests of the Brigantia area is or was usually a huge oak. Near Blubberhouses, a quarter of a mile north of the Harrogate–Skipton road, for example, is a splendid, contorted, ancient but still living oak which is said to be the last tree of the Forest of Knaresborough.

According to Samuel Jefferson (*History and Antiquities of Leath Ward*, 1840) and the *Historical Guide to Carlisle and District*, 1881, last century the swainmote court (a pre-Norman institution) of Inglewood Forest in north-west Brigantia was still being held every St Barnabas' Day at High Hesket, where the forest dues were paid to the lord of the forest. The court was held in the open air at a spot marked by a stone table placed before a large thorn tree, which was known as Court-Thorn. Thorn trees are common marker points on leys and also figure large in folklore. John Premnay in *Country Life* (24 May 1973) remarks: 'Even today fairy thorns are regarded with circumspection in Ireland.'

A mile or so north of High Hesket, the road through Inglewood Forest crossed Wragmire Moss. Of this, Bishop Nicholson of Carlisle in 1715 wrote: 'In 1354 a grant was made of 40 days' indulgence to any that should contribute to the repairs of the highway through Wragmire and to the support of John de Corbrig (presumably Corbridge-on-Tyne), a poor hermit living in that part.' And in that part, on Wragmire Moss, until 1823 there existed a great oak known as 'the last tree of Inglewood Forest'. Jefferson says that it was 700 or 800 years old, and that it was recorded for more than 600 years as a boundary mark between four parts of the Forest – at Jefferson's time, the manors of the Duke of Devonshire and the Dean and Chapter of Carlisle, and the parishes of Hesket and St Cuthbert's, Carlisle.

'The oak has become considerably decayed in its trunk', says Jefferson, 'but fell from sheer old age 13th June 1823. Perhaps de Corbridge counted his beads beneath its shade.' Perhaps, indeed, other religious ceremonies once took place there. Clearly if the tree marked a boundary when it was only 100 years or less old, it presumably succeeded (perhaps as an acorn) an earlier great tree. Meanwhile, Jefferson made good use of his opportunity. The fallen oak, it seems, did not bleed. 'It was remarkable for the beauty of the wood – the writer has a cabinet, the panels of which are made of the heart of this fine oak tree which was marked in a similar manner to satin wood.'

John Jackson, in a lecture on Inglewood in 1897 to the Cumberland and Westmorland Association for the Advancement of Science and Literature, disagreed with Jefferson's description of the Wragmire Oak as the last tree of Inglewood. He cited three existing oaks in the Rose Holms, between Rose Castle and Dalston, one of which at a height between 5 and 6 feet from the ground had a girth of 21 feet, the second 18 feet and the third 13 feet 6 inches, all of them 'magnificent ruins'. He also mentioned an oak called the Barras Tree in the parish of Dalston, near Hawksdale Lodge; a venerable oak 21 feet in girth by the roadside between Hawksdale and Rose Castle; and a magnificent oak at Armathwaite Castle, carefully bound with iron hoops to hold it together.

Perhaps some of the traditions of these and some other forest giants have been forgotten. But the carved Tree of Life Stone on Snowden Carr is not an isolated phenomenon. The enchanted nymph-trees of the forest of *Jerusalem Delivered* have a close counterpart of which Fairfax, though scarcely Tasso, may well have been aware. Here we return to where we came in, in the area of the Cresswell Caves near Worksop in south-east Brigantia from which Neolithic and even Late Palaeolithic cultures may have spread. A little west of Cresswell is Staveley, and a mile and a half west of that is The Hagge. Clarence Daniel records that The Hagge was once famous for its 'mandrake tree' – a venerable oak which tradition claimed had been a focal point of Druid worship and ritual, and which was guarded by a vicious ogre.

It was said to be the only oak in Derbyshire which bore mistletoe . . . as recently as 1808. It had the sinister reputation of being semi-human, screaming and bleeding when its branches were severed and even speaking with the voice of prophetic doom. The tree was chained together and supported by a timber fence, then, later, a mound of earth and stone, but on December 12th, 1883, it became the victim of a terrible gale and was blown down.

A lady who lives in the Forest of Bowland, in west Brigantia, has a talisman hanging beside her front door. It consists of a piece of limestone roughly the shape of a horse-collar, some 8 or 9 inches long, 5 inches wide and 2 inches thick, with a large natural hole worn by water through its middle.

'I have three sisters,' she told me, 'and each of us has one of these hanging by the door. Gypsies never call on any of us. They see that stone from the gate and go by.'

It is a dobbie-stone, intended to ward off witches and evil spirits, especially dobbies. In this book dobbies have appeared briefly twice before: in the description of St Helena, the haunted cottage on the North York Moors, and in that of the old track going past Bush Howe and up White Fell near the Black Horse of the Howgill range. Dobbies and the dobbie-stones which thwart them are not confined to the north of England. A blood-stock horse-breeder in Sussex has a dobbie-stone – which he calls by that name – hanging up by his stable door; and if one of his mares has a black foal, it is called a dobbie. But the tradition is very strong in Brigantia.

In a snap survey one morning in the eastern part of Settle I found eight houses each with a wall decorated on top with water-worn limestone rocks. In each case the rocks included a dobbie-stone cemented in close to the gate or door. One house had a row of rocks on a lintel over the door, and the middle rock had two 'eyes', one above the other – a rarity. Returning home, I found that my own house had a dobbie-stone on each side of the gate. Some of these stones are known to have been where they now are for at least sixty years.

Bogg relates a story about Kereby, a village on the lower Wharfe near Bardsey and East Keswick. One of the best swimmers in the area was one Jim Dale, but while he was seeking to ford the Wharfe he fell victim to the local water-kelpie. 'This water fiend', says Bogg, 'generally presented itself to the belated traveller in the shape of an old, shaggy-haired pony near to some well-known crossing place on the banks of a river.' If the traveller mounted the supposed steed 'it instantly sprang with a wild shriek of laughter into the deepest whirlpool'. That is a good description of a Celtic *each-uisge* (water-horse) or Brigantian dobbie. The word is thought to be cognate with 'Dobbin' and may have for its first element the Celtic *dhu*, 'black'.

In the Sedbergh area of Brigantia there is considerable evidence of something like a surviving dobbie-cult centred on the Black Horse of Bush Howe, at the head of the remote, deep-cut valley of Long Rigg Beck. Clouds and their shadows fall often on these hills. When they lift, they reveal for a moment a strange shape high on the flanks of Bush Howe: the dark outline of a huge black stallion that looks like the horses painted by ancient man in French and Spanish caves. It dominates the whole valley.

Some people of the Howgills will tell you 'once you have seen it, then you never pass by without looking'. Others will say 'we never saw it; we don't believe it's there', and you know they are not at ease. Mrs Mary Roslin-Williams, of Lilly Mere House, Sedbergh, asked two young men if they knew anything about the Black Horse. They both swung round, looked straight at it and denied any knowledge of it. 'Never heard of it,' said one. 'We just don't know it is there,' said the other.

Archaeologists are trying to decide whether the Horse was carved out of the hillside by man, or whether it is a piece of natural erosion. The main difficulty is to see it at all. Mrs Williams told me I would be lucky if I got a good view of it – and that if I went right up to it, I should find nothing there at all.

13 The Black Horse of Bush Howe

She was right. On the first visit to the valley, mists came down and the Black Horse could be seen only by those who knew where it was. Next time, there was some hazy sunshine. A whole reel of film was shot off. Something happened to the camera. Not a single picture developed. A third trip went farther, got nearer, and resulted in three very misty pictures, although to the eye the Horse had been quite clear. The fourth occasion was a complete wash-out. It was the fifth — a really determined expedition — that produced results, not all of which were expected or welcome.

Curiously enough, a Ministry of the Environment inspector found it impossible to photograph the Black Horse. I have had the same sort of experience with the incised pillar at Long Preston. John Premnay in the *Country Life* article cited earlier quotes the *Irish Press* whose photographer, Eddie McDonnell, was sent to photograph a 'fairy shoe' which was kept in a locked glass case:

> The strangest thing was that whenever he attempted to do so, the glass clouded over, only clearing when he stopped. He did succeed in taking one photograph between the cloudings when he asked a child to hold the glass case. When the film was developed, however, the shoe itself now looked as if covered by a cloud.

A dobbie is described as a big, black, horrible, misshapen thing that 'slips about'. It is much more likely to be seen out of the corner of the eye, if at all, than straight ahead. Around Sedbergh several old houses, Copplethwaite Hall and Bleaze Hall, for instance, are said to have a dobbie, and there are bridges and fords where the black thing affrights travellers. You protect yourself and your house with a dobbie-stone. A very good one lies in the window of Askew's shoe-shop in Sedbergh. It came from a farm near Cautley Spout. The farmer would not part with it while he lived. 'I haven't finished with it yet,' he said.

North-west Brigantia has a special sport: girning. It consists of pulling the most frightening face possible, through a horse-collar. There are girning championships. Mrs Williams wonders whether it might have something to do with the horrible misshapen thing. Both girning and the dobbie may have reference to the Black Horse of Bush Howe. If ever a huge mountain object could be said to slip about, this is it. For a start, like the unmentionable heads, it is almost totally unrecorded.

There are a number of books about Sedbergh and the surrounding area. Some of them go into considerable details about the Howgill Fells. At least one of them refers specifically to Bush Howe. None of them makes the slightest mention of the Black Horse. Yet I remember it being pointed out to me when I was a boy, half a century ago. It does not appear even on the 2½-inch Ordnance Survey map. But the Black Horse is on the frontier of the old Celtic kingdom of Rheged.

An ancient poem of Rheged refers to the Three Horses of Britain. One of them is Du y Moroedd, otherwise Black Moro or 'the Black One of the Sea'. Bromwich (*Trioedd Ynys Prydein: The Welsh Triads*, 1961) refers to this horse in connection with a genuine historic invasion of North Wales from 'the North', i.e. probably the still Welsh Cumbria. Du y Moroedd was said to have carried seven men to Benllech in Anglesey (on the island's north-east coast) from an unidentified 'Benllech of the North'. The Long Rigg Beck valley forms an enormous notch, and the Black Horse is in the line of sight along a very narrow 'ray' out to sea off Morecambe; it reaches landfall somewhere near Benllech, Anglesey. 'Llech' may be interpreted as 'ley'. Perhaps Benllech of the North was Bush Howe.

According to tradition, 200 years ago the Black Horse was used as a landmark by smugglers sailing into Morecambe Bay, 20 miles away. This was one of the points to be checked on my fifth expedition. It called for a crafty approach. Instead of walking straight up the valley of the Long Rigg Beck, I tackled it from the flank, climbing the ancient path up White Fell and coming along the summit to reach the Black Horse from above. As I set off up White Fell, I could see two horses cantering down from Bush Howe. I tried to photograph the Black Horse from there, but instantly it clouded over. From there on it was not in the line of sight.

Walking along the summit, I found the Black Horse suddenly quite near. But it was not clear, even now. The strange shape seemed to be dissolving at the edges in places, almost like a wind-blown cloud as it turns to rain. Across the head of the gully I walked on to Bush Howe itself and started off down the steep slope to the Horse. My feet skidded on the dry bent-grass and I found myself tobogganing on trousers which in seconds became hot. I dug my feet in.

I stood on the Horse's head. There was nothing whatever to see except a waste of black stones, the dark Silurian shale of which the Howgills consist. No shape at all could be distinguished. The Horse had slipped from my grasp at the last second.

Morecambe Bay? There was nothing in that direction except the sun shining through thick mist. Pacing out the waste of stone, I found the Black Horse was about 140 yards long and 120 high. Perhaps it had shrunk — I would scarcely have been surprised. The return journey was by the long valley bottom.

At the point where the ancient track up White Fell crosses the beck, I was aware of being observed. Behind, not far away, were the two horses watching me go. One of them was a piebald mare, the other a young stallion; except for a white flash on his nose, he was pure black. I was not at that time aware that these hills are grazed by black Fell Ponies, of a breed created when the Romans introduced Friesian horses to cross with the small ponies of the Brigantes.

There are or were a considerable number of dobbies in a wide region surrounding the Black Horse. Not many evil spirits, however, are recorded as having a bus service established to take the public to see their manifestations. Dr Thomas Gibson of Orton says (*Legends and Historical Notes of North Westmoreland*):

> This part of the country, about 30 years ago [i.e. about 1857], was startled by the phenomenon of a strange occurrence at an isolated farm-house called the Orton Dobbie — something like a spirit-rapping business on a large scale. It drew for many weeks people from long distances to make out the cause of it, but it was never really bottomed, and the occurrence is now looked upon by some as a real visitation of the unseen while others think it was augmented or arranged by the residents for pecuniary profit, if not by them originated. A coach was run, with 'Orton Dobbie' inscribed

thereon, on Brough Hill Fair. The manifestation ceased after continuing a few weeks.

In the same area the belief in witchcraft continued strong. Dr Gibson described an old man at the village of Winton who always carried a rowan-tree staff, and who used to wear a hare's foot on one side of his beaver hat and a piece of rowan bark or leaf on the other. A well known local rhymester, the mason Joe Steel, told Dr Gibson that when he was digging an ashpit in a house near the ford in Ravenstonedale belonging to Squire Thompson, he found a bottle full of crooked pins which he conjectured had been buried to keep the witches away — apparently not long before, as the children had been ill with a fever and cows had cast their calves. But that was nothing much for Dr Gibson, who wrote:

We were acquainted with a schoolmaster who roasted the heart of a chicken stuck full of pins, with fastened doors, at midnight, and he vowed that the witch came to the door and promised she would not molest him again. Her offence was that she had bewitched a calf so that it died, and the schoolmaster — no fool either, in other matters — thoroughly believed it.

Bogg says that in the eighteenth century there lived on Carlton Moor, on the Yorkgate at the eastern end of Otley Chevin, one Hannah Green known as the 'Lingbob Witch' or just as 'Lingbob', famed for recovering lost or stolen property:

Among her customers were very aristocratic personages, and it was no uncommon sight to see carriages standing at the door of Lingbob's cottage during the many years she carried on the profession of witchcraft and goods reclaimer. She is said to have amassed a fortune of over a thousand pounds. Her daughter, also named Hannah, succeeded her in this lucrative business, but she was not so successful as her mother.

A Pendle witchcraft exhibition was held for the summer of 1972 at Towneley Hall, an old mansion owned by Burnley Corporation. It was organised by the then Curator, Mr John Blundell. A few days before it was due to open, he found on his desk a letter written on blue notepaper which said:

Dear Mr Blundell – Having read some of your views regarding the witch country hereabouts and your ideas of making it a tourist centre, I really agree with this. Even Burnley Town Council ought to help and then take some of the profits and put it to help bring local rates down. I am sure the old white-witches of yester-year would agree with this. I wish you every success in getting many of the instruments that old witches used, so as to put them on view to this generation.

May I say that the old witches' powers were very effectual. These powers are used by witches in this area today, just as they were then, and help people in need. I know this is so. I am not putting my name and address on this letter, but the events over the years concerning me – I could write a book on these Things. From – Blessed Be – A Student.

That letter became the newest exhibit in the display. Near it was a written charm, found in 1934 in an old farmhouse called Westfield, overlooking Leeshaw reservoir at Oxenhope, near the Brontës' home at Haworth. Originally the paper was sealed, and rested in a cavity between a joist and a beam. Much of the text seems to be gibberish, but it begins:

Ominas   X   Laudet   X   Mapon

which is probably intended to mean: 'Everybody Praises Mapon.' Mapon was the Celtic god of youth and happiness who became Romanised into Apollo and survived in the *Mabinogion* as one of Arthur's company in the story of *Culhwch and Olwen*.

When I was researching into some of the aspects of Brigantia, I had occasion to interview a highly educated lady. After we had talked at some length about folklore I had a strong mental signal.

'Miss So-and-so,' I said, 'are you a witch?'

There were several seconds of silence.

'Well, no – but – ' and that phrase has stuck in my mind ever since. She explained.

Miss So-and-so lived in a house which stood secluded in considerable grounds at the end of a drive. At the entrance to the drive were two large ornate gate-posts, and to one side was a lodge, which had its own garden and which was occupied by Miss So-and-so's employees. A woman of the village had formed the habit of entering the drive and helping herself to the fruit and vegetables which were the property of the employees. The woman had been warned many times, caught and expelled from the drive, but still came back whenever she felt like it.

'Then one day I caught her at it, picking apples from the tree. I took her out, past the gates, and then I drew a line with my stick in the dust from one gatepost to the other, and I said: "From this day onwards you shall never be able to cross this line." And you know, she never could.'

On the carved frieze of the wall above me as I write, in a house that was built at the time when the seventeenth-century witch-hunts were scarcely over, are two representations of the Horned God of the witches. There is a much older Horned God at Isurium, the capital of Brigantia, nowadays named Aldborough. Dating from Romano-Celtic times, the stone figure is several feet high, carved in high relief within a hollowed-out niche in the stone.

Ross says that the cult of a horned god – equated sometimes with Mars, sometimes with Mercury or a Silvanus type of deity – is 'particularly well documented in areas which are part of the large region occupied by the Brigantes. . . . For this reason, it is proposed to refer to this deity as the horned god of the Brigantes.'

And there it stands. The figure is weathered because it stood in the open air for centuries; even so, it is fairly clear that in this case the Celtic god was probably assimilated to Mercury. The statue is not in the open now. It shelters at the west end of the nave in Aldborough Church, probably not many yards from the position it occupied as the centre of perhaps the main shrine in the capital of Brigantia. It is at once evidence of the priceless heritage which the Church throughout Brigantia has so wisely preserved, and of the continuity of faith through many changes of sacred names, rituals and theological concepts to the present day from the most distant past.

Something like this must have been in the mind of Wordsworth in 1821 when he contemplated Long Meg and her Daughters beside the River Eden in northwest Brigantia:

14 The Horned God of the Brigantes in Aldborough (Isurium) Church

> A weight of awe, not easy to be borne,
> Fell suddenly upon my Spirit – cast
> From the dread bosom of the unknown past,
> When first I saw that family forlorn.

But it was better expressed by old Col. Fetherstonhaugh of Kirkoswald in his book *Our Cumberland Village*:

The annual service at Long Meg, when reverently attended, is a Christian acknowledgement of a link with old paganism in a common doctrine of re-birth as the goal of humanity. So whether it is Long Meg, or the now practically obliterated Gray Yauds on King Harry Common, we have combined

15   Aldborough Cross

civic and religious centres of men holding a faith which died out not so long ago, and with which we have a common link.

>   Jenny Twigg and daughter Tibb,
>   Jenny with her black cat Gibbe,
>   Jenny, Jenny, Jenny Dibb,
>   Long the thread you spin.

APPENDIX

BLAKEY TOPPING

Following are the details of the twelve alignments on Blakey Topping mentioned in Chapter 1.

1 Sil Howe 852028; Widow Howe; tumulus 868962 and Grey Stones; Blakey Topping; Standing Stones; various tumuli in Dalby Forest and on to the south. This alignment is orientated on 4 degrees west of Magnetic North, $10\frac{3}{4}$ miles east of Line 'A' through the Ralph Crosses.

2 Blakey Topping; Bride Stones 874913; between two tumuli 873896 and 876897; Allerston Churchyard 879830; Wintringham Churchyard 885733; tumulus 887700; High Mowthorpe 888689; western edge of tumulus 892647; to Fimber Church 894606.

3 Blakey Topping; between two tumuli on Grime Moor 867923; Whitethorn 861909; virtually along a mile of straight metalled road from 847872 to 843853; along a line of 'earthworks' west of Kirkdale Slack; through the crossroads and church at Thornton Dale 834829; along $1\frac{1}{2}$ miles of the A 169 from Wykeham 809752 to Old Malton Church 798726; along the eastern side of the 'Roman Fort' at Malton; through a tumulus at 783683; and largely along a mile of metalled road from 778667 to 773654 near a 'long barrow'.

APPENDIX

4 Blakey Topping; Smeffell Howe 854915; Lockton Church; the ford at Farwath 829884; 'castle (rems. of)' at Pickering; Little Barugh 760797; Mowthorpe Hill 677691; Sheriff Hutton Castle; moat at West Lilling (and on sheet 97 to Wigginton crossroads, the moat at Nether Poppleton and the nodal point at Upper Poppleton church).

5 Blakey Topping; across earthworks to East Toft Pike; Penny Howe 818896; around earthwork 802886; Cottage Leas 785873; the Hall at Wrelton 768861; Stonegrave Churchyard 656779; Cawton; Grimston Grange 605740; Crayke Castle and Church 561707.

6 Blakey Topping; through the Black Howes 847924; through the middle of Newton-on-Rawcliff; northern edge of tumulus 784890; tumulus 725860; pond at Cartoft 714854; southern edge of Harome; Golden Square 615802; along a mile of metalled road from 609798 through Beacon House to 595791; along the southern lane of Ampleforth village; Newburgh Priory (where it crosses the alignment from Coxwold to Leavening); and Husthwaite Church 519751.

7 Blakey Topping; across earthworks 826919; exactly along the northern edge of the well known Cawthorne 'Roman Camps' from 788903 to 780900; through Cropton; the Low Cross at Appleton-le-Moors 734882; 'Castle (site of)' at Kirkbymoorside 699868; Kirkbymoorside Church; the famous Saxon Gregory's Minster at Kirkdale 677858; alongside 'Double Dikes' to tumulus 570815.

8 This is very close in angle to no. 6. Blakey Topping; earthworks at 832924, 830922 and 826920; just north of Rawcliff Howe and parallel with metalled road for half a mile; through Cropton Castle Mound 755893; Appleton-le-Moors High Cross 734885; the northern edge of 'Castle (remains of)' at Kirkbymoorside 695870; between Helmsley Church and Castle 610839; tumulus 571823; tumulus 548817.

9 Blakey Topping; Low Horcum 844932; through earthworks at 833929; northern end of earthworks or row of tumuli 826928; Keldy Castle 778916; Standing Stone 753910; the famous 'Norman Crypt' church at Lastingham 728904; the middle of Hutton-le-

APPENDIX

Hole 706900; Fadmoor; Nawton Tower 642885; southern edge of 'camp' 506855.

10   Blakey Topping; tumuli 832937; three aligned tumuli 814937; Bee Stone 681931; Harland 668930; tumuli 555925.

11   Blakey Topping; triangulation point 855939; southern edge of the spectacular Hole of Horcum and across Gallows Dike at 848940; Scarfhill Howe 814942; Mauley Cross 796944; Leaf Howe 780945; through the middle of 'Three Howes' (actually four) 715948; triangulation point 702949; just south of Cragg Cottage 681950.

12   Blakey Topping; Wheeldale Howe 767994; Honey Bee Nest 688035; St Helena (a holy well) 683037. This continues strongly on to the next sheet.

BELINUS LINE

Following is a somewhat detailed exposition of the Belinus Line in the section through Brigantia.

It enters Brigantia from the north at about Langholm, through the central crossroads of which it passes. Just east of Carlisle, it runs through the suburb of Stanwix, and crosses the A 1 motorway exactly at the Southgate services centre – crosses it at a narrow angle to the western side of the motorway. Past the Roman fort at NY 442497 it goes by Southwaite Hall to the triangulation point at High Dyke, Catterlen, 480328, past the Newton Reigny earthworks and a long barrow, near the road junction at Celleron, across the existing bridge of Beckfoot 509203, through Butterwick, through Stone Howe, over Sleddale Pike and Whatshaw Common.

Passing exactly by the cairn at NY 543048, it runs (like many ancient and modern routes) beside Hollowgate Farm, and may very easily be examined as a minor metalled road by Whelpside from NY 555009 to 556001. Near Whinfell Tarn it consists of no more than two aligned gates on opposite sides of the road, and at Lambrigg Foot there is a useful bridge but no convincing sign of the line. At Bendrigg Lodge SD 581892 the Belinus Line coincides for a few yards with the metalled road but is otherwise indistinguishable; what is very noticeable, however, is a ley running due east from the Lodge, and in fact this is one of the crossing points in the 'web'.

From here on for many miles the Belinus Line is entangled with the Haweswater–Manchester pipeline. When Manchester was empowered by Parliament to construct this pipeline, the duty was imposed upon the undertaking of preserving and maintaining public rights of way, and a statutory design of gates was laid down. The result is that a remarkably fine series of public footpaths, which would probably otherwise have been lost, all passing through exactly similar concrete-and-iron foot-gates, marks out the Belinus Line's route, although the actual track itself has been largely destroyed. Nevertheless, the track can still be made out at Old Town and passes through a series of pipeline gates through the western side of Kirkby Lonsdale to the ford over the Lune to Nether Burrow.

At Cantsfield 620730 the Line is not easy to see, but in the village green is a prominent circular embankment now bearing three (previously four) magnificent sycamores. South of the village the Line should not be confused with a public path down to a ford over the River Greta. At Ravens Close 625703 the Line is very clear and beautiful, separated from the pipeline only by a magnificent hedge. East of the road junction at 628689 it may be seen running up a hillside marked by gorse bushes. The Line passes by an embanked grove and a well at Park House 635663, goes through the triangulation point at 638646, and at Summersgill Farm becomes what the farmer knows as 'The Long Gutter', where it may be seen ahead for over a mile heading straight for the summit gate on the Salter Road SD 652588.

The gate is a multiple crossing point. It is built into a fence marking the boundary of Lancashire and Yorkshire across the Salter Road, an unpaved drover's road which on this section itself coincides with a ley leading to the node at Blacko Tower near Colne. At the same point a 'Roman road', laid apparently on an earlier track, crosses over on the way from Casterton to the south; and another ley comes up from Hameldon Hill SD 809288 through

Clitheroe Castle, Waddington Church and Newton crossroads (where it is very noticeable).

In this section, from Park House southwards, the Belinus Line is fortunately untroubled by the pipeline, which is diverted to the east and runs through a tunnel under the Bowland moors to emerge near Slaidburn. From the Salter Road gate, however, the Belinus Line is virtually indistinguishable until it reaches High Laithe at SD 659555, where it is a highly picturesque and outstanding feature continuing through Whitendale.

Sugar Loaf is a small but savage-looking hillock beside the road east of Dunsop Bridge, and several leys run through here. The Belinus Line appears to lie through a gap like a broken tooth near the top of the sharp rock, and then down beside a ravine to an area churned up by old tracks. South of Crimpton, at a triangulation point 680467 there is a grove of trees close by where the Belinus Line comes through, highly visible; other leys also cross this point. From the triangulation post along the Line to Browsholme Hall SD 683453 used to be a public path, but the path is now diverted somewhat.

Browsholme Hall, an Elizabethan mansion, is a star feature. The house is built exactly astride the Line, which comes down a wooded hillside, through a gate, across the back approach-lane, into a (modern) doorway, through a chapel (now blocked up), through a modern staircase, through the doors which formerly led to the chapel, straight across the entrance hall (alongside a locked chest containing the legend-haunted skull), out of the front door, over the terrace, through a sundial in the centre of the sward, and across the park.

West of Clitheroe, above the west bank of the River Hodder, a steep road leads up past Riddings Farm. Just above the farm entrance is a waymarker showing a public footpath to Stonyhurst College. This path is the Belinus Line. Walking along it, my wife and I found that a cow was immediately on our left, another cow was 18 inches behind us, and immediately on my right the third 'cow' turned out to be a Hereford bull. This, we felt, was the Bullinus Line. All roads come to an end, however, and after photographing him we climbed a stile into a ravine where the

APPENDIX

Belinus Line, the east–west line from the Penny Stone near Blackpool and at least four other leys all crossed at Kemple End. Very close by, the ravine was also crossed by the pipeline. Beyond the ravine the Belinus Line track could be clearly seen, snicket gate beyond snicket, going towards the eastern side of the college's park.

Southwards the line passes through the public house at 'York' (SD 710337), the triangulation point on Stanhill 724280, another triangulation point at 736237, close to Turton Bottoms (another skull legend here), close to and parallel to Black Lane between Bolton and Bury, across the Ship Canal at Salford at a lock SJ 798975, across the Mersey through the public house at Jackson's Bridge, through Wythenshawe Hall, along the western side of Worms Hill 833828 and down to Alderley Edge – the town centre, not the hill.

Just west of Bell Farm the line passes Eaton at a milestone at SJ 873659, runs east of Congleton (but well to the west of the well known Bridestones), through the Mossley public house, alongside the old railway which in turn is alongside the road from Whitemoor to Lea House, through the Oxhay 892580 between Biddulph and Biddulph Moor, through Abbey Hulton, Bentilee and Adderley Green, and out of Brigantia *en route* for Birmingham and the south coast.

BIBLIOGRAPHY

Ainsworth, Harrison (1965), *The Lancashire Witches*, Nelson, Lancashire, Gerrard.
Alcock, Leslie (1971), *Arthur's Britain*, London, Allen Lane.
Allen, D. Elliston (1968), *British Tastes: An Enquiry into the Likes and Dislikes of the Regional Consumer*, London, Hutchinson (paperback edn, London, Panther, 1969).
Allen, Thomas (1828), *History of the County of York*.
Ashe, Geoffrey (1960), *From Caesar to Arthur*, London, Collins.
Bede, the Ven. (1970 edn), *Ecclesiastical History*, Everyman edn, London, Dent.
Belloc, Hilaire (1913), *The Stane Street*, London, Constable.
Bogg, Edmund (1900), *Lower Wharfedale*, Leeds.
Bord, Janet and Colin (1973), *Mysterious Britain*, London, Garnstone Press.
British Gazetteer.
Bromwich, Rachel (1961), *Trioedd Ynys Prydein: The Welsh Triads*, Cardiff.
Bulmer, T. F. (1901), *History and Directory of Cumberland*, Carlisle.
Burgess, Colin, and Tylecote, R. F. (1968), *Bronze Age Metalwork in Northern England, c. 1000 to 700 BC*, Newcastle-upon-Tyne, Oriel Press.
Burrow, J. A. (ed.) (1972), *Sir Gawain and the Green Knight*, Harmondsworth, Penguin.
Butler, H. E. (ed.) (1937), *Giraldus Cambrensis – Autobiography*, London, Jonathan Cape.
Clark, Grahame (1940), *Prehistoric England*, London, Batsford.
Collingwood, R. G. (1937), *Roman Britain and the English Settlements*, London, Oxford University Press.
Comfort, W. W. (transl.), and Owen, D. D. R. (introd. and notes) (1975), *Chrétien de Troyes: Arthurian Romances*, London, Dent.
Cowling, E. T. (1946), *Rombalds Way*, Otley, William Walker.
Cowling, Geoffrey M. (1967), *History of Easingwold and the Forest of Galtres*, Halifax, Advertiser Press.

BIBLIOGRAPHY

Daniel, Clarence (1973), *Twelve Headless Men and other Derbyshire Ghost Stories*, Clapham, Yorkshire, Dalesman Publications.

Davies, R. T. (ed.) (1967), *Sir Thomas Malory: King Arthur and his Knights* (selections from Malory's *Morte Darthur*), London, Faber & Faber.

Davis, Norman (1967), *Sir Gawain and the Green Knight*, revision of Tolkien-Gordon edn, Oxford University Press.

Denton, Thomas (ed.) (1688), *Chronicle of Lanercost*, copy in Tullie House Museum, Carlisle.

Dibdin, Rev. Thomas Frognall (1840), *Bibliographical Odyssey*, London, Bohn.

Dictionary of National Biography.

Dudley, Harold (1949), *Early Days in North-West Lincolnshire*, Scunthorpe, W. H. and C. Caldicott.

Elwes, H. J. and Henry, A. (1906), *The Trees of Great Britain and Ireland*, Edinburgh, privately printed.

Eyre, Kathleen (1972), *Lancashire Legends*, Clapham, Yorkshire, Dalesman Publications.

Fetherstonhaugh, Col. T. (1925), *Our Cumberland Village*, Kirkoswald, privately printed.

Findler, Gerald (1970), *Legends of the Lake Counties*, Clapham, Yorkshire, Dalesman Publications.

Furness, William (1894), *History of Penrith*, Penrith, privately printed.

Geoffrey of Monmouth (1963 edn), *History of the Kings of Britain*, Everyman edn, ed. Charles Dunn, London, Dent.

Geoffrey of Monmouth (1966 edn), *History of the Kings of Britain*, ed. Lewis Thorpe, Harmondsworth, Penguin.

Gibson, Dr Thomas (1887), *Legends and Historical Notes of North Westmoreland*, London.

Giles, J. A. (1848), *Six Old English Chronicles*, London, Bohn, new edition 1901.

Grainge, William (1863), *Nidderdale*, London.

Grainge, William (1882), *Daemonologia* (ed. of Edward Fairfax's *Discourse of Witchcraft*), Harrogate, privately printed.

Grzimek, Bernhard (1967), *He and I and the Elephants*, London, André Deutsch.

Guest, Lady Charlotte (1906), *The Mabinogion*, 1st Everyman edn, London, Dent.

Hargrove, E. (1832), *History of Knaresborough*, Harrogate.

Historical Guide to Carlisle and District (1881).

Howson, William (1850), *Illustrated Guide to the Curiosities of Craven*, London, Whittaker.

Jackson, John (1879), *Notes on Inglewood Forest*.

Jackson, Sidney (1973), *Celtic and Other Stone Heads: First Series*, privately printed, published in association with Lund Humphries, London.

Johnston, G. (1853), *Botany, Terra Lindisfarnensis*, vol. 1, London.

Jones, Gwyn, and Jones, Thomas (transl. and ed.) (1949), *The Mabinogion*, Everyman edn, London, Dent.

BIBLIOGRAPHY

Kendall, P. F., and Wroot, H. E. (1924), *The Geology of Yorkshire*, Leeds, privately printed.
Kurvinen, Auro (1951), *Sir Gawain and the Carl of Carlisle in Two Versions*, Helsinki.
Leland, John (1971 edn), *Itinerary in England and Wales*, ed. Lucy Toulmin Smith, Arundel, Centaur Press.
MacCana, Proinsias (1970), *Celtic Mythology*, Feltham, Hamlyn.
Madden, Sir F. (ed.) (1839), *Sir Gawain and the Green Knight*.
Malory, Sir Thomas (1883 edn), *Morte Darthur*, ed. Sir Edward Strachey, London, Macmillan.
Malory, Sir Thomas (1886 edn), *Malory's History of King Arthur*, ed. Ernest Rhys, London, Walter Scott.
Malory, Sir Thomas (1893 edn), *Morte Darthur – King Arthur*, ed. John Rhys, London, Dent.
Matthews, William (1966), *The Ill-Framed Knight: A Skeptical Inquiry into the Identity of Sir Thomas Malory*, Cambridge University Press.
Michell, John (1973), *The View over Atlantis*, London, Garnstone Press.
Mitchell, W. R. (1973), *Yorkshire Ghosts*, Clapham, Yorkshire, Dalesman Publications.
Moeller, S. (1904), *Routes et lieux habités à l'âge de la pierre et à l'âge du bronze*, Copenhagen.
Neill, Robert (1966), *Mist over Pendle*, London, Hutchinson.
Neill, Robert (1967), *Witchbane*, London, Hutchinson.
Nicholls, Rev. W. (1883), *History and Traditions of Mallerstang Forest and Pendragon Castle*, Manchester.
Nicolson, J. and Burn, R. (1777), *History of Cumberland*.
Oxford Dictionary of English Christian Names, London, Oxford University Press.
Percy, Thomas, Bishop of Dromore (1765), *Reliques of Ancient English Poetry*, ed. G. Gilfillan, Edinburgh, 1858.
Piggott, Stuart (1960), *Approach to Archaeology*, Harmondsworth, Penguin.
Piggott, Stuart (1965), *Ancient Europe*, Edinburgh University Press.
Pinto, Edward H. (1969), *Treen and other Wooden Bygones*, London, Bell.
Potts, Thomas (1613), *Wonderful Discoverie of Witches in the County of Lancashire*, reprinted Chetham Society, 1845.
Powell, T. G. E. (1966), *Prehistoric Art*, London, Thames & Hudson.
Proceedings of the Society of Antiquaries.
Raistrick, Arthur (1962), *Green Tracks on the Pennines*, Clapham, Yorkshire, Dalesman Publications.
Raistrick, Arthur (1964), *Prehistoric Yorkshire*, Clapham, Yorkshire, Dalesman Publications.
Raistrick, Arthur (1972), *The Romans in Yorkshire*, Clapham, Yorkshire, Dalesman Publications.
Rivet, A. L. F. (1958), *Town and Country in Roman Britain*, London, Hutchinson.
Ross, Anne (1967), *Pagan Celtic Britain: Studies in Iconography and Tradition*,

BIBLIOGRAPHY

London, Routledge & Kegan Paul.
Saklatvala, Beram (1967), *Arthur: Roman Britain's Last Champion*, Newton Abbot, David & Charles.
Scott-Giles, C. W. (1946), *The Road Goes On*, London, Epworth Press.
Screeton, Paul (1975), *Quicksilver Heritage*, Wellingborough, Thorsons.
Smith, A. H. (1961–3), *Place-Names of the West Riding of Yorkshire*, 8 vols, Cambridge University Press.
Smith, Rev. William (1881), *Old Yorkshire*.
Speight, Harry (1906), *Nidderdale from Nun Monkton to Whernside*, London, Stock.
Tolkien, J. R. R., and Gordon, E. V (ed.) (1925–36), *Sir Gawain and the Green Knight*, London, Oxford University Press.
Transactions of the Cumberland and Westmorland Antiquarian and Archaeological Society.
Treharne, R. F. (1975), *The Glastonbury Legends*, London, Abacus.
Underwood, Guy (1969), *The Pattern of the Past*, London, Museum Press.
Victoria County History of Cumberland.
Von Eschenbach, Wolfram (1961 edn), *Parzifal*, ed. Helen M. Mustard and Charles E. Passage, New York, Vintage Books.
Walbran, John R. (1851), *A Guide to Ripon*, fifth edn, Ripon, William Harrison.
Walbran, John R. (1863), *Memorials of Fountains Abbey*, Surtees Society, Andrews, Durham, and Whittaker, London.
Walbran, John R. (1841), *Genealogical and Biographical Memoir of the Lords of Studley*, Ripon, limited private edition.
Walbran, John R., 'Yorkshire Genealogies', MS, York Minster.
Wardale, E. E. (1923), *Old English Grammar*.
Watkins, Alfred (1927), *The Old Straight Track*, London, Simpkin.
Weiss, Roberto (ed.) (1962), *Edward Fairfax: Godfrey of Boulogne or the Recoverie of Jerusalem*, Arundel, Centaur Press.
Whitaker, Dr T. D. (1st edn 1805, 3rd edn 1878), *History and Antiquities of the Deanery of Craven*, Leeds.
Wildman, S. G. (1971), *The Black Horsemen: English Inns and King Arthur*, London, Garnstone Press.
Wright, Joseph (1970), *English Dialect Dictionary*, London, Oxford University Press.
Yorkshire Archaeological Journal.
Young, Arthur (1771), *A Six Months' Tour through the North of England*, London.

INDEX

Aberford, 22
Aberystwyth, 93
Abraham's Hut, 25–6
Acaster Malbis, 21
Acoras Scar, 130–1, 140
Addingham, 24
Adel Crag, 140
Agravaine, Sir, 100
Agricola, 44–5
Aiketgate, 100
Ainsworth, Harrison, 172
Airedale, 143
Aislaby, 23
Albanians, 8
Alcock, Leslie, 11–12
Aldborough (Isurium Brigantum), 19, 45–6, 84, 186, 197–8
Alderley Edge, 31, 206
Alfred, King, 54
Alkeld, Alkelda, 'Saint', 114, 117–18
Allen, D. Elliston, 10, 93
Allerston, 201
Almondbury (Camulodunum), 55–6
Ampleforth, 202
Ana (One Howe) Cross, 25

Ancient Europe (Stuart Piggott), 8
Aneurin, 57
Anglo-Saxon Chronicle, 54
Anketill, 86
Annales Cambriae, 54
Appleby, 87
Appleton-le-Moors, viii, 23, 138–9, 142, 202
Appleton Roebuck, 21
Archflamens, 47
Arfderydd, 56
Arkendale, 24
Armathwaite, 150, 188
Arthington, 24
Arthur, 10, 48, 50, 53, 55–61, 68–9, 70, 72–5, 84, 95–7, 100, 149
Arthuret, 56, 108
Arthur's Pike, 56
Asenby, 24
Ashe, Geoffrey, 57
Askham (Westmorland), 105
Asselby, 21
Attila the Hun, 162
Auterstone, 56
Avebury Ring, 33, 144, 169
'Avoidance feature', 124, 146, 154–5, 162–3, 167, 190–5

INDEX

Bainbridge, 60
Baldwin, Bishop, 100
Bale, John, 88
Balin and Balan, 63
Banier, Sir, 100
Bankwell figurine, 119–20
Bardsey, 190
Barkston Ash, 21, 24
Barmoors, 17
Barnoldswick, 24
Barugh, 202
Basques, 8, 118–19, 131
Bassenthwaite, 151
Beacons, 142
Beal, 21
Beamsley, 25, 164–5
Beckermet, 7
Bede, the Venerable, 48, 54
Bedevere, Bedivere, Sir, 75
Bee Stone, 17, 203
Beezley, 60
Bek, Anthony, 157
Bel, Beli, Belenus, Belinus, 24–5, 27–32, 34, 169, 203–6
Bell Hall, 86
Bendigeidfran, 29, 32, 97, 148, 161
Bendrigg Lodge, 203–4
Benllech, 193
Berbers, 8
Bibliographical Odyssey (Rev. T. F. Dibdin), 90–2
Biddulph Moor, 9, 95, 206
Bidston Hill, 6
Bilton, 21
Binchester (Vinovia), 48
Birds, magical and sacred, 67, 147–67
Birkenhead, 6
Birmingham, 31, 206
Birrens, 3–4
Birstwith, 24
Bishopthorpe, 21
Bispham, 24
Black Hameldon (Lancashire), 24

Black Horse, the, 18–19, 32–3, 124, 134, 189–94
Black Horsemen, The (S. G. Wildman), 56
Blacko Tower, 19, 204
Blackpool, 25, 206
Blakey Ridge, 17
Blakey Topping, 17–19, 23, 25, 32–3, 86, 201–3
Blanchemains *see* Owain
Blencathra, 151
Bogg, Edmund, 4, 122–3, 128, 190, 195
Bog Hall, 17
Bolton Priory ('Abbey'), 112, 114, 139, 155–6, 162–7
Boothferry, 21
Bord, Janet and Colin, 6
Boroughbridge, 32, 45, 144
Bors, Sir, 100
Botton, 23
Boudicca, 39, 43–4, 165
Bournemouth, 27
Bowland, Forest of, 60, 159, 189, 204
Bowness-on-Solway, 108
Bradshaw, 160
Braganca (Portugal), 3
Braint, River, 121
Bramham, 24–5
Bran the Blessed *see* Bendigeidfran
Brayton, 21
Bregenz (Austria), 3
Brennus, Brennius, 28–9
Brent, River, 121
Breunor le Noire, Sir, 66
Brewster, Sam, vii, 58–62, 92
Brian de les Isles, Sir, 66
Brid *see* Bride
Bride, 5–8, 49, 70, 110, 183
Bridekirk, 7, 151
Bride Stones, 5, 9, 95, 201, 206
Bridewell, 5, 49
Bridget *see* Bride
Brigantia: area and realm, 2–13,

211

INDEX

Brigantia—*cont.*
  38–51, 118; goddess, 3, 7, 9, 110, 118
Brimham Rocks, 32–3, 125–8
British Tastes (D. Elliston Allen), 10, 93
Bromwich, Rachel, 30, 193
Bronze Age, 3, 5, 7, 12, 16, 31, 36–7, 40, 120, 148
Brougham, 61, 159–60
Brown, Robert, 16, 30
Browsholme Hall, 24, 159, 205
Brutus, Brut (traditional first king of Britain), 76
Brydekirk, 7
Brydock *see* Kirkbride
Bugthorpe, 21
Bull Stone, 141
Bulmer (village), 86
Bulmer, T. F., 68, 78
Burgess, Colin, 36
Burnett, Hugh, 15
Burnsall, 113
Burrell Green, 75–8, 87, 107
Burton Agnes Hall, 159
Burythorpe, 21
Bush Howe, 19, 189, 193–4
Butcher Hill, 24
'Butler', 73–5
Butterwick, 17, 203
Button Hill, 21

Cadbury Castle, 55–6
Caesar, Julius, 42, 147, 151
Caithness, 28, 30
Calaterium *see* Galtres
Caldbeck, 104
Calderbrook, 24
Calgarth Hall, 158
Cambridge University Library, 85
Camden, 86, 122–3
Camelot, 55–6, 95
Camulodunum *see* Almondbury

'Canonisation', 9
Cantsfield, 204
Capes, hooded, 42
Cape Wrath, 27
Caractacus *see* Caratacus
Carados, Sir, 71
Caratacus, 42–4, 51
Carle of Carlisle, 68
Carlisle (Luguvallium), 4, 31, 40, 55–6, 82, 100, 203
Carrawburgh, 112, 116, 154, 158
Carterton, 31
Cartimandua, 19, 39, 41
Cartmel, 155
Cartoft, 17, 202
Castle Eden beaker, 83
Castle Haugh, 25
Castle Hewen, 68, 82, 100, 104, 150
Castle of Wonders, 58, 61, 64, 103
Castlerigg (Keswick), 144
Castlesteads, 105
Castleton, 23
Castley (Wharfedale), 24
Catterick, 57
Cauldrons, 71, 79, 118
Cawood, 21
Cawthorne, 202
Cawton, 202
Caxton, 84–5, 88, 90–2
Celtiberians, 12
Celtic and Other Stone Heads: First Series (Sidney Jackson), 154
Celts, viii, 2–3, 5–11, 28–9, 31, 35–46, 57, 64–5, 70–1, 79, 84, 89, 113, 118, 140, 147, 153, 185, 190
Cerdic, Cerdig, 12, 42, 51, 71
Cernunnos, 110, 156–7, 169
Chapel-en-le-Frith, 159
Chapel Haddlesey, 21
Charbuckle Harescheugh, 81
Charles I, King, 184
Chattox, 173
Chaucer ('Wife of Bath's Tale'), 100

212

INDEX

Cheshire, 3, 84, 95, 133
Chester, 42, 44, 89
Chevin, the, 140–5, 195
Chop Gate, 5–6
Chrétien de Troyes, 59, 62, 66
Christianity, 47
Chronicon de Kirkstall, 164
Clapdale Castle (farm), 165–6
Clapham family, 162–6
Clark, Lt Col. Edwin Kitson, 15
Claxton, 21
Clifford (Wetherby), 21
Clifford, Anne, Countess of Pembroke, 61, 64
Clifford family, 162–6
Clifton (Penrith), 72
Clifton (York), 18–22, 31–3
Clinschor, 59, 62, 64
Clitheroe, 19, 30, 205
Cockatrice, 150–1
Cockerham, 25
Cockersand Abbey, 25
Coifi, 47–8, 118, 120
Coinage, 42
Cold Harbour, 17
Collingwood, R. G., 37
Colne, 19, 25, 204
Congleton, 6, 9, 95, 206
Coniston Cold, 114
Constable Burton, 24
Constance, Lake, 3
Constantine the Great, 47, 49, 112
Constantius, 47, 49
Copgrove, 153
Copy Hill, 25
Corbridge (Corstopitum), 4
Cornwall, 30, 37, 48, 57, 112, 156
Corstopitum *see* Corbridge
Cote Male Taile, Sir Le, 66
Cottage Leas, 202
Coventina, 112, 154, 158, 171
Cowling, E. T., 105, 140–5
Cowling, Geoffrey M., 11, 85, 157
Cowthorpe, 24, 146, 186–7

Cowton, 24
Coxwold, 17, 23, 86, 202
Cragg Cottage, 203
Craven, 104, 112–13, 164–6
Crayke, 17, 202
Cresswell, 34, 104, 188
Cropton, 23, 202
Cross Fell, 78, 150
Crossley, James, 179–80
Cross o'Greet, 60, 63
Crowther, Mrs Patricia, 92, 169
Culhwch and Olwen, 96, 196
Cumberland, 3, 22, 57, 75, 104, 144
Cumberland and Westmorland Antiquarian and Archaeological Society *Transactions*, 77–9
Cup-and-ring stones, 32, 140, 142, 145–6, 183
Cuthbert, St, 73
Cuthbert's Well, 73, 107
Cynfarch *see* Kenverchyn

Daemonologia (William Grainge), 122–3, 175–83
Danes Hills, 21
Daniel, Clarence, 158–9, 162, 188–9
'Danish', 117–18
D'Armagnac, Jacques, 89
Darnton, Abbot, 156–7
Darrel, John, 172
Darrington, 21
Davis, Norman, 97
Dead Man's Hill, 128–30
Dee, River, 88, 96, 120
Deepdale, 59
Deighton, 21, 23
Demdike, 173
Demonology (King James VI of Scotland), 172
Dent, 59
Dent, Major J. G., 85
Denton, Thomas, 40, 50, 161, 169
Derbyshire, 3, 104, 158–9, 189

INDEX

Destruction and Conquest of Britain (Gildas), 54
Devil's Arrows (Boroughbridge), 32, 45, 141–2, 144
Dibdin, Rev. Thomas Frognall, 90–2
Dickey o' Tunstead, 158–60, 162
Dinas Faelawr, 93
Diocletian, 47
Discourse of Witchcraft as it was enacted in the family of Mr. Edward Fairfax, of Fuystone, coun. Ebor see Grainge, William
Dobbies, 124, 189–95
Dodholm, 21
Dodsworth, Roger, 166
Doe, River, 60–1
Doublers, 143
Dragon's blood, 185
Draughton (Skipton), 25
Dringhouses, 21
Druids, 38, 124, 126, 128, 152, 186, 189
Dumnocoveros *see* Dumnoveros
Dumnonian Peninsula, 30
Dumnoveros, 41
Dunnington, 21
Dunscar Farm (Castleton, Derbyshire), 158
Dunsop Bridge, 24, 205
Dunvallo Molmutius, 29
Durham, 3, 47, 56

Eamont, River, 66, 69, 72
Earthen platforms, 144
Earth Hill, 21
East Keswick, 190
East Riddlesden, 24
Eboracum *see* York
Eburacum *see* York
Ecclesiastical History see Bede, the Venerable
Eden, River, 59–60, 64–5, 68–9, 75, 79, 82, 87, 103, 107, 121–2, 150, 198
Edenhall, 69, 72–6, 87, 107, 124
Edstone, Great and Little, 17
Edward I, King, 161
Edward IV, King, 88
Edwin, King, 12, 47
Egton, 26
Ellerton, 21
Ellingstring, 24
Elmet, 10, 12, 51
Elwes, H. J., and Henry, A., 186
Embsay, 25
Englewood, Engylwode, etc. *see* Inglewood
Epona, 109, 151; *see also* Modron
Eriú, Irish goddess, 9
Eschenbach, Wolfram von, 59–60, 62
Escomb, 47–9
Escrick, 21
Esholt, 25
Eshton, 112, 115–16
Esk, River, 22
Ewan Caesario *see* Owain
Ewan Close, 69, 103
Excalibur, 10, 75
'Eye of God', 153
Eyre, Kathleen, 159–60

Fadmoor, 203
Fairfax, Edward, 122, 172, 174–85
Fairfax family, 10–11, 122, 174
Fairy, fairies, 37–8, 73, 78, 94–5, 104–5, 107, 113, 133, 135, 187, 192
Farnham (Yorkshire), 155
Fetherstonhaugh, Col. T., 81, 107, 151, 198–9
Fewston, 114, 170, 175, 182
Figurines, 119–20
Fimber, 17, 201
Findler, Gerald, 159
Firbolgs, 95; *see also* Biddulph Moor

214

INDEX

Flagg Hall (Derbyshire), 158
Flambers Hill, 25
Flamborough, 140
Flamens, 47
Fletcher, Elizabeth, 178
Flintshire, 89, 96
Foggathorpe, 21
Ford Perilous, the, 59–63
Forest Hill, 21
Foulridge, 24
Fountain Line, 21
Fountains Abbey, 84, 134, 156, 167
Fourstones, 63
Fulford, 21
Furness, Peter, 16
Furness, William, 70–2
Fylde (Lancashire), 161

Galahad, Sir, 67
Gallois, 59
Galloway, 59
Galloway Gate, 59–60, 63–4
Gallows, 17
Galtres, Forest of, 11–12, 46, 85–6, 157
Gareth, Sir, 100
Garrowby, 21
Garstang, 24
Gateforth, 21
Gate Helmsley, 21
Gawain, Sir, 59, 62, 64, 69, 95–100, 103–4
Ge, 110
Genealogical and Biographical Memoir of the Lords of Studley (J. R. Walbran), 85–90
Geoffrey of Monmouth, 27–31, 47–8, 54, 57, 93, 157
Gerald the Welshman (Giraldus Cambrensis), 92–3
Germanus, St, 52–4
Giant's Cave (on the Eamont), 66, 69, 72, 74, 103, 107

Giant's Chambers (on the Eden), 103
Giant's Grave (Penrith), 69
Giant's Graves (Haweswater), 105
Gibson, Dr Thomas, 151–2, 158, 194–5
Giggleswick, 22, 114, 117–20, 154, 171
Gildas, 54
Gisburn, 173
Glassonby, 103
Glastonbury, 33, 49, 59, 152
Gloucester, 30, 59, 75
Godfrey of Boulogne, or the Recoverie of Jerusalem (Edward Fairfax) see Weiss, Roberto
Gododdin, 57
Golcar, 24
Golden Hill, 21
Golden Square, 202
Golland, Rev. C. E., 74, 83
Goole, 21
Gormire, Lake, 106
Graffa Plains (Brimham), 33, 126
Gragareth, 36, 59
Grail, 67, 74–5, 79, 81, 96, 108
Grainge, William, 122, 134, 170, 174–83
Grassington, 44, 112, 130
Great Habton, 23
Green Knight, the *see* Gawain
Green Man, the, 95, 156–7, 169
Greenwell Spring, 171–2
Greta, River, 60
Grey Yauds, 82, 107, 198
Grimshaw, Arthur, 94
Grimston Park, 21, 202
Gros Veneur, Le, 157
Grzimek, Bernhard, 14
Guide to Ripon, Fountains Abbey, Bolton Priory and Several Places in Their Vicinity (J. R. Walbran), 125, 155–6, 163–4, 166–7
Guinevere, 96, 98, 100, 135

INDEX

Gwalchmai *see* Gawain
Gweiz prelljus, li see Ford Perilous

Hambleton Street, 106
Hameldon Hill, 204
Hammerton Hall, 25
Harden Hall, 24
Haresceugh Castle, 18–19, 78–82, 87, 149
Hargrove, E., 139, 156
Harland, 203
Harlow Hill, 25
Harome, 202
Harrington, Cyril, 165
Harrogate, 25
Hartoft End, 23
Hartside Pass, 78
Haweswater, 31, 77, 104, 204
Haxby, 21
Headless bodies, 97, 129
Heads: carved, 35, 112, 114–18, 153–7, 162–7; severed, 97, 112, 158, 161, 164; *see also* Skulls
Healaugh, 21, 23
Heaton, Bradford, 154
Helen, St (mother of Constantine), 49, 110, 112, 116, 122–3
Helena, St (cottage), 17, 189, 203; *see also* Helen
Heligar Pike, 25
Hell Gill, 60–1, 64–5, 121–2
Hellifield, 24
Helmsley, 17, 202
Helm Wind, 78
Hemingbrough, 21
Henges, 45, 56, 69, 104–5
Hen hunt, 151–2
Henry III, King, 86
Henry V, King, 164
Henry VI, King, 75–7, 87
Henry VIII, King, 68, 166
Hen Stones, 147–8
Herd Howe, 23

Herne the Hunter, 122, 157
Heslington, 21
Hewen *see* Owain
Heworth, 21
Hexham, 63, 138
Heyfell, 158
Higgin, Anthony, Dean of Ripon, 91
High Hesket, 68, 100, 146, 187
High Mowthorpe, 201
High Street (mountain and track), 105, 150
High Studley, 84–5, 92
High Way (Mallerstang), 64–5
Historical Guide to Carlisle and District (1881), 7, 187
History and Antiquities of the Deanery of Craven (Dr T. D. Whitaker), 113, 164–5
History and Antiquities of Leath Ward (Samuel Jefferson), 187
History and Directory of Cumberland (T. F. Bulmer), 68, 78
History and Traditions of Mallerstang and Pendragon Castle (Rev. W. Nicholls), 121–2
History of the Britons (Nennius), 54
History of Cumberland (J. Nicolson and R. Burn), 70
History of Easingwold and the Forest of Galtres (G. M. Cowling), 157
History of the Kings of Britain see Geoffrey of Monmouth
History of Knaresborough (E. Hargrove), 139, 156
History of Penrith (William Furness), 70–2
Hob, Hobgoblins *see* Fairy
Holes through stones, significance of, viii, 128, 138–9
Hollowgate Farm (Shap Fell), 30, 203
'Hollow-ways', 40
Holtby, 25

216

INDEX

Honey Bee Nest, 203
Honorius, Emperor, 52
Horcum, 203
Horned God of the Brigantes, 197-8
Hornington, 21
Horse, Black, cult *see* Dobbie
Howgill Fells, 19, 124, 190, 193-4
Howk Stream, 104
Howsham, 21
Howson, William, 113
Huddersfield, 24, 55
Humber, 28
Huntington (York), 21
Husthwaite, 17, 202
Hutton Conyers, 84-6, 89
Hutton-in-the-Forest, 95, 103-4
Hutton-le-Hole, 202-3
Hylton Floghen Manor, 87, 151

Iberia, Iberians, 8-13, 118
Iceni, 39, 43
Ilkley, 141-5
Illustrated Guide to the Curiosities of Craven (William Howson), 113
Illustrium Maioris Britanniae Scriptorum (John Bale), 88
Ine, King of Wessex, 11
Ingleborough (Rigodunum), 36, 44, 59, 61-2
Ingleton, 60-1
Inglewood, Forest of, 40, 69, 87, 95, 104, 146, 152, 187-8
Insh, 31
Irthington, 4
Isis Parlis, 74
Isurium Brigantum *see* Aldborough
Itinerarium Cambriae see Gerald the Welshman

Jackson, John, 188
Jackson, Sidney, vii, 6, 35, 154
James VI of Scotland and I of England, 92, 170, 172, 184
Jefferson, Samuel, 187
Jenghis Khan, 162
Jenny, persistent name, 135-7, 140, 142, 199
Jenny Dibb or Dibble, 136, 175-8, 182-3
Jenny-Green-Teeth (water-weed), 135
Jenny Hurn, 137
Jenny Twigg and her Daughter Tib, 32, 134-5, 138, 140, 145
Jenny's Foss, 135
Jenny's Gate (Dead Man's Hill), 136
'Jew Stone', 121-2
Jones, Gwyn, 93
Jutland, 15

'Kail-pot of guineas' tradition, 79
Kay, Sir, 66, 100-1
Keasby, 25
Keighley, 24-5
Keldy Castle, 202
Kellfield, 21
Kellington, 23
Kemple End, 18-19, 24-5, 30-1, 206
Kendal, 32
Kendall, P. F. and Wroot, H. E., 26
Kenverchyn (Cynfarch), 67, 149
Kettlewell, 44, 130
Kexby, 21
Kidson, Frank, 94
Kincraig, 31
'King Harry', 'King Harry Waste', 198
Kingsdale, 59-60
Kirby Misperton, 23
Kirbymoorside, 16-17, 202
Kirby Wispe, 24
Kirk, significance of word, 104-5
Kirkbride, 7
Kirkby Lonsdale, 106, 139, 204
Kirkby Malham, 114-17, 154

INDEX

Kirkbymoorside *see* Kirbymoorside
Kirkby Thore, 108
Kirkdale, 17, 202
Kirk Deighton, 25, 91
Kirkham, (Fylde, Lancashire), 161
Kirkham Priory (Yorkshire), 17, 86
Kirkoswald, 76, 78–9, 81, 107, 150–1, 155
Kirksanton, 106
Kirkstone, 105, 150
Kitson Clark, Lt Col. *see* Clark
Kittredge, G. L., 87
Klingsor *see* Clinschor
Knaresborough, 113, 146, 187
Knipe Scar (Shap), 105
Kokoarrah, 18
Kurvinen, Auro *see* Carl of Carlisle
Kynheure *see* 'King Harry'
Kynverch *see* Kenverchyn

Lady of the Lake, 58
Lairg, 31–2
Lammersyde Castle, 79
Lancashire, 3, 6, 19, 84, 95, 170, 181
Lancashire Legends (Kathleen Eyre), 159–60
Lancashire Witches, The (Harrison Ainsworth), 172
Lancelot, Sir, 58, 66, 95–6, 100
Land of Wonders, 58–9, 62
Lanercost, Chronicle of see Denton, Thomas
Langcliffe Hall, 148–9
Langho, 24
Langholm, 31, 203
Lastingham, 23, 202
La Tène, 8, 36–7, 39
Laytham, 21
Lead, and lead-bronze, 36, 45–6, 120
Lead Church (near Leeds), 21
Leaf Howe, 203
Leavening, 17, 202
Ledger, Philip, 15–16

Ledston Hall, 21
Leeds, 2, 24, 89, 113
Lees, Dr Arnold, 123–4
Lefebure, Molly, 76
Legends and Historical Notes of North Westmoreland (Dr Thomas Gibson), 151–2, 158, 194–5
Legends of the Lake Counties (Gerald Findler), 159
Leland, John (topographer), 68, 84, 88, 123
Leppington, 17, 21, 23
Levens Hall, Lucks of, 75, 82
Leyland *see* Leland
Leyland (Lancashire), 24
Leys, 14–34, 141, 144, 177, 186–7, 193
Life of Germanus, 54
Lilling, East and West, 17, 202
Lincolnshire, 3, 137
Linton (village), 112
Lionel, Sir, 96
Lister, Thomas, 173–4
Little, Hugh C., 78–80
Llewellyn ap Gruffydd, 50, 161
Lloyd, A. L., 94
Llyn Cerrig Bach, 5
Lobley Hall, 24
Lockton, 202
Lodestone *see* Magnetite
Logres, 95
Londesborough, 21
Longden Castle, 25
Long Marston, 21, 25
Long Meg and Her Daughters, 82, 107, 144–5, 186, 198–9
Long Preston, 115, 153–4
Lower Wharfedale (Edmund Bogg), 4, 122, 190, 195
Lowther, 105, 108
Lucan, Sir, 75
'Lucks', 73–83, 108
Luguvallium *see* Carlisle
'Lullaby' rescue-song, 37–8, 94

218

INDEX

Lune, River, 138, 204
Lydgate, 24

Maben *see* Mapon
Mabey, Peter, 15
Mabinogion, mabinogi, 50, 62, 67, 97, 186, 196
Mabon *see* Mapon
Macbeth, 172
Maelor *see* Mailoria
'Maelor, English' *see* Mailoria
Maelor's Castle *see* Dinas Faelawr
Magnetite, 26, 34
Maidenkirk, 24
Mailoria, 88–9
Malarie *see* Malory
Maledisant, damsel, 66
Maleore *see* Malory
Malkin Tower, 173–4
Mallerstang, 61, 64, 79, 121–2
Mallory *see* Malory
Malmutius *see* Dunvallo Molmutius
Malore, Anketill *see* Malory
Malory, Sir Thomas, 55, 58, 63, 65–6, 84–93
Malton, 17, 86, 201
Mamutine Laws *see* Dunvallo Molmutius
Manchester, 31, 204, 206
Mandrake Tree, 189
Mapon (Mabon, Maben), 109, 128, 196
Mappleton, 25
Mardale, 'Kings' of, 77
Marriage by capture, 38–9, 94
Marriage of Sir Gawain, 68–9, 95
Matthews, William, 87
Mauleverer, family, 85
Mauley Cross, 203
Maxen Wledig, 50
Meaux (East Yorkshire), 164
Meilerius, 93
Melbourne, 21

Melmerby (Westmorland), 149–50
Merlin, 57, 157, 185
Merlin (romance), 84–5
Meugher, 130–1, 140, 147
Michael, St, 70, 82, 103, 107, 146, 150, 153–4, 156, 186–7
Middlesmoor, 129–30
Miles Hill (Leeds), 113
Miley Pike, 23
Milford, North and South, 21, 24
Millfield Project, 15
Mist, magic, 185
Mist Over Pendle (Robert Neill), 173
Mockerkin, 106
Modron, 109, 179
Moeller, Dr S., 15
Molmutius *see* Dunvallo Molmutius
Moon, Prior Richard, 166–7
Morcant *see* Morken
Morecambe Bay, 24, 27, 193–4
Moreton-in-the-Marsh, 31
Morgan le Fay, 58, 67, 99, 102–3, 106–7, 113, 185
Morken, King, 106
Mórrígan, 148
Morte Arthur (alliterative poem), 84, 95
Morte Darthur, 55, 58, 63, 65–6, 70–1, 84–93
'Mother, the', disease, 178–9
Mounsey, William, 121–2
Mountain ash *see* Rowan
Mount Grace Priory, 23
Mount Pleasant, 17, 21
Mowbreck Manor (Lancashire), 161
Mowthorpe, 17, 86, 202
Mulethorp *see* Mowthorpe
Muncaster, 'Luck' of, 75–8, 81, 87
Murton, 21
Musgrave family, 73, 76, 87
Mustard, Helen M., and Passage, Charles E., 60
Myrddin, 57

219

INDEX

Mysterious Britain (Janet and Colin Bord), 6

Nawton, 203
Needfire, 133
Neil, Robert, 173
Nennius, 54
Nether Haresceugh, 81, 87, 107–8, 150
Neuchâtel, Lake, 8, 12, 171
Newburgh Priory, 17, 202
Newby Wiske, 24
Newhall (Fewston), 174
Newton Kyme, 24
Newton-on-Rawcliffe, 202
Nicholls, Rev. W., 121–2
Nicolson, J. and Burn, R., 70, 74
Nidd, River, 125, 128, 130, 187
Nidderdale (William Grainge), 134, 170
Nidderdale from Nun Monkton to Whernside (Harry Speight), 129, 139
Ninekirks *see* Ninian, St
Ninian, St, 71
Ninth Legion, 12, 45–6
Normans, 9, 40, 54, 64–5, 73
Northallerton, 24
Northumberland, 3, 56, 63
Northumbria, 47, 106
Nottinghamshire, 3
Nun Appleton, 21

Oaks, 34, 68–9, 86, 154, 157, 185–9
Ob, *see* Fairy
Old Byland, 23
Old Straight Track, The (Alfred Watkins), 14–16, 27
Old Wife Ridge (Heyshaw Manor), 139
Old Yorkshire (Rev. William Smith), 125–6

Ostorius Scapula, 42–3
Our Cumberland Village (Col. T. Fetherstonhaugh), 81, 107, 198–9
Ouse, River, 11, 19
Overton, 21, 89
Owain of Rheged, 57–8, 65, 68, 100, 149

Pagan Celtic Britain (A. Ross), vii, 7–9, 35–6, 110–11
Palamides, Sir, 55–6
Paradise Lodge, 21
Parisii, 5, 37
Park Rash, 44, 128
Parsifal, 59; *see also* Peredur
Parzifal *see* Parsifal
Passage, Charles E. *see* Mustard, Helen
Pelagius, 1–2, 51–3, 56, 107–8
Pendle, 170, 179, 184, 196
Pendragon Castle, 61, 64–6, 79
Pennines, 6, 36, 42, 44–5, 78, 95, 144
Pennington, Sir John, 76, 87
Penny Howe, 202
Penny Stone (Bispham), 19, 24–5, 206
Penrith, 19, 40, 56, 68–70, 78, 87, 95, 144, 159
Penwortham, 24
Percy, Bishop, 75, 99
Peredur, 62, 102; *see also* Parsifal
Petillius Cerialis, 44–5
Pickering, 16, 202
Picts, 8
Piggott, Stuart, 8
Pike Howe, 23

Rhys, Ernest *see* Malory
Rhys, John *see* Malory
Ribblesdale, 115, 140–1, 159–60
Ribchester, 60, 141
Ribston Hall, 25, 85

220

INDEX

Richmond (Yorkshire), 57
Richmond, Sir Ian, 59
Rigodunum *see* Ingleborough
Ripon, 45, 84–5, 90–2, 111, 113, 134, 138, 144, 153, 170
Rivet, A. L. F., 37
Road Goes On, The (C. W. Scott-Giles), 50
Robin Hood, 169
Robinson, Henry, 170–2, 174–6
Robinsons in Pendle witches case, 173
Rocking-stones, 139–40
Roman Britain and the English Settlements (R. G. Collingwood), 37
Romanby, 24
Romans, 12, 30, 36–53, 54, 72, 111, 152
Romans in Yorkshire, The (Dr A. Raistrick), 46
Rombalds Moor, 105, 140–3, 174
Rome, 28, 32, 43, 51
Romillies Moor, Romleyes Moor *see* Rombalds Moor
Rock Barugh, 17
Rosedale, 25–6, 34
Ross, Dr Anne, viii, 7–9, 35–7, 110–11, 116–18, 120, 122, 138, 147–8, 185–6, 197
Rowan, 132–3, 136, 174, 183, 195
Rudgate, 122–3
Rudston, Rudstone, 142, 144, 155
Rufforth, 21
Rufus, King William, 40
Ruiton 'sand and salt' people,
Ryther ferry, 21

Sacrifice, actual or vestigial, 7, 118, 129–30
Saklatvala, Beram, 10, 55, 70–1, 75
Salford, 31, 206
'Salt and sand' people *see* Ruiton

Salter Road, 18, 24, 204–5
Sandhutton, 24
Santa Claus, 169
Saracens, 55–6
Saxons, 9, 10, 12, 40, 47, 51, 54–5, 69, 79, 106, 118, 131–2, 149
Saxton, 21
Scarfhill Howe, 203
Scotland, 3–4, 44, 46, 63
Scott-Giles, C. W., 50
Scow Hall, 25
Screeton, Paul, viii, 16
Scurff Hall, 21
Seaton Ross, 21
Sedbergh, 19, 190, 192–3
Selby, 21
Semmerwater, 106, 115
Seohín seó, lú ló leó, 37–9, 94
Settle, 22, 115, 119, 189
Seven, River, 23, 26, 34
Severn, River, 30, 120
Shakespeare, 11, 122, 157, 172
'Shaking bottles', 72–3, 82
Shap, 30, 108
Sherburn-in-Elmet, 21
Sheriff Hutton, 202
'Shoheen, Sholo' *see Seohín seó*
Shrove Tuesday, 151
Sil Howe, 17, 23, 201
Silures, 9, 42
Singletonthorpe, 25
Sir Gawain and the Carl of Carlisle (Auro Kurvinen), 97, 185
Sir Gawain and the Green Knight, 95–100, 103–4; *see also* Gawain, Sir
Siwards How, 21
Skell, River, 157, 170
Skewkirk Hall, 21
Skipsea Castle, 25
Skirpenbeck, 21
Skulls, 158
Slaidburn, 25, 205
Slaid Hill, 25

INDEX

Smeffell Howe, 202
Smith, Rev. William, 125–6
Smithson, Rev. Nicholas, Vicar of Fewston, 175, 182
Snainton, 23
Snowden Carr, 25, 183, 188
Solway Firth, 7, 27, 46
Son of the Rocks, 128
South Otterington, 24
Southowram, 24
Spaldington, 21
Speight, Harry, 129, 139
Stainton, 23
Stamford Bridge, 21
Stanwick (North Yorkshire), 41, 44–5, 57
Stanwix, 31, 203
Staveley, 113, 188
Steeton, 21
Steven, Sir, 100
Stockbridge, 21
Stockton-on-Tees, 23
Stone circles, 108, 142, 186; see also Grey Yauds, Long Meg, Castlerigg
Stonegrave, 202
Stonehenge, 33, 59, 144, 169
Storwood moat, 21
Studley see High Studley
Submerged towns, etc., 167
Sugar Loaf Hill, 24–5, 205
Summersgill Farm, 204
Sunrise Farm, 25
Sutton-on-the-Forest, 21
Swaledale, 11, 45, 150
Swastika Stone, 32, 140, 143–5
Swinsty Hall, 170–2, 174–6

Tacitus, 9, 44–5
Ta Dyke, 44, 51
Taliesin, 57
Talkin Tarn, 107
Tallentire, 150–1
Tal-y-Llyn shield, 119–20
Tarn Wadling, 68, 82, 99–103, 107
Tarquin, Sir see Turquine
Tasso, 172, 174, 180, 184–6
Tempest family, 85, 89–90
Temple Hill, 21
'Temples', 106, 120, 126, 144
Terrington, 86
Thames, River, 30
Thirsk, 23
Thorganby, 21
Thornton Dale, 201
Thornton Force, 60
Thornton-in-Cleveland, 23
Thorpe, Lewis see Geoffrey of Monmouth
Thorpe, Margaret, 176–8
Thorpe Fell, 24
Threlkeld Place (Cumberland), 159, 161
Thunderstones, 108
Thursden, 24
Tib see Jenny Twigg
Timberbottoms Farm (Lancashire), 160
Timble, Timble Gill, 106, 170, 176, 182
Tin, 36, 120
Tockwith, 24–5
Tolkien, J. R. R., 95
Topcliffe, 24
Top of Blaze Moss, 25
Town and Country in Roman Britain (A. L. F. Rivet), 37
Towton, Battle of, 75, 87
Towton Spring, 21
Tow Top Kirk, 104–5
Tree of Life Stone, 25, 145–6, 183, 188
Treen and Other Wooden Bygones (Edward H. Pinto), 80
Trees, magical and sacred, 67, 146, 185–9

INDEX

Trees of Great Britain and Ireland, The (H. J. Elwes and A. Henry), 186
Trent, River, 137
Tricephalos, 155
Trioedd Ynys Prydein: The Welsh Triads (Rachel Bromwich), 30, 193
Tristram, Sir, 55–6, 100
Troyes, Chrétien de *see* Chrétien de Troyes
Tullie House Museum and Library (Carlisle), vii, 78
Tunstead Farm (Derbyshire) *see* Dickey o' Tunstead
Turquine, Sir, 67, 71
Turton (Lancashire), 160, 206
Twelve Headless Men and other Derbyshire Ghost Stories (Clarence Daniel), 158–9
Twigg, Jenny *see* Jenny
Twisleton Glen, 61
Twisleton Lane, 60
Twisleton Scar, 60
Twiss, River, 60–1
Tylecote, R. F. *see* Burgess, Colin
Tyne, River, 46
Tyverinton *see* Terrington

Upleatham, 17, 23
Upper Hapton, 24
Ure, River, 45, 130
Urien, King, 57–8, 65, 67–9, 100, 102, 106, 149
Urswick Tarn, 107
Uther Pendragon, 64, 85
Uwaine, Sir *see* Owain

Venutius, 41, 43–5, 51
Vinaver, Eugène, 89
Vinotonus, 51, 104, 130
Vinovia *see* Binchester
Volisius, 41

Waberthwaite, 22, 25
Waddilove, Dean of Ripon, 90
Waddow Hall, 70, 159–60
Wagner, Richard, 59
Waite, Margaret, 178
Wakefield, 24
Walbran, J. R., viii, 85–90, 125, 128, 155–6, 163–4, 166–7, 180
Walburn Hall, 18–19
Wall, the Roman, 46, 63
Walter, Archdeacon, 28
Walton–Walshford pocket, 10–12, 84, 89, 122, 146, 174, 186
Walwein *see* Gawain
Walwen *see* Gawain
Wardley Hall (Worsley), 160
Warrington, 21, 24
Wars of the Roses, 75, 85, 87–8, 162–5
Warthill, 21
Wash, the, 2
Washburn, River, 5, 7, 139, 170, 174, 181, 184
Wass, 23
Watkins, Alfred, 14–16, 27
Wawain *see* Gawain
Wear, River, 48
Weiss, Roberto, 172, 184–5
Well (Yorkshire village), 111
Wells, 17, 49–50, 62–3, 72–4, 77–8, 81, 103, 107–8, 109–24, 150, 171
Welsh, 50, 54, 65, 84, 141, 193
Wensleydale, 44–5, 106, 117, 130
Wesham (Lancashire), 161
Westby, John, 161
Westmorland, 3
Wetherby, 4, 21, 112
Whale Jaw Hill, 141
Wharfedale, 44, 105, 112, 114, 120, 122, 130, 139–46, 174, 190
Wheeldale Howe, 203
Wheeldrake Howe, 86
Whernside, 59, 63
Whinstone, 26

223

INDEX

Whitaker, Dr T. D., 113, 164–5
Whitby, 23
White Mount (London, the Tower), 97
Whitendale, 205
Whitethorn, 17, 201
Whitley, 23
Widow Howe, 201
Wighill, 21
Wig Stones, 131–5, 140, 147
Wilberfoss, 25
Wild Boar Fell, 64
Wildman, S. G., viii, 6, 9, 56
Wildon Grange, 17
Willitoft, 21
Wintringham, 201
Wirral, 2, 95–6, 120
Wisemen, 176
Witchbane (Robert Neill), 173
Witchcraft in Yorkshire (Patricia Crowther), 92
Witches, 92, 136, 168–83, 184–99
Witches' manna *see* Jenny-Green-Teeth
Wonderful Discoverie of Witches in the County of Lancashire (William Potts), 172
Wooding, Michael, 165–6
Wookey Hole, 112, 158, 171
Wrelton, 23, 202
Wren, 135–6
Wroot, H. E. *see* Kendall, P. F.
Wykeham, 201

Yanwath, 69, 72
Yarm, 23
Ynglewood *see* Inglewood
Yoden claw-beaker, 83
Yore, River *see* Ure, River
York (Eboracum, Eburacum), 11–12, 19, 21, 41, 44–8, 85, 141, 173, 180–1
York Minster Library, vii, 85
Yorkshire, 1, 2, 3, 6, 15, 35, 61, 84, 95, 104, 170
Yorkshire Genealogies (J. R. Walbran), 87, 89
Ysbidinongyl, 103
Yvain *see* Owain
Yverdun, 8